*Evil is unspectacular and always human,*
*And shares our bed and eats at our table.*
**W.H. Auden**

# HELL HATH NO FURY

## 13 MORE SPIRITS OF DEPRAVITY AND DESPAIR

### 2

## BY TROY TAYLOR

AN AMERICAN HAUNTINGS INK BOOK

# HELL HATH NO FURY 2
## 13 MORE SPIRITS OF DEPRAVITY AND DESPAIR

© Copyright 2022 by Troy Taylor
All Rights Reserved.

ISBN: 978-1-7352706-9-2

Published by American Hauntings Ink
228 South Mauvaisterre Street - Jacksonville Il - 62650
www.americanhauntingsink.com

Cover Design by April Slaughter
Interior Design by Troy Taylor

Printed in the United States of America

# TABLE OF CONTENTS

INTRODUCTION -- 7

## DEPRAVITY

"THE GHOST IN THE ATTIC" ---- 10
WALBURGA "DOLLY" OESTERREICH

"THE MURDERED DUTCHMAN" ---- 25
AUGUSTA NACK

"LONELY HEARTS KILLER" ---- 66
MARTHA BECK

"THE PHANTOM FLAPPER KILLER" ---- 89
MARGARET HELDMAN

"THE WORST WOMAN ON EARTH" --- 103
LIZZIE HALLIDAY

"THE GIGGLING GRANNY" --- 126
NANNIE DOSS

"THE TRUNK MURDERESS" --- 139
WINNIE RUTH JUDD

# DESPAIR

"GENERAL INDIGNITIES" ---183
ELSA LEMP WRIGHT

"THE LADY OF THE LAKE" --- 205
HALLIE LATHAM

"WEEPING MAY ENDURE FOR A NIGHT" -- 218
NELL CROPSEY

"THE WOMAN WHO LOST HER HEAD" --- 241
DOROTHY EGGERS

"VICTIM OF THE KILLER PRIEST" --- 259
ANNA AUMULLER

"STRANGE LOVE" --- 288
ELENA MILAGRO HOYOS

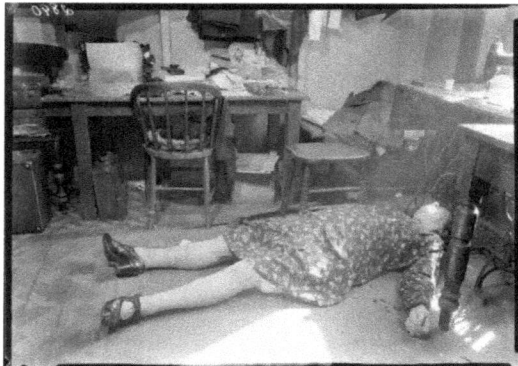

# INTRODUCTION

*It did not occur to them that a woman could be dangerous. How foolish they were.*
**Ken Follett**

The underestimation of women always takes me back to the Rudyard Kipling poem that I quoted in the introduction to the first book in this series - a poem that stresses the fact that no matter what we might think, the female of the species is always "much deadlier than the male."

In far too many ways - and for too long -- society has overlooked the achievements of women. We have overlooked them in business, politics, science, education, war, literature, and, yes, even when it comes to murder. They have claimed more than their share of victims throughout America's history, and yet we have failed to offer them the notoriety that we have given to men.

This is a grave mistake, for the murders committed by women are usually more terrifying than anything a man can imagine.

Women kill for money, revenge, love, and sometimes, just for pleasure. They have left behind dead lovers, murdered husbands, slaughtered roommates, innocent children, and lingering spirits. They are serial killers, the insane, and the vengeful, who still demand attention long after death.

Women are also victims and, sometimes, enduring ghosts - reminders that the hands of man can be cruel and begging for their stories to be told.

They are women lost, disappeared, misguided, spurned, wicked, put-upon, vicious, neglected, misunderstood, sinister, haunted, devious, mistreated, murdered, and spectral - and women you will never forget.

When I wrote my first book about women who prey on others - and those who have been preyed upon - I knew there were too many stories for a single book. There were simply too many stories that deserved to be told.

Some of the macabre tales within these pages may not tell stories of the supernatural, but they are so strange, so dark, and often so gruesome that they had to be included.

All are tales of terror, bloodshed, suffering, death, and murder - and continue to be tales that are not for the faint of heart or the weak of stomach.

As I have already made clear, a woman can be dangerous and should never be underestimated. I'll stress once more that Shakespeare told us that "Hell hath no fury like a woman scorned...."

Don't forget it.

**Troy Taylor**
**Spring 2022**

# PART ONE:
# DEPRAVITY

# "THE GHOST IN THE ATTIC" WALBURGA "DOLLY" OESTERREICH

This house had ghosts, too.

That's the only thing Fred Oesterreich could imagine would explain the strange sounds that he'd heard at night - the creaking of the floorboards, the soft footsteps, the rustling in the ceiling. There seemed to be someone - or something -- with his wife and himself in their two-story Los Angeles home. He couldn't imagine what else it would be other than a resident specter. Had the same ghost followed them here from Milwaukee?

Fred was convinced he was losing his mind. The wealthy German businessman, who had made his fortune by manufacturing aprons in Milwaukee, had recently moved to Los Angeles to get away from the ghosts. To think the spooks had followed him to the West Coast didn't frighten him – it made him angry. The rich, loud, and overbearing man was determined not to be run out of this new house by a denizen of the spirit world.

He'd get to the bottom of what was going on this time if it was the last thing he ever did.


The story of Walburga Oesterreich truly begins in 1903, nearly two decades before her husband, Fred, began hearing strange sounds in the attic of their California home. At that time, Walburga - better known by her nickname of "Dolly" - was 36 years old but looked much younger. She was of average height but had a trim, voluptuous build, sultry smile, and eyes that managed to get her in a lot of trouble. When her story eventually became known, she was often described as a "nymphomaniac," which may or may not have been accurate because there was one man that Dolly was not passionate about - her husband, Fred.

Fred owned a factory that made aprons in their hometown of Milwaukee. A few years older than Dolly, Fred was the epitome of a German businessman who had fought his way to the top from immigrant beginnings. By 1903, he was worth at least $250,000, and while he prospered, he watched every cent and devoted nearly every waking moment to his business. He was loud, crude, cruel to his employees and wife, and often intoxicated.

Dolly could have dealt with all that but what she could not tolerate was that Fred was also clumsy and unsatisfying in bed. Dolly had appetites, and her husband failed to meet them. She often berated Fred so loudly and violently about his conjugal failures that neighbors were sometimes compelled to call the police.

It was not surprising that Dolly would find a lover. What was a shock was that he was a worker in her husband's factory, a small, frail-looking young man named Otto Sanhuber.

Otto had been a foundling, left at a Milwaukee orphanage with no idea who his biological parents were and when he had even been born. He was quiet, painfully shy, friendless, and was barely five feet tall, with a sallow complexion, receding chin and hairline, and weak blue eyes that looked out from cheap spectacles. In the summer of 1903, he was thought to be 17 years old, so he applied to apprentice as a sewing machine repairman at Oesterreich's factory.

For whatever reason, Otto caught Dolly's eye, and she saw many hidden possibilities. She later said that he reminded her of her late son, Raymond, who died before he could reach Otto's age.

Which makes everything that happened next even creepier, in my opinion.

At first, her interest in the boy was motherly, and Otto admired how she stood up to her domineering husband, who terrified most of the factory workers. Soon, though, he stopped seeing her as a mother figure, and Dolly began to realize that Otto had hungers that matched her own.

According to most accounts, she summoned Otto to her home to "service a sewing machine" one day. When he arrived, he found the lady of the house wearing nothing but a silk robe. She led him off to her bedroom to inspect the damaged appliance.

Otto serviced it - and then he serviced Dolly.

Dolly, to her delight, discovered that her instincts were correct. Between the sheets, the boy was much more of a man than her husband.

All went well for some months. Otto continued to sneak over to the Oesterreich home whenever the husband was away. They took a "weekend" trip to St. Louis that lasted nine days and never left their hotel room.  Dolly was satisfied by the odd young man. Fred continued to work and drink, and everyone seemed to be happy.

But then, in 1907, the first signs of trouble appeared. A busybody neighbor informed Fred that his wife was seemed to be having a suspicious amount of trouble with her sewing machine. Fred confronted Dolly about her visitor, but she calmly asserted that such stories were all lies. She put on such a convincing display of wounded outrage that Fred backed off, apologizing for even bringing it up. He drank more and put the whole idea out of his mind.

Dolly was torn. She couldn't risk the loss of her marriage - or at least Fred's money - and she couldn't lose Otto either. If only she had a place where she could keep Otto where he could be entirely out of sight, still come and see her, but not be spotted by anyone else.

She suddenly thought of the perfect place - the attic of the house.

There was a small cubbyhole in the attic, conveniently above the master bedroom, that could only be entered through a small trap door in the ceiling. Dolly decorated it with a cot, a table, a chair, a chamber pot, and other household items. She told Otto to quit his job at the apron factory. And when the day came that they were sure Fred was safely out of the way, she installed her lover in his new place, which was right above the Oesterreich bed.

Otto obediently settled into his new life. When Fred was away at work, Otto would come downstairs and take care of everything that needed tending to in the house. He took great pride in his talent for washing floors, preparing food, doing laundry, and, of course, taking care of Dolly's many physical needs. When Fred returned home in the evening, he huddled in his attic room, reading by candlelight.

Otto spent his time devouring adventure novels that Dolly got him from the local library. After reading hundreds of cheap novels and pulp magazines, Otto decided to try some writing of his own. Dolly got him a post office box, and, using a pen name, he scribbled stories of excitement, adventure, and sex, often set in the Orient. Dolly typed them up and mailed them off to the pulp magazines, and they started to sell. Dolly opened a bank account for the attic dweller who now had a career in pulp fiction.

Otto was perfectly happy in his bizarre life. So was Dolly.

On the other hand, Fred became sure that he was losing his sanity. Often at night, he heard strange noises coming from the ceiling. Food he could swear he had seen just a short time before would suddenly be gone. His cigars began disappearing. Once, when he was in the backyard, he swore he saw a face in the attic window.

Dolly sighed and suggested her husband consult a doctor. He was slipping, she told him, after too much work, too much drink, and not enough sleep. The only entrance to the attic was over their bed. No one could be up there. She even let him pull on the door, which Otto had locked from the inside. It didn't budge, she told him, because no one had been up there for years.

Fred didn't see a doctor, and after that, when he heard a cough from the ceiling, noticed footsteps, or saw that some leftovers had vanished from the refrigerator, he kept silent. He was convinced their house was haunted, but he knew no one would believe him.

The odd sounds continued until Fred became so rattled that he insisted they move to a new house, so Dolly found one with a large attic. When the Oesterreichs moved, so did Otto.

At first, Fred thought he was safe from the ghosts, but soon, they returned. He heard soft noises in the night, and his food and cigars continued to vanish. Dolly's hints about his drinking and his need to seek medical help ensured that he kept his complaints to a minimum.

In 1913, the Oesterreichs moved again. Otto came along, much to the delight and relief of Dolly, setting himself up in another attic room. The three might have remained in Milwaukee for good, except one night in 1918, Otto got careless. While Fred and Dolly were out with neighbors for the evening, Otto came downstairs to have dinner. He was sitting in his underwear in the kitchen when Fred and Dolly returned unexpectedly early.

Fortunately for Otto, Fred was drunk. He escaped with only a beating before Fred stumbled off the bed, convinced that he had surprised a peculiarly dressed burglar. Still in his underwear, Otto was locked out of the only home he had. He hid in a park and returned the following day after Fred had left for work.

Otto came up with a new plan. World War I had started, and Otto told his lover that he would join the army and serve his country. But Dolly had plans of her own - she needed Otto's services more than Uncle Sam did. Dolly gave him the money he had earned as a writer and told him to use the money to go to Los Angeles. They would keep in touch via a post-office box, and she would persuade her husband to move there as soon as she could.

As always, Otto did as he was told. He took the next train to L.A. and got a job as a porter in a hotel, staying in touch with Dolly through his old post office box in Milwaukee. Rather than enjoying his new-found freedom, though, Otto missed his quiet, safe place in the attic and the private little world he had built with his writing and with Dolly.

In a few months, Dolly, true to her word, convinced Fred to sell off his holdings and Milwaukee and expand to Los Angeles. Otto was so excited that when he learned the arrival time of their train, he watched it approach Union Station with binoculars from the Elysian Street Bridge.

Within a short time, Fred had bought a controlling interest in a garment factory downtown, and Dolly had found a charming home on a small hill overlooking Sunset Boulevard. It had an attic right above the master bedroom, and Otto worked nights for two weeks creating a comfortable and secure spot there.

Life went on, just as it had in Milwaukee.

That is until the night of August 22, 1922. Late that night, neighbors reported ominous crashing noises coming from the Oesterreich house. When several gunshots followed these sounds, they called the police.

Officers arriving at the scene found the body of Fred Oesterreich on the living-room floor. He had been shot several times with a .25-caliber revolver.

They could hear knocking and crying coming from the hall closet and opened it to find Dolly inside. She seemed frightened but was unhurt. She told them that she and her husband had come home and surprised a burglar in the house. The intruder shot her husband and then locked her in the closet to prevent her from calling for help. As far as she could tell, the only thing missing seemed to be Fred's diamond-studded watch.

Detectives seem to have sensed from the beginning that there was something a little off about Dolly's story -- not to mention something a little off about Dolly herself -- but without any evidence to show she was involved, Fred's murder went unsolved.

Meanwhile, Dolly had Fred's complicated estate to settle. She needed an attorney and chose Howard Shapiro to sort things out. Their relationship soon went beyond attorney and client, and they became lovers. To show her appreciation for Shapiro's hard work, Dolly presented him with a gift - an expensive diamond-studded wristwatch.

"It had been my dear husband's," she said. This watch was previously presumed stolen, but Dolly claimed that she found it under the couch cushions in the living room a week after the murder but was too distraught to tell the police. An attorney who sleeps with his clients doesn't have many rules, so Shapiro started wearing the watch.

As you might imagine, this was a bad idea.

Dolly put her home up for sale -- too many bad memories and all that -- and bought a smaller one on Beachwood Drive. It had a lovely attic, which made Otto happy, and he soon moved into it.

One day, Dolly gave a large envelope to another of her gentlemen friends, an actor named Ray Bellows. When he looked inside, he saw that it contained a .25-caliber revolver. Dolly explained that she kept the gun for self-protection, but since "dear Fred" was killed with a similar weapon, it might be awkward if the police found it in her possession. She asked him to get rid of it for her.

Bellows asked no questions and obediently dropped the weapon into the La Brea tar pits, where he thought it could never be found.

Dolly had gotten away with everything - or so she thought at the time.


Chief of Detectives for the LAPD, Herman Cline, had never forgotten about Dolly Oesterreich. He felt in his bones that she had something to do with her husband's murder, but he couldn't prove it. He kept the case open, even as it became colder and colder over the following year.

There were little things that ate at him. For one, there was the gap between the floor and the bottom of the closet door, in which Dolly had been locked. The gap was wide enough to accommodate a large key easily -- like the one found several feet in front of the locked door when the cops arrived. He theorized that Dolly had shot her husband, locked herself in the closet, and then skid the key across the floor. Cline was sure she'd done it for the money. He'd found out that Fred's estate was worth more than $1 million.

Cline thought it was a simple motive, never realizing just how complicated it would turn out to be.

Cline took a trip to Milwaukee to snoop around on his own dime, where he found several witnesses who recalled that Fred and Dolly argued and bickered constantly and had a terrible marriage.

He still didn't have enough to make an arrest - but he soon would.

About a year after the murder, Cline bumped into Dolly's lawyer, Herman Shapiro. He noticed Shapiro's wristwatch and asked him about it. Shapiro stated that Dolly had given it to him, repeating Dolly's story about finding the watch in the couch cushions. Cline didn't say much, but he filed the information away.

A few weeks later, it came back up when Ray Bellow decided to talk to the police about the gun. He and Dolly had quarreled and broke things off. Now he felt obliged to tell the police about the weapon he had tossed into the tar pits. The police carefully searched the edge of the tar pits and, by incredible chance, found the envelope with the gun inside. It had landed just a few inches short of the pits. The gun was rusted by recognizable.

Detective Cline went straight to the house on Beachwood Drive and arrested Dolly for murder. Even so, he still didn't have the whole story. That wouldn't be revealed until Dolly demanded to see her lawyer a few days later. When Herman Shapiro arrived, she begged him to go to the bedroom closet of her home, find the trap door in the ceiling that led to the attic, and knock softly three times.

She tearfully claimed that her mentally challenged half-brother was hiding there, and without groceries, he would starve. Shapiro was supposed to tell him that she had to go away on a business trip, but she would see him soon.

Shapiro, confused, did as he was asked. When he rapped on the trap door, Otto's thin face emerged. When he heard Dolly's message, Otto sighed and commented, "It's too bad that she has been so upset over something that I did."

Otto, desperate for a conversation with someone other than Dolly, prodded Shapiro with questions. The attorney eventually admitted that Dolly was in jail. Otto wept, telling the attorney that she was only there because she had been protecting him.

Once he started talking, Otto couldn't stop.

While Shapiro sat in astonished silence on the floor of Dolly's closet, staring up at the man who had lived in six different attics, Otto poured out the details of his 20 secret years with Dolly, including what happened on the night of Fred's death.

The Oesterreichs had come home drunk and, as usual, arguing violently. This time, though, it seemed worse than expected. Otto feared for his lover's safety and decided he'd had enough of Fred Oesterreich. While still upstairs, he heard a crash and then a thump as Dolly hit the polished wood of the living room floor. In fact, she had merely slipped on a throw rug, but Otto didn't know that. He assumed that Fred had knocked her down. He grabbed Dolly's gun and rushed into the living room with this belief. Like a hero straight out of his adventure stories, he confronted Fred, "Unhand this lovely woman!" Otto cried.

Unimpressed by Otto's gift for dramatic dialogue, Fred lunged at him. Otto panicked and, without thinking, shot him in the chest.

Otto and Dolly realized their only hope was to make the murder look like a robbery. Dolly took Fred's watch and hid it in some couch cushions. Then, she locked herself in the closet and shoved the key through the crack underneath the door while Otto fled the house.

Shapiro was fascinated - and out of his depth. He was a civil attorney and realized that this case needed an expert. He helped Dolly hire Frank Dominguez, one of the best criminal lawyers in the city. Shapiro told Dominguez to go to Dolly's house and tell the guy hiding in her attic to get out of town - fast.

Once again, Otto did as he was told. He left town, changed his name to "Walter Klein," and eventually settled in Vancouver. Dominguez then went to the district attorney and demanded Dolly's release. He claimed that with no witnesses, no confession, and a weapon that was too corroded to be traced to the murder, there was no case against his client.

Dolly was released from jail. She settled into a life without Otto but with the money from Fred's substantial estate to ease the pain.

Otto married and eventually returned to Los Angeles. He got a job as a night janitor in an apartment house, which suited him. After spending all those years in an attic, he had a distaste for being out in the daylight. He and Dolly had parted ways, and their story seemed to be over.

But with a story like this, could it really end so easily?

In 1930, Dolly and Herman Shapiro had a falling out. He had learned, among other things, that she was cheating on him with her business manager, Ray Hedrick. Angry, the attorney wanted revenge.

One day, he walked into the district attorney's office and filed a complaint against Dolly for threatening his life. Because of that, he wanted to file a formal affidavit about the death of her husband. He told everything he knew about Dolly, which was plenty, and she and Otto were both indicted for murder when he finally finished.

Not content with having informed on his old flame, Shapiro also filed a lawsuit against Dolly, alleging that she had violated an agreement to assign some of her insurance claims to him. Ray Hedrick's wife, Geneva, brought her own legal charges against Dolly for alienation of affections.

In front of a grand jury, Dolly denied everything but was nevertheless indicted for murder. Her defender was Jerry Geisler, who managed to get separate trials for Dolly and Otto.

Otto told the grand jury the same story he gave Shapiro years before. Perhaps he felt nostalgic for his attic and figured a closed-in jail cell would be the next best thing.

He rambled on about being Dolly's love slave, threatening him with punishment if he didn't make love to her. When he was too tired or too sick to have sex, she starved him until he agreed to do so. In addition to sex, he also cleaned the house, cooked, and did Fred and Dolly's laundry. He spoke in a quiet, sobbing voice, and jurors strained to hear every juicy detail.

He was charged with murder, which had no statute of limitations, and went on trial first. His lawyer persuaded him to retract his confession, so the only evidence against him put before the jury was Shapiro's account of the murder. The defense could scornfully dismiss this account as a fantasy invented by Dolly's disgruntled ex-boyfriend.

Even so, Otto was found guilty of manslaughter. This left everyone with an interesting legal problem on their hands. Fred had been shot eight years before Otto went on trial. The statute of limitations for manslaughter ran out after three. Thanks to the delay, Otto had to be released.

Once he was out of jail, he disappeared for good. There are no records of what happened to him next. With any luck, he found a comfortable attic and spent the rest of his days there.

The district attorney had been unable to build a case against Dolly for murder, so she had been indicted for conspiracy instead. The defense presented by Jerry Geisler was simple: Otto was to blame for everything. After Fred's death, she had not come forward with the truth because explaining her unconventional private life might have been embarrassing.

Dolly Oesterreich was just too much for the jury. They found themselves unable to reach a verdict. The district attorney, hoping new evidence might someday come to light, kept the case against her open for six more years until he finally gave up and dropped the charges.

Dolly lived uncharacteristically quietly in Los Angeles until she died in 1961. She had married Ray Hedrick just two weeks before her death, leaving him with what was reported to be Dolly's multi-million-dollar estate.

The story of the "Ghost in the Attic" had finally ended, but what lesson it can teach us is anyone's guess. An old radio show used to assure us that "crime doesn't pay," but, in this case, it certainly did.

# "THE MURDERED DUTCHMAN" AUGUSTA NACK

On the hot and sticky New York City afternoon of June 26, 1897, a handful of boys were swimming in the East River just south of an abandoned dock at the foot of East Eleventh Street.

Two of the boys, Jimmy McKenna, 13, and Jack McGuire, 14, saw a bundle of some kind in the water a short distance away. They couldn't tell what it was, but it looked like a bundle of some sort of merchandise, perhaps carefully wrapped by one of the fine downtown stores. The two boys swam eagerly toward what they thought would be a prize and snagged the package. Its bright covering turned out to be oilcloth, carefully tired with good, strong twine.

One of their compatriots offered a knife when they got to shore, and the string was cut. Jack McGuire pushed the blade into the oilcloth and tried to cut the package open. The blade became stuck, and he struggled to remove it.

As he did, he caught a glimpse of something white inside - and then the package began to bleed.

The oilcloth was torn away, revealing another layer beneath of dirty burlap. Jack kept cutting and found another later of dry, coarse brown paper. He yanked it away, and then the gathered boys froze for a moment.

In the package were two human arms attached to a muscular torso.

When the police arrived about 30 minutes later, they had to fetch the bundle out of the river again - the boys had thrown it into the water in disgust - and officers put in a call to the coroner's office to let them know that medical students were up to their usual pranks. The city had five medical schools that were allowed to use cadavers, and parts of them showed up in the unlikeliest of places, much to the delight of the medical student pranksters.

But these body parts didn't turn out to be part of a prank.

When the morgue driver arrived, the police officers got a better look at the remains. The head had been severed cleanly from the neck, almost on a line with the shoulders. It was so clean that it was no surprise that officers believed the work had been done by an expert, or student, who was used to amputation instruments.

The work of removing the legs had not been as carefully accomplished. They had been severed from the trunk just below the abdomen, leaving marks that looked like the legs had been hacked away.

The chest had been marked and scarred peculiarly. The flesh had been lifted from the bones just below the left breast and cut off cleanly all the way across the chest to a point almost on a line with the shoulder. The cut was even and laid open to expose several of the ribs. To the untrained eye, this seemed to suggest again that the corpse had come from a dissecting table.

A story that appeared in the *New York Telegram* suggested that the trunk belonged to a man in his prime of life, weighing 180 pounds and having big and powerful arms. The flesh was clear and white, indicating a man in good health. The hands were small, though, and the fingers smooth, suggesting they were not the hands of a man who did manual labor.

A small blue mark was found on the man's left palm. It looked like it was a burn, not a tattoo mark, for there were no regular formations to it.

The oilcloth that had been wrapped around the body was new and had never been used. The twine was white and very heavy. The paper on the inside of the package was heavier than normal, and it was suggested that it was a type used in hospitals, which strengthened the theory that medical students had been at work.

But not everyone agreed. It was also suggested that the removal of the legs and the flesh on the chest had been carried out to destroy tattoo marks or other marks that might help the police identify the body.

With these questions swirling, the arms and torso were taken to the morgue.

By the time Bellevue superintendent Dr. Thomas Murphy and medical examiner Dr. George Dow arrived at the morgue, there were already reports from the afternoon papers - the *Evening World, Evening Journal,* and *Evening Sun* - waiting for information about the remains. The Telegram had beaten all of them to the punch since a reporter happened to be nearby when the body was discovered in the East River. It was a time of frantic competition between the New York dailies, and the other papers had a lot of catching up to do.

Dr. Murphy closely examined the package, muttering to his colleague, "There is a mystery here."

Dr. Dow nodded. He felt the skin's texture and lifted an arm to examine where the flesh had been excised from the chest. A reporter had noted that the cut at the neck had looked clean, but Dow disagreed. "No medical student would have done this," he announced. It was no medical school cadaver. This man had met with foul play.

And he had one more announcement for the startled room of reporters, "The man of which this formed a part was alive 24 hours ago."

When the "ghastly find" at the East River's docks appeared in the newspapers, it caused a sensation in the city. There had been many murders in New York before, but this one got everyone's attention for one simple reason - the newspapers turned it into the "murder of the century." Fighting was fierce among the city's various newspapers, and it had been a slow news week. This meant that reporters were looking for something sensational, and now they had it.

Both the *World* and the *Herald* were skeptical about the likelihood of the police finding whoever wrapped and dumped the body. "The finding of the upper portion of the headless trunk of a man in the East River yesterday furnishes a mystery that will not easily be solved," the *World* reported and added, "All indications point to an atrocious murder. There is, however, no apparent clue by which the identity of the victim may be discovered, or his slayer brought to justice."

The *Herald* reported, "There is nothing to tell when or where the crime was committed, whether on land or on sea, and there is not one chance in a million that the identity of the victim will be discovered." A few people had surmised the body had been dumped at sea, but if it had, the police said, the dead man could not have been a sailor because there were no calluses on his hands.

The *Journal* added its own thoughts, but they were usually just to disagree with anything printed in the *World*, a paper that Charles Pulitzer had purchased in 1883. The *World* overshadowed all its competitors until a newcomer, William Randolph Hearst, began challenging Pulitzer with the *Journal* in 1895. Hearst was trying to take over Pulitzer's grip on the evening news by imitating all the older man's tricks to stay on top - and then some. By 1897, despite retaliation by Pulitzer, Hearst was gaining ground, and the feud between the two men actually affected crime in the city - or at least the solving of crimes.

When a *World* or *Journal* reporter found a valuable clue at a crime scene, he would grab it and bring it back to his newspaper. If reporters had reached the dock before the police that day, the officers at the scene would have attached no significance to the chunk of flesh missing from the dead man's chest. They would have assumed that a reporter had carried it away.

Reporters from the World and the Journal developed their own leads, paying more money to informants than the police did. Then they would follow the leads, "arresting" suspects -- if they didn't appear too dangerous -- and extort confessions from them. And they'd publish these confessions as "scoops."

This practice occasionally became awkward when it turned out that a reporter abducted an innocent party, but there weren't many mistakes that a few bucks couldn't square. Neither paper begrudged coughing up some cash to cover excessive zeal. In making "arrests," the reporters usually represented themselves as detectives, who had badges and pistol permits. However, when printing the story, their papers always said they had "made the arrest as citizens."

It should be no surprise that some reporters became better detectives than the real thing, so the NYPD would put tails on the leading newspapermen when a big case broke. Naturally, there were exchanges of information between friends in the two professions, by which cops helped reporters to discredit rival reporters and reporters helped cops to discredit rival cops.

It was in this climate that the murder of the unknown man had occurred and would eventually be solved - to the shock of the readers who were glued to every twist and turn of the story.

On Sunday, June 27, a second parcel was found, wrapped in oilcloth, on the Bronx side of the Harlem River - roughly 10 miles from where the other had shown up.

Two boys who were out berry-picking with their father had stumbled across it. It had been apparently tossed from Undercliff Avenue, a winding carriage drive on the side of a hill.

When the parcel was opened at the High Bridge police station in the Bronx, it had yielded another section of a corpse. The captain there had dispatched it to the morgue to be matched up with the East River section.

"If the pieces fit, it's the same stiff," the man on the desk said. "If it's part of a different stiff, then the guy with the red oilcloth has murdered them both."

Reporters rushed to the morgue to discover that the two fragments of the body matched as neatly as a jigsaw puzzle. The section from the Bronx included everything from the abdomen to a point above the knees where the saw or knife had been used again to detach the legs. The legs hadn't turned up yet.

By that evening, the body was claimed for the first time. Clara Magnusson arrived at the morgue to state that the body might belong to her brother-in-law, a 34-year-old Danish scrap metal dealer named Max Weineke. He had been missing for more than a month. But when Clara looked the body over, she realized that it wasn't him. The dead man had a scar on his left hand that she didn't recognize.

The mystery continued.

The police made efforts to trace a red and gold pattern that was found on the oilcloth in which the body parts had been wrapped. Medical men weighed in with theories about the murder and the body's condition, suggesting that some of the discolorations were caused by bruises, perhaps from a beating.

Andrew L. Drummond, a 22-year veteran of the Secret Service that now ran a detective agency in the city, suggested that the killer was a Spaniard or a Cuban. It should be noted that the United States was then on the brink of war with Spain over their treatment of the Cuban people. He suggested the dead man had been killed for revenge, "for some wrong to his wife or sweetheart. Then, in an unguarded moment, the man was killed, and his body cut up for disposal by one or several men."

Drummond's theories were more fodder for the papers, which also drew comparisons between the murder and the work of Jack the Ripper, hinted at cannibalism, told people to be on the lookout for a deranged butcher or carpenter, and encouraged people to look for the dead man's missing head.

More than anything, though, the editors railed against the police and their inability to solve the crime - or at least the man's identity. The *Evening Sun* took a thoroughly dim view of the case and assailed the police. "Indications in Mulberry Street this morning pointed to the conclusion that the police had not yet waked up to the serious import of the case," it grumbled.

In addition to searching for the missing head, Pulitzer's *World* trumpeted a new idea: "The *World* will pay $500 in gold for the correct solution of the mystery concerning the fragments of a man's body discovered Saturday and Sunday in the East River and in Harlem," an announcement read. "All theories and suggestions must be sent to the City Editor of the *World*, in envelopes marked 'Murder Mystery,' and must be exclusively for the World. Appearance of the solution in any other paper will cancel this offer of reward."

Hearst refused to be outdone. As soon as the World hit the streets, the Journal published an "extra" issue that offered a $1,000 reward for "clews, theories, or suggestions that will solve the unique murder mystery of the East River."

More misidentifications of the dead man followed, and then the *World* decided to include the opinions of the "two most famous palmists in America." Both papers had already been plastering close-up details of the dead man's hands on their front pages, hoping someone might recognize them, and now the *World* was taking things a step further. "Queen Stella" and "Cheiro" - the two palm readers - analyzed the photographs of the palms, noting that he had a "tragic hand" and "business capacity in a higher degree." It was also noted that "through his domineering disposition and rashness in speech he must have made one or more deadly enemies."

The part about "enemies" and "tragedy" seem a bit obvious since the hands belonged to a murdered man, but editors and the public ate it up.

The analysis from the palmists marked the beginning of the World covering the occult aspects of the case, which included appeals to another palm reader (a man who was smuggled into the morgue), a phrenologist (slightly handicapped by the absence of the head), a clairvoyant, a physiognomist who could glean information from faces (working from a photograph of the supposed victim after his identity became fairly certain), a handwriting expert, and, finally, a spirit medium.

None of the paranormal approaches to solving the murder led anywhere, and neither did the contests to solve the crime for $500 or $1,000. Letters by armchair detectives printed in the newspapers make for interesting reading, even more than a century later.

They wouldn't lead to the crime being solved, but something else would - a bar of soap.

Ned Brown was a young reporter for the World when he got involved in the murder case. Like most reporters of the time, Ned did his own sleuthing, but he was too young and too inexperienced to be trailed by police detectives, hoping he stumbled across a clue.

When he visited the morgue on the day the first part of the body had been discovered, he felt that there was something familiar about the hands of the corpse. He was sure that he'd seen how they looked somewhere before. After some thought, he realized the muscled arms and soft fingers could be found in one place - among the muscled masseurs of the city's Turkish baths. The baths were where revelers would go after a long night of hard drinking in Midtown. With rooms heated to 120 degrees, they were thought to not only evaporate the alcohol but also cure all kinds of other ailments.

Ned had been known to work off a few shots at the Murray Hill Baths, a Times Square establishment with a steam bath, massage room, and long swimming pool. It billed itself as the "Most Handsome and Perfect Baths in the World," but locals had another name for it - "The House of a Thousand Hangovers."

Ned dropped in, and after signing up for a steam bath and massage, he asked one of the attendants if any of the masseurs had slacked off and not shown up for work that week.

"That would be Bill," one of them told him. "He took Friday off because he was going to look at a house in the country with his girl, or so he said. Guldensuppe is his name."

The attendant added that Guldensuppe hadn't been seen since then but that someone had called in sick for him on Sunday. The other attendants all assumed that he was off getting drunk somewhere."

When Ned asked what he looked like, the attendant told him he was "built like a big Dutchman. He has the upper half of a woman tattooed all over his chest." The man had been a sailor when he was younger. He lived somewhere around Thirty-Third and Ninth Avenue, a German and Irish neighborhood of low brick tenement houses.

Ned hit the pavement and talked to bartenders throughout the neighborhood, explaining that he was looking for an old pal. A saloon cook finally sent him to an apartment over Werner's drugstore, where Bill was living with the landlady.

Ned now had to figure out how to get into the apartment. Thinking fast, he managed to get $10 from his editor to buy a suitcase filled with expensive 25-cent soaps. He then started making his way around the neighborhood, posing as a salesman with a 5-cent trial offer. The women he spoke with knew good sandalwood and verbena soap when they smelled it, and at such a cheap price, they didn't care if it was a trial offer or stolen. Word made it around the neighborhood in a hurry, and Ned had no problem unloading the bars of soap. But it wasn't money he was after. He wanted the word to get around about the soap, which would make it easier to sell it to the women above the drugstore. He took a short break in a nearby tavern, letting the gossip travel faster, and then he went directly to No. 439, the apartment over Werner's.

Ned climbed the stairs and rang the bell at the door. In the center of it was a brass nameplate that read:

## AUGUSTA NACK
## LICENSED MIDWIFE

He knocked and heard a faint commotion inside. The door opened to reveal the midwife herself, a dark-haired woman in her late thirties. She was heavy, with a broad, flat face, pale skin, and small eyes. She was wearing an apron over her dress, and there was a smell of cooking sauerkraut in the air. Its memory would leave Ned with a distaste for the stuff for the rest of his life.

Ned started his spiel about the soap, but she interrupted him. "You didn't give me any!" Augusta said angrily, and Ned understood why she seemed upset. She must have heard from other women about the soap salesman in the neighborhood and had felt slighted that he hadn't visited her.

"I would have sworn I'd been to every flat in the house," Ned said. "But guess I wasn't, or I would have remembered you sure."

Augusta sneered at him. "Give me the soap now."

"I'm sorry, Madam, but I'm afraid I can't," Ned said. "You see, I have to get a report for my company on what each lady thought of the soap. That was the purpose of our special offer."

"Leave it and come back tomorrow," She commanded in her thick German accent.

"I'm sorry, Ma'am, but I can't do that either," Ned said. "Tomorrow I'll be working up in Yonkers." Then he tried to look as if he had just had a bright thought and said, "But happen to have a couple of bars left over. If you could give the soap a trial now while I wait, I'd be glad to let you have one."

She considered this for a moment. "All right," she grumbled, "give me the soap."

Ned took a step toward her, fumbling in a pocket and being careful not to give her the soap until he was inside the apartment. He knew she wouldn't shut the door in his face before he gave her the sample. She took a step back, and Ned moved forward into the space. He handed her the bar of soap, and she sniffed it.

Ned continued, "I've actually got two left and since I'm putting you to all this trouble, I'm going to let you have both of them, if you like the first one. But I get awfully thirsty, climbing stairs all day in this heat, and I wonder if I might ask you for a glass of water before you start washing your hands."

Augusta grudgingly agreed and directed him to sit down in a black upholstered chair. He looked around while she went into the kitchen for some water.

Within a few days, the newspapers were going to describe the contents of Augusta Nack's apartment in much more detail than

Ned was able to during that visit, but his eyes were drawn to one item that subsequent reporters were never going to see.

Ned later wrote, "Leaning against a lamp, on a kind of a knickknack stand, there was a studio photograph of a big blond guy with little turned-up mustaches under his nose–a kind of Dutch version of a sport. The minute I saw it, I was sure I had seen him around, without ever knowing his name."

Augusta brought him a glass of water, and he gulped it down thirstily. He then sent her off to wash her hands, suggesting that she take the time to soak her hands in the lather for the full effect. When he heard the water running in the rear of the apartment, he snatched the photograph of the blond man from the table and shoved it into his jacket.

He wanted to run but knew it would look suspicious if he did. Instead, he waited for Augusta to return. When she did, she handed him a dime for both bars. She liked the soap but did not want to be quoted for any ads. She planned to return to Germany soon, she said.

She didn't notice that the photograph was missing.

Ned concluded his "business" and hurried out the door. He stopped when he saw an angry-looking man coming up the narrow stairs in his direction. This man was smaller than the missing man - whom Ned assumed was Bill Guldensuppe - and this man had a brown mustache. His eyes were deep-set and glaring, and he seemed furious to see Ned standing at the doorway to the apartment. He grabbed Ned by the shoulder and twisted him around in front of Augusta Nack, who was still in the doorway. He demanded in German to know who Ned was and then berated her for answering the door. He said he'd told her not to let anyone in.

Augusta began to explain who Ned was, adding that if the man didn't stop making noises, the neighbors would come to see what was the matter. Finally, he pushed Ned toward the stairs and slammed the door. More shouting followed, and then Ned heard a slap.

He later recalled, "I ran down the stairs and kept going. From the way those two had acted, I was sure that I had the right man's picture and that they were the ones who had killed him."

With a photograph that he believed was Guldensuppe in his jacket and the glare of the other man still in his memory, Ned returned to work at the *World* the following morning. He was dead certain that he had the solution to the mystery. The only problem turned out to be - the paper couldn't tell anyone.

Not yet anyway.

The city desk vetoed the idea of going straight to No. 439 Ninth Avenue and "arresting" Augusta Nack and the man with the mustache before the torso had been positively identified as Guldensuppe. It would have been easy to visit the Murray Hill Baths, collect a couple of the big Dutchman's colleagues, and take them to the morgue, but this would have been hard to keep quiet from the competition.

The following night, one of the paper's senior reporters, Gus Roeder, got in touch with a Murray Hill masseur that was off duty, Joseph Kavanagh, and took him to the morgue. This resulted in a brief story on the second page of the *World* that said, "Dead man said to be William Guldensupper, a Turkish bath attendant." The story went on to say that police detectives had confirmed this while acting on the information provided by one of the man's co-workers. At the Murray Hill baths, someone had informed the police that Gildensupper - the name was spelled a half dozen different ways in the newspapers when the story first broke - had not worked there for three months.

On July 1, the World broke the story, taking credit for the dead man's identification, which it had printed with little fanfare and less conviction. The original lack of enthusiasm was because on Tuesday night when Roeder was taking Kavanagh to the morgue, another identification had come out that was more plausible because it was a cabinetmaker named Theodore Cyklam with an injury on his left hand just like the one the corpse had. The factory's superintendent where Cyklam worked saw the scarred finger and was convinced that it was Cyklam or part of him at least. It turned out that he was wrong.

The *World* was not.

The *New York Herald*, though, had their own scoop on Wednesday. They didn't have the murdered man's name, but they did have a tip from a cop at the Mulberry Street station. In a column on the front page, it was printed:

**MURDERED BY JEALOUS HUSBAND**

"It was reported early this morning that the victim of the murder had been identified . . . and suspicion pointed to a jealous husband," the text below the small headline read. "It was said that the man was a shampooer in an uptown Turkish bathhouse, who has been missing for a few days. This man, it is said, had been living with a baker's wife."

Augusta Nack's husband, Herman, was, in fact, the driver of a bakery delivery wagon, but he had not particularly resented it when his wife left him. After the identification of Guldensuppe, he considered himself very lucky to be all in one piece.

He was, however, hunted like a criminal for at least one day.

It would be reporters from the *Journal* who recklessly pursued Herman Nack. The *Journal* - by its own account - had singlehandedly solved the mystery. Its reporters had identified the body, interviewed Augusta Nack, and had informed the police of the developments in the case. Why had the paper not reported it sooner? The editors didn't want to get into the many reasons. Still, on Wednesday, they turned the front page over to an idealized image of Augusta Nack's head with a caption that papers now would consider reckless disregard of the law of libel -- "Mrs. Nack, Murderess!"

After looking for Herman Nack's bakery wagon all night, Journal reporters finally found him at 11:15 in the morning at the corner of Fortieth Street and Ninth Avenue.

"Mr. Nack?" one of the reporters called out. Nack was in the driver's seat, and the two Journals reporters tried to climb up the steps.

"What do you want?" Nack replied.

When he was told the police wanted to see him, Nack pushed the two men off the steps, whipped his horses, and drove off down Ninth Avenue.

The two reporters were in hot pursuit on bicycles, calling for him to stop. They flew down the street, toward the Garfield Drug Company on Thirty-Fourth, where a patrol officer was waiting for a soda to take the edge off the heat. He saw one of the reporters attempt to jump onto the wagon and then saw Nack hit the man with his whip. The officer joined the chase just as the other reporter jumped onto the wagon and tried to wrest control of the vehicle from Nack.

Finally, the policeman caught up with the wild trio and halted the wagon. Nack struggled as they forced him onto the group, and the policeman snapped handcuffs onto his wrists. The patrolman made the collar - not the Heart reporters who had been attempting to make a citizen's arrest.

Herman Nack was taken in on suspicion of murder - a murder he soon proved he didn't commit.

But first, he had to be questioned. He admitted that he was married to Augusta Nack -- or had been. They were still married on paper because they'd never divorced but no longer lived together.

He also knew William Guldensuppe. Bill had been their boarder, and Augusta ran off with the man when their marriage fell apart. He hadn't seen the man in months.

Nack carefully detailed his alibi at the time of the murder, and it was verified by the owner of the Astoria Model Bakery. He'd work all day and that night, led all the customers of Strack's saloon in belting out an entire set of drinking songs.

Detectives knew Herman Nack wasn't their man. But they already had another suspect in mind. Detectives were already at the apartment of his wife, Augusta. They had arrived just in time to stop her from boarding the next steamer for Hamburg, Germany. She was quickly arrested and taken to Mulberry Street.

Placed in Captain Stephen O'Brien's office, the midwife looked more like a wronged woman than a suspect in a murder case. She was 38 years old and a German immigrant who had been living with William Guldensuppe for 16 months.

She had married Herman Nack in 1883 in Germany. Together, they came to the United States, where Herman had failed at several jobs - pottery workers, bologna store proprietor, and grocer - because of his drinking. He had left her, their children were dead, and now she worked as a midwife and occasionally took in boarders, one of whom had been Guldensuppe.

The last time she had seen him had been the previous Friday when they had argued about money. She had withdrawn some funds from her bank and had given them to him. After that, he went out, and she had not seen him since. After he had not returned by Monday, she decided to go to Germany to see her mother, who was sick.

She did not believe that he was dead because she had received telegrams from him - one on Sunday and one on Tuesday, asking her to send him his clothes. She had refused. Finally, a "disreputable man" showed up at her door, asking for the clothing, and she put them in a brown valise and handed over his belongings. "That was the last I heard of him," she said.

After her statement, Captain O'Brien motioned to a woman who had been hidden just outside of his office door. Her name was Pauline Riger, and she owned a dry goods store in Astoria. She had been listening and identified Augusta as the woman who had bought an oilcloth that matched the material wrapped around the severed pieces of William Guldensuppe. "I am sure of her," she added.

When confronted with her connection to the murder, Augusta maintained that it was impossible. She was not a killer, and William was still alive.

While Augusta protested her guilt, Captain O'Brien received word that new evidence had arrived at headquarters. It had been fished out of the Brooklyn Navy Yard.

O'Brien ushered Mrs. Nack to the door, where two severed human legs were in the middle of the hallway. They had been sawn halfway through and then snapped off.

"Do you know these?" he asked the woman.

The legs looked hideous. They had been rotting in the river for five days and were still nestled in a bundle of oilcloth. O'Brien waited for the woman to dry out or break down, but the midwife merely turned to him with a blank expression on her face.

"How should I know?" she asked him.


While Augusta remained at police headquarters, unwilling to talk, the police picked through her apartment. Detectives opened and rifled through the boxes she had packed to return to Germany. They were searching for clues, but it was not an easy job. She'd been busy washing down the apartment before the move. Was it in hopes of getting her deposit back, or was she washing away evidence?

Amid the cases of crockery and clothing were photographic albums, letters, and telegrams. All of it was seized as evidence, whether it had a story to tell or not.

In the neighboring tenements and stores, resourceful reporters conducted their own searches and found plenty of stories. Into almost every story crept the name of a third man -

known only as "Fred." He had been seen around the neighborhood and had once rented a carriage on Augusta's behalf. He was shorter, moodier, and darker than William Guldensuppe and had also been a boarder with Mrs. Nack for a time. She had been friendly with both boarders until last February when Guldensuppe had beaten his rival so severely that he had moved out.

But "Fred" had been seen recently. Had he come back? And if so, why? The detectives in Augusta's kitchen thought they had the answer to that question. One of them reached into a hiding spot in a cupboard, and his hand emerged holding a butcher's knife, a broken saw, and a revolver.

When held up to the light, they appeared to be coated with a spray of blood.


The newspapers had already identified Augusta as "Mrs. Nack, Murderess!" but real evidence was starting to stack up against her. A telegram that she claimed was sent to her by Guldensuppe had his name misspelled - it had been signed by hand. Detectives looked through her bank accounts and found no sign of the money she claimed to have withdrawn for him. But then it turned up - hidden in her corset. A jail matron found it there during a search.

Captain O'Brien met with reporters, pleased to have the likely murder weapons on his desk, a dozen identifications of the body, and a prime suspect behind bars.

"Do you believe Mrs. Nack killed the man whose body is now in the morgue?" one reporter asked him.

"If that body belongs to William Guldensuppe, I believe she did, or is implicated," O'Brien replied. "She has a temper - an awful temper, I believe." He hesitated to offer any specifics about her capacity for violence. Still, he didn't need to - it had already been in the papers that Herman Nack claimed his wife had repeatedly threatened to kill him.

"She is strong enough?" another writer asked.

"Oh my, yes," O'Brien chuckled. "She has arms larger and more muscular than mine."

But Augusta Nack, as violent as she may have been, didn't act alone when she took the life of William Guldensuppe. Over the next few days, it became clear to reporters that "Fred" was not Augusta's former husband, but a man named Martin Thorn.

"Thorn" was the Americanized version of the man's real name, "Torzewski." He had been born in German Poland and worked as a journeyman barber, a silent, moody man who, like Guldensuppe, lived off women who would support his carefree life. For years, he had hired furnished rooms from women. If he learned that his landlady had money, he would make advances to her. He had a particular fondness for widows, and he even went so far as to advertise in German-language newspapers for them. Augusta Nack had started listing herself in the city directory as a widow - a claim that would have been news to Herman Nack - so she probably looked perfect to Nack. There was just one thing in his way - her lover, Guldensuppe. Eventually, the larger man had driven away his rival, but Thorn would come back to see Augusta on days when the masseur was at work.

Soon, every policeman - and every reporter - in town was looking for Thorn. He was nowhere to be found. Rumor was that he had safely gotten away on a ship to Germany, but he was actually living in a cheap hotel with money that he'd gotten after pawning Guldensuppe's watch and clothing.

Detectives tracked down one of Thorn's old co-workers, Constantine Keehn, who related the story Thorn had told him about the confrontation he'd had with Guldensuppe. He said Thorn had tried to shoot the other man, but his pistol didn't fire. He ended up with a smashed nose and blackened eyes and vowed to Keehn that he would use a pistol the next time around. The barber repeated what Thorn told him to the detectives, "I'll catch him sometime when he isn't expecting me, and then I'll fix him."

Thorn had "fixed" Guldensuppe, but where had the murder been committed?

It would be the newspapers that would alert the authorities to the place where the bloody murder of William Guldensuppe had taken place.

And they did it by accident.

It happened because Augusta's picture was plastered onto the front page of every newspaper in the city. It was hard to miss, and a woman in Woodside, Long Island, didn't miss it. She identified Augusta Nack as a stout woman who, with a male companion, had rented a house from her in what was then a sparsely settled neighborhood. Her companion matched the description of Thorn. The house had outside drains, which leaked, and the neighbors' children now recalled that the pipes had run "red water" for two days. A farmer's ducks had drunk some of that water and became sick.

Four Manhattan detectives and a reporter from the World - who'd finally gotten the jump on the Hearst men - took a trolley to Woodside, a sleepy community of lonesome farmhouses and overgrown swampy lots. There was a general store that sold hay and groceries, and the only entertainment in town was a bowling alley. The local police captain led them to the rental house in question at 346 Second Street.

The street held little more than a dairy, a flower nursery, and three new, cheap wood-frame two-story houses. It seemed a remote place, but it was actually just one block from the New York and Queens County trolley line. A couple of blocks in the other direction was Jackson Avenue, a straight shot down to the East River ferries. It was an excellent place to get in and out of quickly if you were coming from the city.

As the men walked up to them, a scowling woman stepped out of No. 344 and introduced herself as Mrs. Hafftner. She was the caretaker for the three houses. The owners, Bualas, ran a wine shop in the city.

And yes, someone had rented No. 346 lately - a couple from the city who gave their name as "Mr. and Mrs. Frank Braun." She identified a photograph of Augusta Nack as "Mrs. Braun."

The couple had signed a one-year lease, but they'd disappeared after coming to the house just a few times.

She unlocked the door to No. 346, and the detectives went inside. It was a dreary place. The walls of the seven vacant rooms were coated in brown paint and only a small amount of light leaked through the windows.

Someone had been there recently, they knew. In the ashes of the stove were the remains of a man's shoe. Only the steel shank was left. A scorching fire had consumed the leather.

On the southeast side of the upstairs was the bathroom. It contained a large zinc tub, but it was spotless and clean - perhaps too clean. There was no dust on the floor. Kneeling down, a detective found a spatter of dark spots between the tub and the wall and some hard-scrubbed sections of flooring around them. Something had soaked into the wood that had been nearly impossible to clean. Using a borrowed carpenter's plane, they shaved samples from the floor that they would send to the Loomis Laboratory at New York University for analysis. One of the detectives followed the drain line to a ditch outside and scooped up a bucket of mud at the mouth of the pipe. It would be sent to the lab, too. Advanced forensic detection was decades into the future, but they would at least be able to tell if the substance collected was blood.

A crowd gathered outside as the men dug in the cellar and probed a cesspool searching for Guldensuppe's still missing head. Word had spread, even as far as back to the city, which sent reporters from other papers scrambling for trolleys and ferries.

Reporters questioned the onlookers. Why yes, they had heard a strange cry last Friday night, some said, something like "Help! Help! Murder!" One of them had even looked outside to investigate but hadn't heard anything else.

One of the morbid curious remarked that she had recently seen another man with Mr. and Mrs. Braun at the house. In fact, she added, it had been last Friday. She'd seen two men go inside, but come to think of it, she only remembered one of them coming out.

While detectives were searching what would come to be called the "Den of Murder" in Woodside, other officers - and reporters, of course - were still searching for Martin Thorn.

But Thorn didn't seem to understand the idea of remaining hidden. As if he felt that his revenge against Guldensuppe didn't mean anything if he kept the details to himself, he decided to tell someone what happened. He walked into a barbershop where a man he knew was working and told him the whole story -- swearing him to secrecy, of course.

The other barber, John Gotha, went home in a cold sweat after hearing the story and told his wife, who went straight to the police. Against her husband's wishes - he didn't want to inform on an old friend, he said, but likely feared being Thorn's next target - she told detectives everything.

Detectives coerced Gotha into making a date to meet Thorn at Spear's Drug Store at the corner of 125th Street and Eighth Avenue for 9:00 on the evening of Tuesday, July 6. Inspector O'Brien was there in disguise and a legion of his detectives in various disguises. To judge by subsequent newspaper accounts, each detective was trailed by a reporter. Thorn was waiting, and O'Brien arrested him.

On July 8, the *New York Sun* shocked its readers with the account that Thorn had passed on to Gotha.

Augusta had gotten tired of Guldensuppe, and Thorn hated him, so they decided to get rid of him for good. Looking for a place to commit the crime, they chose the house in Woodside. It was isolated, and no one knew them there.

Guldensuppe - knowing that part of Augusta's work as a midwife involved her providing abortions - had pressured her to find a location where she could operate as a business. When the time came to kill, she told him that she could make even more money with a "baby farm." She would take in illegitimate children and sell them to couples who could not have their own. There were no laws against that sort of thing at the time, but there were laws against abortion. Augusta also told Guldensuppe that she knew of a good spot for the business in Woodside and lured him there to see it.

Thorn was waiting at the house when the couple arrived on that fateful Friday. He had a razor, one of his tools of the trade, in his coat, and he'd purchased a new revolver. On the way to Woodside, he stopped in a hardware store and had also bought a new saw. On a previous visit to the house, he and Augusta had left plaster of Paris, oilcloth, cheesecloth, cord, twine, and other supplies they thought might come in handy.

When Augusta and William arrived, Thorn was hiding in a closet near the second-floor stair landing. He waited there only in his underwear and socks. He had removed his other clothing because he didn't want to get blood on them. He prepared himself when he heard the gate outside click shut - a prearranged signal. Augusta suggested to Guldensuppe that while she went and looked at the outhouse, he should go upstairs and see what he thought about the arrangement of the rooms. She had already seen it, she told him.

William did what she said and marched up the staircase to the second floor. When he peered into the first bedroom off the landing, Thorn opened the closet door behind him and shot him in the back of the neck.

The burly man immediately went down. The shot was fatal.

Once he stopped moving, Thorn dragged him into the bathroom and managed to heave him up over the edge of the tub. He cut Guldensuppe's throat with his razor and then began cutting him apart, severing his head, his arms, and legs from his torso. He hacked away the tattoo on the man's chest, hoping it would make him harder to identify.

The butchery completed, Thorn ran hot water into the tub, washing the blood down the drain, where it seeped outside and made a pool for the ducks.

He then encased the dead man's head in a block of plaster of Paris. He planned to throw it into the river, and he wanted to make sure that it would sink. He wrapped the other pieces in paper and oilcloth, avoiding the time-consuming process of soaking them in plaster. It was a mistake that he admitted later that he regretted.

With Augusta's help, the gruesome bundles were tied into neat bundles and taken aboard a trolley to the Long Island slip of the Greenpoint ferry. Out on the water, the head sank immediately, but when they saw that the parcels containing the legs and the upper torso were floating, they decided to hold on to the one with the lower torso.

The day after the murder, they hired a carriage from an undertaker near Mrs. Nack's apartment and drove to the Bronx, where they got rid of that bundle.

That should have been the end of it. They should never have been caught, Thorn said. He imagined spending the rest of his life with Augusta Nack.

But how long would that life have been if one day she decided she was tired of him, too?

Thorn and Mrs. Nack were indicted for murder by a New York County grand jury on July 9th, but the indictment was found faulty because the crime had been committed in Queens County. They were reindicted there, and trial dates were set.

Very little was happening with the actual case, but the newspapers managed to keep interest high by chronicling the ongoing search for William Guldensuppe's head. Swimmers, fishers, and even deep-sea divers had searched the river along the ferry boat route, but they'd found nothing.

Rumors spread - likely by reporters - that Thorn hadn't dropped the head into the river after all. It was still out there somewhere, just waiting to be found. Rewards were offered, and the hunt was on.

Men and boys searched around the house in Woodside and dug holes all over the yard. They wandered the woods, the alleys, the back streets, checking in garbage cans, old boxes, and empty barrels. The papers kept everyone apprised of the search.

A boy found a plaster-caked head in Branchport, New Jersey, panicked, and threw it into a local stream. Despite scores of news stories about "little Tommy Cooper" and his terrible find, the police couldn't turn it up again. A reporter from the *Herald* found out why - Tommy Cooper wasn't a real person. The story was a hoax.

Three more boys claimed to have seen a head floating by the 117th Street Boathouse, but no one could find it again. Ferry passengers were frightened by a "decomposing mass" in the water, but it turned out to be the head of a dead fish. One day, a janitor from the Upper West Side ran into his local precinct station, screaming that he'd found the head. It turned out to be a medical school's teaching skull.

But when a seven-year-old Woodside girl found an actual chunk of plaster in a ditch, things seemed more promising. The police broke it open and found a head inside - a head of cabbage.

Another Woodside child discovered a brown derby hat with a bullet in it in an area that had been searched at least a dozen times before. Hearst's and Pulitzer's men fell under suspicion for having planted both the hat and the head of cabbage.

Yet, for all their stories and practical jokes, every newspaper seemed to come up empty when it came to finding Guldensuppe's head. And Martin Thorn refused to offer any hints.

He knew that if the man's head wasn't found, then there was a chance the body in the morgue wasn't his. And if he wasn't dead, the Thorn might just get out of this mess alive.

Augusta and Thorn both stood trial. Thorn's attorney was William "Big Bill" Howe, and he was no ordinary lawyer. His office was the best-known in the city and operated 24 hours a day across the street from the Tombs, New York's infamous criminal holding cells. Howe's firm was a cash-up-front operation that served as counsel for the Whyo Gang, the Sheeny Mob, the Valentine Gang, and every pickpocket and safecracker operation in Manhattan. When 78 brothel madams were arrested in a one-night sweep, everyone named Howe as their attorney. He was a 300-pound tornado of indignation who was dressed as loud as his voice, with diamond rings on every finger. Howe had personally defended 650 murder and manslaughter cases in four decades and wasn't accustomed to losing.

"You cannot prove a *corpus delecti* by patchwork," he told anyone who would listen. "And I shall prove the body in the morgue is *not* that of William Guldensuppe!"

During the trial, Howe badgered witnesses, called evidence into question, loudly proclaimed his client's innocence, and constantly shouted that Guldensuppe wasn't even dead.

The newspapers had tried desperately to keep the case alive. Once the trials started in November 1897, they were back in their element, writing about every word, gesture, and facial expression that occurred each day.

Thanks to the rampant publicity, the courthouse had thousands of ticket requests. There were seats for 72 reporters, and space was left for ten telegraph lines.

During the trial, Augusta and Thorn turned on each other. They both said the other was the actual killer, and even the attorneys exchanged sharp words. Howe called Augusta's lawyer, Manny Friend, an "insignificant little imp."

Ultimately, Augusta confessed to the murder, but Thorn did not. Nevertheless, he was found guilty of murder in the first degree and sentenced to death.

Augusta, the woman who had instigated and likely planned it all, was only sentenced to 15 years in prison after pleading guilty to manslaughter to the first degree.

Thorn was sent to Sing Sing, where he waited to die. Finally, on August 1, 1898, he was executed for the murder of William Guldensuppe. He'd made it clear that he was ready to die and sat down in the electric chair on his own, as if, one reporter stated, he was taking breakfast on an ordinary Monday morning.

He prayed with his priest as the guards placed sponges soaked in salt water against his calves and at the base of his neck. Over these, they firmly buckled the cable fittings and the headpiece. A long rubber sash was stretched across his face and around the back of the chair to hold his head in place. His mouth was still visible through a slit in the material.

The priest continued to pray and slipped a small wooden crucifix into Thorn's right hand.

The warden silently nodded to the executioner.

Before Thorn could reply to the prayer, his body was thrown into the straps by a massive shock. His limbs convulsed, and his neck swelled as the power of 1750 volts jolted through him. A thin ribbon of smoke rose from his right calf, and Thorn's body slumped when the executioner pulled the lever back after 59 seconds.

A doctor stepped forward, opened Thorn's shirt, and pressed a stethoscope to his chest as the spectators sat stunned and breathing in air that a *Herald* reporter noted smelled "like an overheated flat iron on a handkerchief."

"This man is dead," the doctor said.

And the execution was over.


Augusta Nack served only nine years in jail. She was released with a flurry of publicity in 1907. Newspaper reporters hounded her as she looked for work as a seamstress or a housekeeper. New York was not the place she remembered. Many of the blocks she once lived on were gone, demolished to make room for Penn Station. Her lawyer, Manny Friend, had died three years earlier. He died on the same day that he'd sent his premium check to his life insurance company, jokingly telling his secretary, "You'd better take it over now, as I might drop dead this afternoon."

Even William Howe, Thorn's attorney, who had been so insulting to her in the courtroom, was gone. His legal practice had been ruined and notorious after the case. He had died in 1902.

Augusta tried to find a hotel where she could live. Her first stop was the Hotel Markwell, but the manager recognized her and told her she was not welcome. She used an alias to check into the Hotel Rand a few blocks later. When reporters followed her there - and exposed her name to another manager - she was asked to leave after only one night.

Hoping to raise money, she tried to sell her story to the *New York Times*, but they turned her down. The *Journal*, however, did not. A large headline on the cover shouted:

## MRS. NACK CONFESSES!

Readers who snapped up a paper to see the story's details discovered that she indeed had confessed - to her love for William Guldensuppe.

She was back to blaming the murder on Martin Thorn, claiming that she didn't know he was at the cottage when she and William had arrived in Woodside. When she saw that Thorn had killed the man she loved, she had fainted, she said. She only awoke to find Thorn kneeling next to her, saying, "Gussie, darling, I did it for you."

After her story appeared in the newspaper, Augusta Nack vanished for a time. She wouldn't emerge again until 1909, and when she did, she did so unwillingly. A murder that involved a beheading prompted reporters to revisit the Guldensuppe case, and they found Augusta hiding in plain sight just blocks from where her old apartment had been.

An article read, "Mrs. Nack has taken the name of Augusta Huber and now manages and owns a small fancy goods store at No. 357 Ninth Avenue."

Within hours, Augusta's identity had been exposed to newspaper readers across the country, including her neighbors and customers. Within a month, her business was shuttered, and her home was abandoned.

Augusta Nack vanished from the public eye again, and this time, it seemed, it was for good.

After all these years, some maintain that there is doubt about whether Augusta and Thorn actually killed Guldensuppe. The newspapers were more concerned about selling stories than the truth and expected their readers to rush to judgment to soothe their hunger for a bloody tale. The evidence was circumstantial, and, thanks to the shortcomings of forensic science at the time, the police were never able to identify the man in the morgue with certainty.

Whoever he was, his head was never found.

William F. Howe was willing to contend until the very end that the pieced-together headless body could have been that of anybody at all.

And perhaps he was right.

But I don't think so. And neither did the veteran police detectives who worked the case. Chief Inspector Ernest Van Wagner later admitted that there had never been any question about these detectives. It had been August Nack who had "designed and planned" the murder of William Guldensuppe.

They also believed that she'd helped carry it out.

Why? That was simple - neither her explanation of the crime nor Thorn's fit the evidence.

When he looked over Guldensuppe's body, the medical examiner found signs of a desperate fight. There was a deep stab wound from a knife that plunged straight down, defensive wounds on his hands where he'd grabbed the blade, and additional glancing and angled wounds. These wounds were clean of any fibers, indicating that he had been attacked while naked.

When Augusta had been arrested, the jail matron had discovered bruises on her arm that appeared to be as old as the day of the crime.

There was also one more thing found in the house that had not been explained - an empty bottle of cabernet wine.

None of this was explained at trial - not in Thorn's story to John Gotha or in either murderer's story on the stand. But it is possible there is an explanation, and it's the only one that fits the evidence.

Guldensuppe was stabbed while naked, and he was stabbed from above when he least expected it. Only one person could have gotten Guldensuppe into the bedroom of an empty house, offered him wine, stripped him naked, straddled his body - and then plunged a knife down into his chest.

Augusta Nack.

Guldensuppe likely reached out and grabbed his killer's arm, leaving bruises, and was also slashed across his hand and clumsily in the chest. That was when Martin Thorn probably came out of the closet and finished off the man with a gunshot to the back of the head.

The house had been cleaned, and no evidence had been left behind that would have made sense to detectives at the time. Years later, though, they would be convinced this was what happened.

Neither Augusta nor Thorn could admit to this scenario. Thorn, a man who impressed his friend John Gotha with his skills with women, could never admit that he had shot his rival in the back after watching him making love with Augusta. Once the two went to trial, each was determined to establish that only the other had been upstairs to commit the murder. They could not admit they'd acted in concert. Even if he suspected what had occurred, the district attorney had no hard evidence of it, so he stuck to the plan that he had.

But those who suspected what really happened could never shake off the chill of seeing a woman as evil as Augusta Nack walk free. In 1938, Chief Inspector Van Wagner wrote that she was still around.

"I saw her last a few years ago," the old detective recalled, "smilingly selling cheap candy in her little store to the unsuspecting and innocent children of her neighborhood."

Although the record has not been found showing when Augusta Nack died, we can rest assured that she did. She may even be resting in peace, her twisted conscience clear of the murder of her former lover.

But Augusta's death - whenever it was - does not quietly end this story. A portion of it lingered, longer than most would like, at the small house in Woodside where William Guldensuppe met his gruesome end.

Even before the trials of Augusta Nack and Martin Thorn began, the house had turned into a tourist attraction. After the news broke of what had occurred there, the sleepy little town began to fill with people who wanted to get a glimpse of the "Den of Murder."

They also wanted to find Guldensuppe's missing head.

They thrashed around in the pasture behind the house, waded into the murky pond, beat the bushes, and jabbed sticks into the weedy roadside ditches. A rumor spread that there was a $1,000 reward for the missing head, and no one wanted to miss out on the chance of finding it.

The authorities did the best they could to keep people out of the house itself. It was a crime scene, after all. Mrs. Hafftner, the caretaker, was nowhere to be found, and the police didn't have a key to the house. When detectives arrived to search the house again, they had to climb inside through an unlocked window.

The house itself, though, remained as vacant and unremarkable as ever.

Or was it?

Months later, during the trials, the judge allowed the jury to visit the Woodside house as part of the proceedings. The jurors and the police traveled to Long Island in a trolley, followed by a parade of reporters and spectators.

When they arrived that day, they found the place had hardly changed. The trees had lost their autumn leaves, and the grass in the yard was tall and uncut, but otherwise, it remained recognizable from the front pages of the previous summer.

The men stomped through mud and ice to get to the porch, and a detective turned a key to let them inside. The door groaned open, and they filed into a parlor darkened by the shutters that had been locked tight over the windows. The air in the unheated house was frigid, leaving their breath hanging in front of them as small white clouds.

In the cellar, they saw the smashed remains of the chimney, a hole still gaping where detectives had smashed it open with hammers, looking for Guldensuppe's head.

They moved through the parlor pausing in the kitchen to look into the iron stove that held the ashes of a dead man's shoes. Their footsteps echoed in the hallways and empty rooms into which the 12 men struggled to fit.

Upstairs, they entered the second bedroom, which remained as it had been, except for the subtle shavings taken off sections of the floor to be examined for blood. The closet door stood open.

They entered the bathroom, and jurors inspected the metal bathtub, leaning down one at a time for a closer look. There were no dents or saw marks to be found. As attorney William Howe had stated, it would have been difficult for one person to do the dismembering alone.

In the backyard, they saw ground furrowed by the diggings of detectives and treasure hunters. They wandered out to the roadside ditch, where ducks swam in the half-frozen water. They saw the same ducks that had become sick from the red drainage that oozed from the house.

The jurors returned to the trolley and silently rode back to the courthouse. The house in Woodside was empty once more.

Or was it?

The house in Woodside never recovered from the events that occurred within its walls. It suffered, much like Herman Nack, the ill-fated ex-husband of Augusta. He lived the rest of his life in shame. He found it hard to hold down delivery jobs whenever his name was recognized. In 1903, six years to the day of Guldensuppe's murder, he calmly abandoned his delivery wagon at the foot of Canal Street and drowned himself in the Hudson River.

Herman Nack, like the house in Woodside, became collateral damage.

The house at No. 346 Second Street sat vacant for years after that last visit from the jury during the murder trial. Its reputation was so fearsome that the owners could never rent it to anyone.

The bedroom where Guldensuppe was murdered was never the same either, for the district attorney had carelessly thrown the room's baseboard away during a fit of evidence room housecleaning. This left behind gaping, open wounds in the walls of the room.

But there were some who refused to be bothered by the events that had occurred in the house.

"We have already put one haunted house out of business," said William Offerman to a reporter for the *Tribune*. He was the president of the Brooklyn Society for the Extermination of Ghosts and Dispelling of Haunted House Illusions. He and his fellow members - "30 young men between the ages of 17 and 23" - were seeking out spirits within 100 miles of New York known for being restless and moaning at midnight.

In 1904, they began a letter-writing campaign to real estate dealers in towns in New Jersey, Westchester, and further up the Hudson River, offering to rent all the haunted houses offered.

None of them believed in ghosts and were willing to spend their time and money to bring other people around to their point of view. Offerman said that if their theories did prove wrong and a ghost should really confront them, they were prepared to make an immediate capture. All his members had proven their bravery and courage, and on their ghost hunts, they carried revolvers and lanterns.

They had recently camped out in an old colonial house on Rockaway Road on the outskirts of Jamaica, where a butcher had committed suicide in one of the upstairs rooms. People refused to live in the house because the butcher returned each night, and his ghost cut his own throat over and over again. "We camped out in the suicide room every night for a week," Offerman claimed, "staying up until long after midnight, but there was never a sign of a ghost."

After spending the week at that house, Offerman and the members of his society made plans for a stay at the house in Woodside, where William Guldensuppe had been killed.

While they reported no ghosts during their stay, their efforts did nothing to rid the house of its reputation for bad luck.

A few years later, a new tenant opened a pet shop in the house, only to die of rabies after a dog bite.

A wine seller named Peter Piernot fared a little better with his shop, especially after he preserved the upstairs bathroom "as it was on the day of the murder" and opened it for customers intrigued by the murder.

In the dead of a late November night, Piernot awakened visiting family members with screams from his bedroom. He wrapped only a blanket around himself and fled the house, jumping onto the next train out of Woodside.

Word was telegraphed ahead, and the police were waiting for him when the train pulled into the next station. Pierpont was taken away and spent the next several weeks in an insane asylum.

No one could get anything out of him at first, and then he began to babble to the doctors - he had run away, he said, from the ghost of William Guldensuppe, who had appeared to him in his bedroom.

The house in Woodside was apparently never vacant at all.

# "LONELY HEARTS KILLER"
## MARTHA BECK

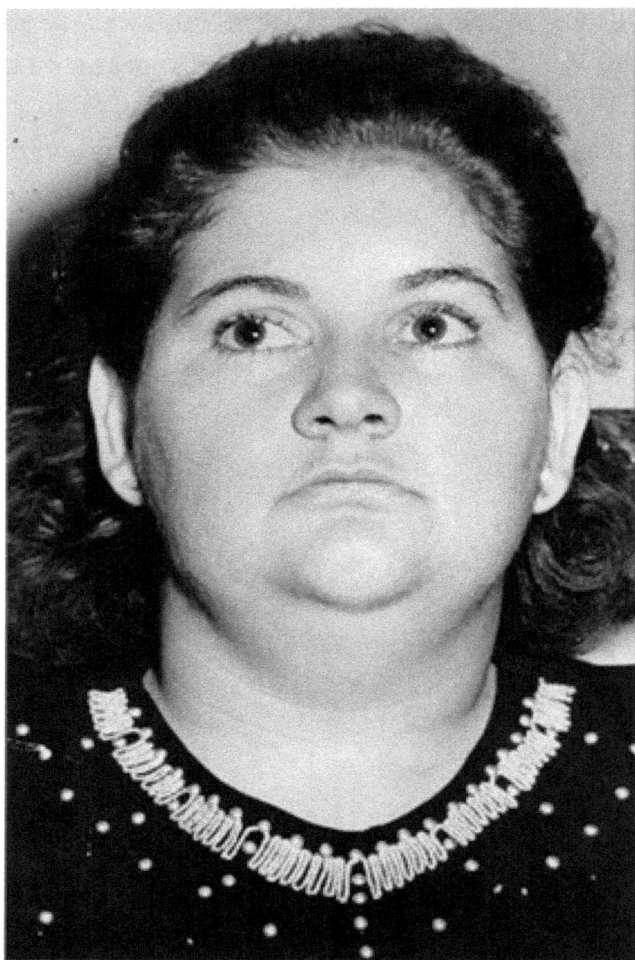

"Lonely hearts" advertisements didn't start when the infamous case of Martha Beck and Raymond Fernandez began being splattered across the pages of detective magazines in the late 1940s - and they didn't end there either.

For decades, people had advertised for love in newspapers and magazines. Many of them were immigrants who only spoke their native tongue, looking for men and women from their own countries with whom they shared a tradition, background, and language.

One such man was Andrew Helgelein, a Norwegian bachelor farmer from Aberdeen, South Dakota, who answered a "lonely hearts" ad from a "comely Indiana widow" in 1906. She was looking for a husband to help run her prosperous farm and spend her money.

Andrew wrote a letter to the widow and told her that he was an experienced farmer with the funds to pay off her mortgage and make her farm an even greater success. He received an immediate reply, asking him to come and visit - and, of course, bring money. She assured him that his money would go much further in Northwest Indiana, and with the right investments, he would be independent for life.

More letters followed, all warm and welcoming and constantly enticing him to come to see the farm. The widow's letters became more urgent when Andrew failed to go to her by September 1906. She implored him to visit before winter arrived, but Andrew still hesitated.

He did not make it down for the lavish Thanksgiving dinner that he had been promised, and soon the widow's correspondence began to reflect a growing impatience. She sent him pressed roses and wrote longingly of a Norwegian Christmas. She drew pen and ink portraits of herself and Andrew snuggling on the couch in front of her blazing fire, warm and snug as snow gently fell outside. The letters ran the gamut of emotions and began to show Belle's desperation.

Nearly 11 months more passed before Andrew could put his affairs in order and before he made up his mind to join the widow on her farm. Her reply letter was ecstatic and ended with the lines:

*My heart beats in wild rapture for you, My Andrew; I love you. Come prepared to stay forever.*

Andrew may not have planned it that way, but he indeed came to stay on the farm forever.

The widow that he had been exchanging letters with was Belle Gunness, one of the most prolific serial killers in American history, and Andrew became the final victim that she murdered and buried on her farm.

The story of Belle, her murder farm, and the "lonely hearts" ads that she used to lure unsuspecting bachelors to her farm made national news, but even so, people continued to meet, court, and marry partners they met through the mail. Gradually, those advertisements evolved into so-called "lonely hearts clubs," which provided names and addresses for a fee. The clubs rose in popularity as it became difficult to meet people in bars and clubs during Prohibition in the 1920s and people had to look for other ways to meet people. The clubs seemed to break down into two categories - middle-aged people looking for love and young people anxious for the "joys of marital life." In 1920s speak, "marital life" meant sex, so the clubs became the era's version of a hook-up app.

But it seemed most club members were those with limited social options, particularly widows and single women, and men past a certain age.

Whatever their reasons, they flocked to the lonely-hearts bureaus by the thousands. The love-starved sent hundreds of thousands of letters through various services, hoping to meet the perfect person each year. Advertisements that attracted as many as 500 letters per day included things like "Rich Widows... Wealthy Widowers!" and hinted at the possibility of landing someone with a six-figure bank account.

The cover charge for most clubs was 25-cents, which was the price of a four-page brochure that contained a snapshot and brief biography of clients looking for spouses. For $3, a client could receive a yearly subscription. The rest was up to the correspondents who exchanged letters - or, as they called it, "engaged in postage stamp flirtation."

It all seemed innocent enough, but as Andrew Helgelein found out in 1906, sometimes the person writing the letters was not what they appeared.

There were numerous accounts of men and women who corresponded with a dozen or more people at a time, accepting gifts, money, and marriage proposals who suddenly disappeared, ending the scam. People lost their fortunes, their hearts, and, inevitably, their lives.

In 1931, the "West Virginia Bluebeard," Harry Powers, began preying on lonely women through lonely hearts ads. He penned dozens of florid love letters from his home, lured women there, and murdered them after robbing them of their money.

The scandal that followed his capture resulted in investigations and temporary injunctions against some of the most popular lonely-hearts clubs. But efforts to close them down permanently met with failure. New ones popped up in the classified ads of newspapers and magazines like weeds and became fixtures in romance and detective pulps.

More scams followed, and when federal authorities did manage to make a case, the story was always given front-page headlines, but the exposure failed to slow down the business end of matchmaking. Lonely hearts simply ignored the cautionary tales of robbery - even murder - and continued to look for love among the ads.

But, of course, that wasn't all they found.

Raymond Fernandez was a brain-damaged Latin lover who was already luring lonely, wealthy women through lonely hearts ads in romance magazines before meeting the woman who sent him entirely off the rails.

They became a match made in hell, and their lives would end together in the electric chair, still professing their undying love.

The woman who managed to catch Raymond was Martha Beck, a lonely single mother from Florida who responded to one of his ads. She soon had him completely under her spell. As for Martha, she was head over heels for Raymond. Together, they would unleash a kind of horror their victims would never have imagined.

Martha would later say that her life began on December 9, 1947 - the day she met Raymond Fernandez - but in truth, she was born Martha Jule Seabrook near Pensacola, Florida, on May 6, 1920.

Allegedly due to a glandular problem - a common explanation for obesity in those days - Martha was an overweight child and went through puberty early. She later claimed that her brother had raped her, and when she told her mother what happened, she was beaten because her mother told her she was responsible. She ran away from home as a teenager and spent some time with a traveling carnival.

Regardless, Martha finished school and became a registered nurse but had trouble finding a job because of her weight. She took a job as an undertaker's assistant and prepared deceased women for burial. Later, she moved to California and worked as a nurse at an Army hospital during the early years of World War II. While living in California, she became pregnant. After failing to convince the father to marry her, she returned to Florida - single and pregnant.

Martha told people that her baby's father was a serviceman she had married and that he had been killed during the Pacific campaign. The town mourned her loss and even published a story about his tragic death in the local newspaper.

Shortly after her daughter was born, Martha became pregnant again by a Pensacola bus driver named Alfred Beck. They quickly married, but it was a disaster, and they were divorced six months later. Soon after that, Martha gave birth to a son.

Unemployed and the single mother of two young children, Martha escaped into a fantasy world, buying romance magazines and novels, and seeing romantic films at the local theater. In 1946, she found work again at the Pensacola Hospital for Children.

For months, Martha had been poring over the lonely-hearts ads that she found in the back of the magazines she read, dreaming of finding the perfect man. So, in 1947, she placed an ad of her own - an ad that was answered by the man of her dreams, Raymond Fernandez.

Raymond Martinez Fernandez was born on December 17, 1914, in Hawaii to Spanish parents. When he was three, his parents moved to California and eventually to Bridgeport, Connecticut. As a teenager, he worked hard on his family's farms but moved to Spain to work for his uncle after a confrontation with his father. There, he married a local woman, Agnesia Robles Alonaso. After the birth of their first child, Raymond returned to the United States, already bored with married life. He stayed until 1935 when his son became ill. He went back to Spain but planned to go back to America as soon as possible.

But that chance didn't come until 1947. Thanks to the Spanish Civil War, he remained with his wife for the next decade, and they had three more children. He eventually abandoned all of them.

During World War II, Raymond served in Spain's Merchant Marine and later claimed to have been a spy for British Intelligence. It's possible this was true. He would have been well-suited for this kind of work with his considerable charm and charisma.

In 1947, Raymond finally decided to return to New York. Shortly after boarding a ship for the United States, a steel hatch fell on him, fracturing his skull and injuring his frontal lobe.

This injury would be used to explain Raymond's change in behavior - and his turning to a life of crime, which began with committing burglaries of homes and stores after he was released from the hospital.

He was arrested after stealing some clothing and spent a year in prison. While there, he allegedly learned magic and voodoo from one of his cellmates and began using his so-called magical powers on the women he started meeting through the lonely-hearts ads. He later claimed that black magic gave him his irresistible power and charm.

One of his victims - Jane Thompson - traveled with him to Spain. He talked her into changing her will, making him the sole beneficiary. She then died under mysterious circumstances. He told one person that she had a heart attack, then told Jane's mother that she had been killed in a train accident. Whatever happened, Raymond wound up with her money.

His schemes continued, and then he wrote to Martha Beck after seeing her ad in a romance magazine.

Martha would describe meeting Raymond as knowing they were a perfect match for one another. After a brief but torrid exchange of letters, Raymond traveled to Florida on December 9, and the lovers spent the weekend together. Three days later, before returning to New York, Raymond proposed marriage, and Martha gladly accepted. Martha stayed behind in Pensacola, preparing for the wedding.

Unable to think about anything but Raymond, Martha lost her job, so she took her two children and followed him to New York. Raymond loved being suffocated by her, and he quickly filled her in on his devious plans to defraud lonely women, using the name

"Charles Martin," --- and Martha then decided that it was her duty to join in the fun. She even gave her children away so she could devote herself to Raymond full-time. She dropped them off at the Salvation Army one day and never looked back.

Raymond then laid out his new plan – she would pose as his sister while he seduced other women through the lonely-hearts ads. Then they would rob the women before going on to their next victim.

Martha agreed, but only if the scheme would remain business, not pleasure. Raymond belonged to her and her alone. Raymond couldn't do anything but agree.

And the violent string of matrimony and murder began.

With Martha sitting next to him, Raymond began writing to five or six women, including Esther Henne, a teacher from Pennsylvania. Around Valentine's Day 1948, "Charles Martin" and his "sister," Martha, traveled to Pennsylvania, where Raymond began wooing the unsuspecting woman. The two got "married" in Virginia, and the three of them returned to New York. The marriage didn't last long. Esther got suspicious and went home. With help from a lawyer, she managed to get back most of the money that the pair had stolen from her.

While this failure was cooling down, Martha and Raymond took a trip, stopping in Miami and Havana and then landing in Chicago in May 1948. They both got temporary jobs while Raymond swapped letters with an Arkansas widow named Myrtle Young.

With Martha standing by as his "sister," he married Myrtle in August. The marriage only lasted a few days, ending when Myrtle left Chicago to cry on her sister's shoulder in St. Louis. The affair turned out to be profitable for Martha and Raymond, netting them about $4,000.

After this, Martha and Raymond traveled to North Carolina, where Raymond romanced another woman on his list. When that relationship didn't work out, the pair drove to Vermont and met with another target, Irene De La Point.

Martha was starting to question Raymond's devotion to her by this point. She decided to teach him a lesson and wrote a letter to Irene, warning her of Raymond's intentions. And then she walked out, leaving her lover stranded in Vermont. She first went to see her mother in Florida and then turned up at a sister's house in North Carolina on November 1. Two days later, Raymond finally tracked her down. He begged for her to come back. After a suitable amount of groveling, she agreed, and they rendezvoused in New York to patch things up.

Raymond already had another victim on his list, and this time, things were going to get ugly.

On January 1, Martha and Raymond traveled to Albany, New York, so that "Charles Martin" could meet a 66-year-old widow named Janet Fay. While Martha remained at the hotel, Raymond met Janet for Dinner. He was still checking her out to see if she had money. Convinced in part by the large diamond ring that she wore, he invited her to stay with him at a house that he had rented in Valley Stream.

During a trip with Janet to New York City, Raymond introduced her to his "sister." The three of them were staying in a hotel when Martha began to get suspicious about what Raymond was up to. Though she encouraged Raymond to keep preying on the lonely woman, Martha continued to insist that he never have sex with any of them. When she found him in bed with Janet, Martha lost her mind.

She hit the woman in the head several times with a hammer, shattering her skull. When that didn't kill her, Raymond finished Janet off by strangling her with a silk scarf. They placed the body in a trunk and temporarily stored it in the basement of Raymond's sister's house in Queens.

The body remained there until January 21, when they rented a house and moved the trunk there. Raymond buried it in the basement before covering it with fresh concrete.

After hiding the body, they fled New York and went west to Michigan, where they would commit the murders that would send them to the electric chair.

On January 12, 1949, a 31-year-old widow named Deliphene Price mailed a letter that eventually led to her death. It was written to a wealthy New York man named Charles Martin. The two had first made contact the previous month through a lonely-hearts ad. Thrilled to receive correspondence from an affluent Manhattan man, Deliphene thought nothing of fulfilling Charles' request for a recent photo and a lock of her hair.

Hoping to make herself seem attractive to a man from the big city, she presented herself as a woman of means, mentioning that she soon hoped to buy a new car and mentions her two-stall garage and her nice home in the suburbs.

She also hints that she is eager to find love. Perhaps a little too eager. She even mailed another letter to Charles before he received her first one.

This will be the biggest mistake of her life.

Born November 4, 1917, Deliphene Price grew up alongside her older sisters - Zora, Zella, and Esther - on her father's 3,000-acre ranch near Palisade, Nebraska. She attended the local high school and graduated in 1934. Her senior photographs show a cute girl with curly brunette hair worn just over her ears and parted on the side, a wide mischievous grin, and smiling eyes. Friends and relatives would always describe her as "old-fashioned," seldom using makeup or wearing pantyhose, stockings, or garters.

After graduating, Deliphene took a job teaching at a small school near home. In the summer of 1942, during a visit with a sister living in Los Angeles, she met and fell in love with a dashing soldier named Rolland Downing. They corresponded for almost two years before getting married during one of Rolland's furloughs in 1944.

After the war, the newlyweds moved to Rolland's hometown of Grand Rapids, Michigan. They lived with his parents while house hunting and then moved into a five-room bungalow on Byron Center Road in Wyoming Township, a small suburban community. A machinist by trade, Rolland worked as a truck driver until he could save enough money to start his own business. On June 6, 1946, the couple welcomed a daughter they named Rainelle.

But Deliphene's life was shattered on a gray November morning when a passenger train struck Rolland's truck, killing him instantly. Rainelle was only 17 months old when her father died, and Deliphene was left to raise her alone on a monthly life insurance payment of $125.

A year after her husband's death, the widow joined a lonely-hearts club - a fact she kept hidden from family and friends. She was still young and pretty, and she ached to find someone to spend her life with.

So, she was thrilled on January 23, 1949, when Charles and his sister arrived at her bungalow on the southwest side of Grand Rapids.

Raymond and Martha would offer two different accounts of what happened after they arrived at Deliphene's house and Raymond began trying to work his "magic" on the woman.

According to Raymond, he'd liked "Dela" - as he called her - more than any other women he'd met through the lonely-hearts ads and contemplated bringing her back with him to New York City. But then an incident occurred that changed everything.

They had started arguing on a Saturday afternoon. Raymond claimed there were two reasons for the fight. The first involved money that Deliphene wanted to withdraw from her bank account to send to her sisters. "But what about us?" he'd asked, trying to manipulate her into not giving away what he saw as his windfall.

The second reason for the spat involved the $150 hairpiece that Raymond had purchased in downtown Grand Rapids. Deliphene didn't like how it had changed his appearance - or so Raymond later told police.

It likely had more to do with Deliphene's sense that something fishy was going on with her new lover and his sister. She had already refused to move her savings into a joint account that he'd suggested they open, and the hairpiece seemed to be one more reason to doubt the man's sincerity.

Deliphene allegedly became hysterical during the argument, and Raymond said she began hurling dishes and silverware at him.

As Raymond was later recounting this story to the police in his confession, he decided to throw his accomplice, Martha, under the bus. He said that Martha was an unwanted hanger-on that he didn't seem to be able to get rid of. "I liked her - but she wouldn't go away," he stated. "She said when I was settling down, she would go away, but she didn't. This last one, Deliphene, was the nicest. She was really a very nice woman. She was the one I wanted. But I didn't love Martha. I couldn't get her off my system. I tried to make her go away, but whatever she wanted she would whimper and cry and make me do what she wanted."

Jealous of Raymond's attention to Deliphene - and fearful she might be replaced - Martha, the trained nurse, convinced the young woman to take some medicine that would help her to calm down. She convinced her to swallow 14 phenobarbital tablets. The dose wasn't lethal, but it did put her into a deep sleep.

Seeing her mother unconscious, Rainelle began to cry. Unable to get her to stop, Martha nearly strangled the girl. Realizing that no amount of smooth-talking would keep Deliphene from going straight to the police about the argument, sleeping pills, and bruises on her daughter's neck, Raymond decided to kill her before she woke up. Using Rolland Downing's army-issue .45, he shot Deliphene in the head - while Rainelle watched the whole thing.

Is that really how it happened, though? Martha offered a slightly different version of Deliphene's death.

Like Raymond, she said the breaking point came when Deliphene reacted to the new toupee on that Saturday afternoon, and a heated argument followed. According to Martha and John Bossler, the shop's proprietor where he'd purchased it, the wig made Raymond look much younger, which must've raised Deliphene's suspicions and triggered the argument.

Martha told the police that the sleeping pills had been Raymond's idea, not hers. Raymond shot her when Deliphene became restless that night, trying to wake up. He had wrapped the pistol in a baby blanket to muffle the sound, but he worried that a neighbor might have heard something, so he wanted to get rid of the body right away. He went down to the basement and started digging a hole in the floor. He had tools and leftover concrete from a project he had recently been working on in the house.

He told Martha to wrap the body up in a blanket. "I tried tying her, but the rope kept slipping," she later recalled. "He, in the meantime, had gone into the basement to dig a hole. The hole kept filling up with water, and I don't believe he dug it as deep as he had planned."

Together, they carried Deliphene's body downstairs, and Martha bailed two buckets of water from the hole before they placed the body into it. Once it was covered, Raymond filled the hole with cement.

After burying the body, Raymond and Martha took Rainelle out for dinner and a movie. By the following day, though, they were unable to pacify her. She cried continually, begging for her mother so loudly that the couple feared the neighbors would be alerted. Trying to calm her, they took her for a drive and promised her a puppy. They stopped at a local pet store and purchased a cocker spaniel, but when the dog accidentally scratched her, they returned it.

The next day, the crying continued, and they began to talk about "putting it down with its mother."

While they were deciding what to do next, Raymond and Martha went to the bank and withdrew all but $500 of the money in Deliphene's account. When they returned to the house, Martha had made up her mind about what to do about their "problem."

Martha later claimed that she initially decided to keep Rainelle and take her back to New York with them. But then she realized that they would have problems with the child's grandparents. There would also be explanations created to explain Rainelle to Raymond's family in New York.

Unable to develop a credible story, Martha decided that Rainelle would have to join her mother.

Raymond told the police, "When we came back, Martha said she was going to drown the baby and took her down into the basement."

Martha undressed Rainelle in the basement and thrust her head into the muddy water that filled the hole where Deliphene had been buried. She leaned forward, holding the child's heels, using her body weight to keep the thrashing little girl from coming up for air. "The baby struggled so much I could hardly hold her," she admitted.

Before she had shoved Rainelle's head into the water, Raymond heard the girl crying in the basement. He told detectives, "I ran down and said, 'Let her be! Don't let her suffer anymore!'"

The sight of Martha holding the girl by the legs and forcing her head down into the murky water allegedly unhinged Raymond, who ran back upstairs.

Martha cruelly called after him, "What's the matter? Why don't you come back down?"

After Rainelle stopped struggling, Martha pulled her out of the water. To be sure she was really dead, Martha battered the little girl's head with a heavy object.

Rainelle never moved again.

After calming himself, Raymond returned to the basement. While he mixed another batch of cement, Martha wrapped the dead little girl with wire, placed her in her father's footlocker, and shoved it into the hole next to her mother's corpse. Raymond dumped a thin layer of wet cement over the whole thing.

And then they went out to the movies.

They returned to the house around 10:00 p.m. and started packing, planning to leave in the morning. They were nearly finished when they heard a knock on the front door. They had planned to flee the area, but they weren't fast enough.

It was the police at the door.


Both Raymond and Martha began to confess at the jail, initially putting most of the blame for their crimes on the other. Reporters quickly filed their stories, and the two killers soon became known coast-to-coast as the "Lonely Hearts Killers."

The police searched Deliphene Downing's home and recovered the bodies of her and her daughter from the basement. Detectives were sickened by their confessions. John Vanderband balled up his fists tightly and muttered to one of the other lawmen, "It makes me want to smash them."

Raymond was soon called on to reveal the location of Janey Fay's body back in New York. He was convinced that he would face the music in Michigan, not New York, so he decided to cooperate with detectives out east. He directed them to the house he'd rented from a man named James Lloyd and told them how to find the body under the basement floor.

Using pickaxes, two officers broke through the recent cement patch and dug down four feet to reveal Janet Fay's body, clad in a bathrobe and with her knees trussed up to her chest, just as Raymond had left her. Her hair was covered in sticky red blood, and it was apparent her skull had been bashed in by a hammer. Bruising around her throat showed that she'd been strangled from behind.

Raymond and Martha made their first court appearance on March 2, 1949. Each of them faced separate warrants for the murders of Deliphene and Rainelle.

Eager to catch a glimpse of the infamous killers, a standing-room-only crowd of mostly women packed into the small courtroom. They craned their necks to see the woman who admitted holding a toddler's head under muddy water until she drowned and saw Martha in a black dress with her lips pursed in irritation.

Raymond looked utterly dejected - and he had cause for concern. The Michigan Attorney General, Stephen J. Roth, had asked for a delay in court proceedings to give New York time to extradite the two killers. Michigan didn't have the death penalty, but New York did. If they were sent there and convicted, it would mean the electric chair.

They only spent a few minutes before the judge that day, but it was enough for reporters. By the following day, Martha and Raymond's photos were plastered across front pages all over America.

The confessed killers became overnight media sensations - especially Martha. Depicted as a monster, Martha's weight became a theme of the stories and was always mentioned prominently in the text, even if it had little or no relevance. Of the two killers, writers pegged Martha as the one with the bloodiest hands and the dominant to Raymond's submissive. Her fits of insane jealously, it was agreed, ultimately led to the murders of Janet Fay, Deliphene, and Rainelle.

A reporter for the *Chicago Daily Tribune* wrote:

*Twice in two months, her jealousy flamed into murderous rage. Twice she took preliminary steps in murder and twice she forced her shrinking consort to finish the job. She was an iron woman, coldly and implacably demanding bloody proof from her lover that his attentions to another had after all only been play acting. He could and did atone - on each of these occasions - by killing the woman for whom his protestations for love had been too realistic for his co-conspirator.*

The press loved to hate Martha Beck.

And so did everyone else. The unflattering photographs made her situation worse. Her blank expression and her vacant stare as she focused on nothing in particular - the product of exhaustion more than apathy - became the face of a malignant force who would kill an older woman, feed an overdose to a single mother, and drown a child in a muddy puddle, all for the love of a man.

And then there was Martha's smile - in reality, a nervous tic that pulled up one corner of her mouth. The odd effect led reporters to conclude that not only did she feel no remorse for her horrific deeds, but she smirked whenever she discussed them.

There was one photograph that showed a very different Martha Beck, though. It was taken after her first interrogation, and it revealed her overcome with emotion with her face buried in her hands. The picture was largely ignored by those who wanted to see Martha as cold and devoid of feelings. Reporters all agreed that she seemed "too human" in that one.

But she might not have if they had looked into the three rings that can be seen on her fingers in the photo - Martha had taken them from the dead fingers of Janet Fay and Deliphene Downing.

When the Lonely Hearts case hit newspapers across the country, inquiries began pouring in from other law enforcement officers who were trying to track down missing women. Authorities from Chicago, Denver, Minneapolis, St. Louis, and other cities wanted to know if Raymond and Martha had hunted in their towns, too.

When Raymond was arrested, he carried a list of names - reportedly numbering 100 - in his jacket pocket. There were 17 entries check-marked on the list. The first name on the list had been Janet Fay, which led the police to fear that 16 other women lay undiscovered in concrete basement tombs somewhere.

The names on the list contained ages, addresses, and perhaps most telling, a dollar amount after each one. Of course, the figures - money that Raymond expected to steal - suggested that he had engaged with at least some correspondence with the women. But had he and Martha killed them, too?

The police began contacting the women on the list, and luckily, they all seemed to be alive. Out of the 17 names, only Janet Fay had ended up under a basement floor.

But if they hadn't been caught, any - perhaps all - of them could have been next.

Raymond and Martha were eventually extradited to New York, where they were put on trial for the murder of Janet Fay. A jury found them guilty, and both were sentenced to death. Packed off to Sing Sing, their dates with the executioner fell on the same day - March 8, 1951.

Both of the killers had filed multiple appeals, but all had failed. Martha even offered to donate her corpse to science if officials would agree to commute Raymond's sentence. No one accepted the offer.

The animosity between the two of them, leading each to blame the other for their crimes, had melted away by the time they landed in prison. Although banned from writing to one another on Death Row, they had found a way to send each other a final love note of sorts on the eve of their executions. They were allowed to make public statements, and each declared their undying love for the other.

They ate their last meals at 5:00 p.m. - Martha had fried chicken, French fries, and a dinner salad, while Raymond had an onion omelet, sliced tomatoes, and almond ice cream. Then they changed into their "death suits." Raymond was given a white shirt and black pants, and Martha wore a house dress. One hour later, a bald patch was shaved into Martha's hair.

Raymond was first into "Old Sparky." When he sat down in the chair, he pulled up his pants legs to maintain a crisp crease in his trousers. It took only three minutes to strap him into the seat, and his body jumped slightly when the first surge of electricity went through his body. Three shorter bursts followed, and he was dead just four minutes after entering the death chamber.

Martha walked into the room just five minutes later. The press couldn't resist one more jab about her weight. "The electric chair was a tight fit," wrote *Daily News* reporter Martin Kivel. A fellow reporter added that "Martha had to wriggle slightly to get her more than 200 pounds between the fatal arms."

A reporter described her final moments:

*Her eyes drifted around the room, and she glanced up as the death mask was lowered. At that moment, a ghostly smile played at the corner of her mouth. She looked to her left where the matrons who had attended her during her long imprisonment were standing. Two matrons, Mrs. Nellie Evans and Mrs. Bessie Irving, were near tears, fighting for control. Martha seemed to sympathize. Her left eyelid dropped in an unmistakable wink.*

A smile and wink? Or were the expressions caused by the facial tics that went with Martha's frayed nerves? The press chose to assume the worst.

Unlike Raymond, Martha's death did not occur quickly. She struggled and strained against the straps as the first jolt hit. Again, at the second shock, she jerked forward. Two more followed before she was finally still.

"I pronounce this woman dead," the prison doctor finally announced.

And the "Lonely Hearts Killers" case was quietly closed.

# "THE PHANTOM FLAPPER KILLER"
# MARGARET HELDMAN

Even though she was quiet and kept to herself, most people on the outbound Canton, Ohio, bus noticed the girl on the cold night of December 6, 1928.

It wasn't just her clothing - a blue chinchilla coat, close-fitting black turban-style hat with a brilliant pin attached, oxford shoes, and gloves - or even her looks. Everyone who recalled her said she was a "beauty." She was around 22 years old with light-brown hair and lovely eyes. What got people's attention was the paleness of her face, her brooding intensity, and how she nervously kept putting her hands into the opposite sleeve of her coat.

She was a young woman with something on her mind.

George Patterson, the bus driver, noticed her, and so did W.E. McCombs, the proprietor of the Rite-of-Way Inn in the small village of Waco, where the bus dropped her off. Both men had seen the same girl the night before. She had gotten off at the Waco stop at 8:10 p.m. and then had turned right around and immediately took the return bus back to Canton. An hour later, she showed up again, only to depart once more on the return bus to Canton. Both men thought she might be a "spotter" for the bus company, checking up on their work.

On the night of December 6, the young woman stepped off the bus and asked McCombs if he would turn on the signal light to announce there was a return passenger for Canton. She had to run an errand, but she would be back in a few minutes. She didn't want to miss her bus.

She then turned, shoved her hands in her sleeves, and started walking up a hill toward a group of houses. Just over the crest of the hill, she walked up the driveway of local man Vernard Fearn, a 35-year-old coal merchant who lived in a new home he had built for his wife, Mary, and his nine-year-old daughter Kathryn.

Mary was making dinner when the young woman knocked on the door. She wiped her hands on a kitchen towel and opened the door.

"Is Mr. Fearn at home?" the woman on the porch asked.

"Yes, won't you come in?" Mary replied.

"No, thank you," the pale girl said. "I'll only be a moment. I'll stay right here."

Mary told Vernard there was someone at the door for him, and she returned to the kitchen.

As soon as Vernard opened the door, the young woman produced a .380 Colt Revolver and calmly shot him five times without saying a word. Three slugs smashed into his chest, another entered his side as he spun around, and the fifth went into his back as he fell on the porch.

The woman then turned, stepped off the porch, and walked down the hill to the Rite-of-Way Inn. She got there just before the return bus to Canton arrived and was on it when it left 10 minutes later after the driver filled the gas tank.

Shortly later, she stepped off the bus at the McKinley Hotel in downtown Canton and disappeared into the crowd of holiday shoppers on the streets.

The "Phantom Flapper Killer," as the newspapers began calling her, vanished into the night.

The Stark County police soon arrived on the scene but had no idea how to discover the mysterious killer's identity. The search had only a few clues to focus on, provided by those who had seen the pretty, quiet girl during her bus trips to Waco on December 5 and 6. But other than her physical appearance and demeanor, they had nothing else to go on.

Within hours, the news spread that the "Phantom Flapper" murder would never be solved.

The dead man's wife, Mary, was little help to Stark County Sheriff Edward Gibson and his detectives. Although Mary and her daughter, Kathryn, had gotten a good look at the girl, neither recognized her.

Drawn to the porch by the sound of the shots, Mary tried to help Vernard as he staggered, bleeding heavily, toward the kitchen. She cradled the dying man in her arms and asked him who had shot him.

"I don't know," he gasped. "I...never saw...her...before."

He died a few moments later, but Mary told the police that she thought she heard Vernard call out to his killer as he was falling, "Why are you doing this? What did I ever do to you?"

With no apparent motive, such as robbery or a feud with an enemy, Sheriff Gibson's men turned the investigation toward Vernard's private life. Although his wife and many of his friends insisted that Vernard had been a man of upstanding behavior and manly virtues, detectives began to think otherwise.

A local boy, Vernard was considered a good man in the Canton area. He had been a good student, played semi-professional baseball, was a veteran of World War I, a hard worker who paid his debts, and a businessman who was active in community affairs.

But as often happens, a man who works hard also plays hard. Detectives discovered that Vernard played very hard when they began canvassing the dance halls he often visited in the months before his death and talking with the many women he spent time with. They didn't find any immediate suspects, but they found that Vernard had flirted with many of the women who hung around the all-night dances and marathon contests he attended. He had gone out on "dates" with many of these women - although by "date," they didn't mean dinner and a movie.

Six days passed without any apparent progress on the case, although Sheriff Gibson and Stark County Prosecutor Henry Harter, Jr. kept promising they were close to making an arrest.

Wild theories made the rounds, filling the gaps left by the absence of actual clues. One story claimed that Vernard had been lured to his porch by the attractive stranger but that a man in hiding had killed him from the front lawn. Another idea was that the phantom killer was a professional assassin from the Canton underworld, hired by unknown persons. Another claimed Vernard was killed by a man dressed as a woman. One more story made the rounds that the young woman was the outraged sister of a girl who Vernard had wronged.

Meanwhile, Sheriff Gibson and Prosecutor Harter kept everyone guessing by taking frequent trips to small towns in Ohio and Pennsylvania to run down supposed sightings of the girl.

But Gibson and his detectives knew more about the "Phantom Flapper" than the newspapers thought - even if they still didn't know her identity.

No matter what Mary said about her husband's saintly life, it was clear the killing had been very personal. Moreover, it was clear that she hadn't cared about getting caught after she pulled the trigger that night. The killer had made three trips to the Fearns' house, going there twice on December 5 only to find he wasn't home. She returned the next night wearing the same clothes, so she wasn't worried about anyone remembering her. It was also clear to them that she was not a person of means, as the police had never known a killer who would take the bus if they had access to an automobile.

So, when not chasing "Flapper" sightings all over the countryside, Gibson and Harter continued to question Mary Fearn, hoping she would reveal whatever sordid secrets Vernard had that cost him his life.

Meanwhile, public interest was stoked by the announcement that Stark County Commissioners were willing to offer a $1,000 reward for the arrest of the "Phantom Flapper." Within days, police officers and the public were harassing every pretty woman in a chinchilla coat or wearing a turban-style hat. On December 12, three young men in New Philadelphia were charged with assaulting a young woman they tried to capture for the reward money. She was not the "Flapper."

But then the strange story ended just as suddenly and as violently as it began.

On Thursday, December 13 - one week after the murder - a car screeched to a halt in front of Sheriff Gibson's office in downtown Canton and began frantically blowing its horn. Gibson ran outside to find Wilbur Heldman, 27, a furnace salesman, sitting in the car. In the passenger seat next to him was his wife, Margaret, bleeding, and near death from a bullet wound to her heart.

Margaret was the notorious "Phantom Flapper Killer."

Gibson jumped onto the running board of the auto and directed Wilbur to speed to Canton's Mercy Hospital, where Margaret died one hour later. Before she passed, she tried to speak, but she could not. She closed her eyes, and then she was gone.

Margaret's story would never be told.

But Wilbur's was and what he told law enforcement officers and reporters seemed to end the week-long mystery. But did it really?

Like Vernard Fearn, Wilbur had grown up in the Canton area and worked there selling furnaces for several years before meeting Margaret Horner in August 1927. Just out of high school, Margaret was young and impressionable and worked as a ribbon clerk at a Canton department store when she was smitten by the older and, seemingly, more worldly Wilbur. They were married just three weeks later after a whirlwind courtship.

But their mutual infatuation didn't last. Their subsequent months of married life were marked by frequent fights, separations, and short-live reconciliations. According to Wilbur, his wife was cold, moody, and an uncontrollable liar. He made every effort, he told the police, but he could not satisfy his unhappy, restless wife.

In September 1928, they had a baby, Emmett, but even that wasn't enough to hold the marriage together. In fact, it made it worse. They moved to the nearby town of Lorain to, as Wilbur claimed, make a fresh start. But friends of the couple insisted it was actually so that Wilbur could establish a 30-day residency there and file for divorce. When they moved to Lorain, Wilbur also took their infant son - which he said Margaret neglected - and placed him in foster care in Canton.

Wilbur told the police that he first suspected something was going on between Margaret and Vernard Fearn in early

November after sneaking a look at some letters that Margaret had written to her mother and sisters. In the notes, he saw that Margaret was telling them that he was about to divorce her because of a man named Fearn. She added that she had met this man at a dance and later agreed to go for a "ride and xxx" with the married coal merchant.

That was enough for Wilbur. He confronted Margaret about her adultery and insisted they move to Lorain and start again.

Margaret left Wilbur on December 2, telling him that she was going to visit her sister, Laura, in Canton. When she returned home on Friday - the day after Vernard was shot - he had asked her how her trip had been, and she replied, "Just fine."

Wilbur grew suspicious over the weekend, though, when he saw the story in the newspapers about the mysterious woman who had murdered Vernard Fearn - a name that was not unfamiliar in Wilbur's home. He also noticed that the man had been killed with an unusual weapon, a .380 Colt, which police said was a difficult gun to find cartridges. As it happened, Wilbur had just such a hard-to-find gun in his sock drawer.

He told detectives that he had looked up from his newspaper and said to his wife, "You know, I believed you killed this man Fearn."

"Don't be foolish," Margaret replied calmly. "Why would I do a thing like that?"

Wilbur - or so he told the police - let the matter drop.

Three days passed, and Wilbur tried to ignore the nagging feeling his wife had committed murder. He told the police that he couldn't ignore them anymore after finding a crumpled note in some trash he was about to burn. The note was dated December 2, the same day Margaret left to "visit her sister." It read:

*I am leaving out of your life forever and I am truly sorry for all the trouble I caused you, and rather than try to go through the rest of my life under a lie I am taking this means to tell you the truth. I can't face you and tell you this, so I am leaving this to explain the thing you don't know.*

*He has made my life hell on earth. He came to my house... he threatened to expose me if I didn't do what he wanted me to... I can't stand the worry any longer and to be away from my baby. So, I do hope you can forgive me and give our baby a good home. Love him even if you don't me for, I do surely love you.*

*Margaret.*
*Please do not tell my mother.*

Wilbur was enraged. He confronted Margaret and told her to put on her coat. They were going to see Sheriff Gibson and added, "If you've done this, you'll have to pay for it."

According to Wilbur, his wife didn't even try to deny it. She did stall for time, though, asking Wilbur to wait until morning, but he was firm, and they left for Canton late in the afternoon on December 13.

It must have been a tense two-hour drive to Canton.

He later told the police that Margaret haltingly confessed to the terrible sequence of events as he drove. She said she had met Vernard at a dance hall before she married Wilbur, but she met with him again during one of the couple's frequent estrangements. They spent time together during many of the all-night hops where Vernard was well known for his flirtations.

One day in 1927, Margaret was hitchhiking home from the Canton library, and Vernard picked her up in one of his coal trucks. Instead of taking her home, he drove her to a remote spot outside town and raped her.

She was too ashamed to tell her husband what had happened, and in the months that followed, Vernard forced her to sleep with him many times, threatening to tell her husband and ruin her reputation if she resisted.

Finally, by the fall of 1928, she had reached her limit. She had decided to kill Vernard. She made two trips to Waco on December 5 and then returned the next night and shot him to death. Although she expected to be caught immediately - which is why she wrote the note to Wilbur - she safely made it back to Canton and then took a bus to Akron, where she stayed at the Bon Hotel before going home on Friday morning.

And here's where the story goes further off the rails.

According to Wilbur's account, Margaret turned to him as they made it to the outskirts of Canton and asked, "What do you think they'll do to me? You don't think they'll be brutal to me?"

Wilbur had no sympathy for her. He was simply too angry. "Well," he answered, "if you don't get the electric chair, I'll miss my guess."

There was a moment of silence, and then Margaret said quietly, "Be sure to take good care of the baby."

"Better than you ever did," Wilbur snapped at her.

Just as they passed the "Welcome to Canton" sign, Margaret reached into her coat, pulled out Wilbur's Colt revolver, and shot herself in the chest.

The sound was deafening in the close confines of the automobile.

The bullet entered Margaret's lung, penetrated her heart, smashed through her back, and embedded itself in the metal frame of the front-seat upholstery.

"Oh Margaret, don't die!" Wilbur cried. Sideswiping several cars in his haste, he sped to the Sheriff's office and then to Mercy Hospital.

Wilbur's account seemed to wrap things up for Sheriff Gibson and the reporters hanging around Canton, writing what they could about the story.

But just as soon as the case was resolved, it started to unravel.

Margaret's mother and sisters were outraged that Sheriff Gibson would just so readily believe Wilbur's story. They demanded - and received - a second autopsy of Margaret's body, conducted by doctors in Pennsylvania, where the family lived and where she had been taken for burial. Although that postmortem agreed that Margaret died from a single bullet wound to the heart, her family refused to believe Wilbur's story. Margaret would have never committed suicide, they said.

Public opinion, which had initially favored Wilbur, began to sour toward him as the days passed. The reasons that Margaret shot Vernard depended entirely on Wilbur's version of events. There had been no corroborating witnesses to what she told them in the car that day.

The Stark County authorities and the public also wondered what kind of man would insist on taking his wife to the police before getting her a lawyer or at least checking out her story. And why had he gone to Sheriff Gibson's office after Margaret shot herself instead of the hospital?

Within a week of Margaret's death, the police and much of the public had started to believe that Wilbur was at the very least a terrible husband, if not a lying murderer who had killed his wife to protect his own reputation.

Two days later, Wilbur was arrested and held as a witness for a hearing into the deaths of Vernard Fearn and Margaret Heldman.

But the hearing mostly just damaged the reputations of the two dead principals. Despite previous statements, it turned out that Sheriff Gibson and Mary Fearn had suspected Margaret was the "Phantom Flapper" from the start. So had Margaret's family. Her father had come to Canton during the week after she died. There was talk of clandestine communications and negotiations between Margaret's family, the authorities, and Mary Fearn.

It looked as though Wilbur, embarrassed by his wife's actions, which he claimed led to her rape and continued assaults, had killed her.

The hearing ended with Wilbur being charged with "moral murder" and held for indictment by a grand jury. Prosecutor Harter said that he believed Wilbur had either shot his wife himself during their last car ride or deliberately frightened her with his brutal talk about the electric chair, making her pull the trigger herself. Wilbur's behavior was made even worse by the fact that no jury in Ohio would have convicted Margaret after hearing the story that she was only able to tell her husband.

Even so, no one really believed that Wilbur would be convicted on the existing evidence against him - and they were right.

Harter's case fell apart when he failed to produce two witnesses who, he claimed, could disprove Wilbur's assertion that Margaret shot herself on the way into town.

As the weeks passed, the story faded from the headlines, and finally, on April 11, 1929, after spending four months in jail, the grand jury refused to indict him, and Wilbur walked out of the courtroom a free man.

But was he an innocent one?

We'll never know, just as we will never know the entire story of what happened between Margaret and Vernard Fearn. Mary Fearn apparently had suspicions about her husband and Margaret, but whether they were based on fact or rumors is unknown. If Vernard raped Margaret and then coerced her into having sex with him in the months that followed is also unknown, but his truck was seen frequently outside of Margaret's home while Wilbur was away. This could be evidence of her story - or evidence of a consensual affair.

How much her husband knew about what was going on is also a mystery, although both he and Mary Fearn knew or suspected a lot more than they initially told the police.

What finally caused Margaret to kill Vernard is a secret that died with her. Did she fabricate the story she told her husband? Did she kill Vernard because he blackmailed her into continuing to have sex with him - or because he wanted to break it off?

Did Margaret kill herself because she feared going to jail? Or did Wilbur kill her or at least terrorize her into doing it herself?

All we can really be sure about is that Margaret Heldman - the "Phantom Flapper Killer" - took her secrets to the grave.

# "THE WORST WOMAN ON EARTH" LIZZIE HALLIDAY

In 1888, a cell door at the Eastern State Penitentiary slammed shut behind a woman who called herself Lizzie Brown. She served two years for the crime of arson in the imposing institution, and for most of her sentence, she was a model prisoner. But then, two years before her release date, she began acting strangely, even unhinged.

Lizzie was taken to an asylum, and after doctors confirmed her insanity, they looked after her until her prison sentence had expired.

She was no closer to being sane when she was released.

Lizzie made her way up the east coast to New York to hunt for work. In a small town called Newburgh, she met Paul Halliday, who was looking for domestic help. He'd been married before and fathered six children, one of whom was mentally disabled and still lived with his father on the family farm. Lizzie told Paul that she had arrived in America from Ireland just six weeks earlier, and he hired her, agreeing on a salary of $40 a month.

It wasn't long before Paul realized that it would be cheaper to marry Lizzie and have her work for free than to pay her. Besides, he didn't mind the thought of her as his wife. There was something oddly charming about the young woman. The two were soon wed, and Halliday's children would later describe their marriage as one of "peculiar influence."

Lizzie's time as Paul's wife must have been a nightmare but it seemed that no matter what she did, he refused to blame her. In the spring of 1891, Paul came home one day and found that his house had been reduced to a smoking pile of ashes. Standing near the ruins, Lizzie casually informed him that his disabled son had died in the fire. The brave boy had died trying to save her from the flames.

Or so she said. This story didn't make much sense when fire officials found the boy's bedroom door in the rubble, and it was clearly locked. Lizzie herself was carrying the key. And yet, Paul stayed with her.

Less than a month later, Lizzie burned down his barn and mill, telling him he needed a new one anyway. Soon after, she ran off with another man, determined to become a horse thief. She was arrested and thrown in jail. Behind bars, she immediately started tearing her hair out and screaming at anyone who would listen - as well as at invisible people who weren't there. Her mad behavior caused her to be acquitted on the grounds of insanity, and she was sent across the river to the Matteawan State Hospital for the Criminally Insane.

Paul Halliday scoffed at this. Lizzie was "perfectly sane," he objected. But the doctors at the asylum disagreed with him. They kept her for a year and then released her into Paul's custody. She was cured, they assured him. She'd be no more trouble.

Their unusual marriage continued for the next year - without any mysterious fires - but then, one day, Paul disappeared.

Lizzie told her neighbors that her husband was simply away on business, but some of them noticed odd happenings on the Halliday farm a few days before he "left on his trip." They had heard eerie sounds, loud noises, and figures creeping around at night.

Besides that, there was just something strange about Lizzie. The neighbors didn't really trust her.

So, one day while Lizzie was away, they decided to search the farm. There had been no word from Paul, and they feared the worst, wondering if they might find a body hidden there somewhere.

They were right to fear the worst, but they didn't find a body there - they found two.

Lizzie Halliday had been born Elizabeth Margaret McNally in County Antrim, Ireland, in 1860. Her parents and nine siblings immigrated to New York when Lizzie was still a toddler. She grew up to be a troublesome child. Her brother, John, later recalled, "She was inclined to so much quarreling that the family disowned her for years. She could not stay in a place any time when working out on account of her violent temper."

Lizzie was strong and unpredictable. On one occasion, she attacked her father, and on another, she badly beat her sister, Jane. If she did show love, it was with wild passion. When she returned home after a long absence to find that her father had died, she flung herself on his grave and tried to dig him up with her bare hands, weeping about how she had been unable to say goodbye.

She had little education, but she was cunning. She was always on the lookout for money and could usually find it. She presented a poor impression to most of her employers, though. Lizzie wore strange clothes, was subject to mood swings and could be so unpredictable that she frightened people, even grown men. Once she threw a knife at a young man who was teasing her. When an employer tried to correct her baking methods, Lizzie ran screaming to the authorities, claiming the woman had assaulted her.

She was a frequent visitor to the police station. The cops were either hauling her in for assault, or she showed up on her own, threatening to press charges against someone - like two little boys who pointed toy pistols at her. However, when she was in a good mood, she could be found at religious services and revivals, lost in the throes of music, song, and prayer.

Lizzie was a strange mix of appearances. She was short but very physical, with lovely pale Irish skin. But she had a very large nose and a high forehead that caused her to be mocked by others. She was called "repulsive" by a neighbor, and her landlord once referred to her as "naturally ugly."

But she didn't seem to have any trouble finding husbands. Between jobs, she got married, and between marriages, she found jobs. At 15, she married a Greenwich, New York, man known by the alias Ketspool Brown - his real name was Charles Hopkins. Both were terrified of the other throughout their marriage. Lizzie told her family that Hopkins wanted to murder her, and Charles told his doctor, "I am afraid of her. She has threatened my life."

They had a son together, and childbirth sent Lizzie into a depressive spiral. She visited her sister and complained that she heard nonstop singing in her head and saw flashing lights around the room. At one point, she sat mending a dress and cried, "What's the use of living?" and tore up the garment.

Hopkins died of typhoid fever three years into their marriage, and Lizzie worked her way through three more marriages - none of them were happy ones.

In 1881, she married pensioner Artemus Brewer, but he died less than a year later. Her third husband, Hiram Parkinson, left her within their first year of marriage. Lizzie then married George Smith, a war veteran who had served with Brewer. After a reported failed attempt to kill Smith by putting arsenic in his tea, Lizzie fled to Bellows Falls, Vermont. There, she married a younger man named Charles Playstel, but she vanished two weeks later after he confessed to Lizzie that he had "pounded his first wife to death."

In the winter of 1888, Lizzie resurfaced in Philadelphia at a saloon on 1218 North Front Street that was run by the McQuillans, fellow Irish immigrants that she knew from her childhood.

Going by the name "Maggie Hopkins," Lizzie set up a shop but was later convicted of burning it down for the insurance money, destroying several neighboring buildings in the process.

After serving two years at Philadelphia's Eastern State Penitentiary - and the asylum - Lizzie was released only to find that her son had disappeared. She never saw him again, but stories say he was later institutionalized, having inherited a bit of his mother's madness.

In 1889, now using the name "Lizzie Brown," she became the housekeeper for Paul Halliday, the twice-widowed, 70-year-old farmer from Burlingham, New York. They later married, and their time together was marred by Lizzie's sporadic "spells of insanity," which resulted in his house burning down, the death of his son, and the destruction of his barn and mill. On another occasion, Lizzie took a team of Paul's horses and had a neighbor help her drive them to Newburgh, New York, where she sold them.

Lizzie then ran off, stole more horses, was arrested, and eventually ended up in an asylum for a time.

A year later, in early August 1893, Paul disappeared. Lizzie claimed that he had traveled to another town to do some masonry work, but friends and family members didn't hear from him. His absence didn't stop Lizzie from getting into more trouble.

A few miles from the Halliday farm lived the McQuillan family - yes, members of the same family that Lizzie had stayed with in Philadelphia. It should be noted that Lizzie believed that it had been the McQuillans that turned her into the authorities after the suspicious fire. Although the family that lived near the Hallidays - Tom, his wife, Margaret, and their daughter, Sarah - knew nothing of the events in Philadelphia.

On August 26, a woman arrived at their farm in a wagon and introduced herself as "Mrs. Smith." She was looking to hire a cleaning lady, she said. Even though a visiting friend told her that Mrs. Smith seemed odd and urged Margaret not to take the job, Margaret volunteered, brushing off the advice she drove away with Mrs. Smith, teasingly calling out, "Goodbye, if I don't see you again!"

A few days later, Mrs. Smith was back at the farm. This time, she was in a panic. She exclaimed that Margaret had fallen from a ladder and desperately wanted to see her daughter. Tom wanted to go himself, but Mrs. Smith was adamant - Margaret wanted to see only Sarah. The two of them quickly drove away in the wagon together.

When two days passed with no word from his wife or his daughter, Tom became suspicious and went looking for Mrs. Smith's house. He quickly realized that she had given the

McQuillans a false name. No one knew who he was talking about when he asked about the mysterious "Mrs. Smith."

Meanwhile, Lizzie's neighbors and Paul Halliday's sons started to suspect something wasn't right about Paul's disappearance. He had been gone too long, and Lizzie's excuses were becoming harder to believe.

And that's when her neighbors got the shocks of their lives in her barn!

The local police obtained a search warrant, and they arrived at the farm on September 4 for their own search. When they came to the door, they found Lizzie busy cleaning a bloodstain from the carpet. When she spotted them, she sprang up and roared in a fit of anger. She threatened to kill anyone who entered her home. The police chief ignored her, and Lizzie snatched up a board and smacked him with it, screaming that she would "cut his heart out!"

Undeterred, Lizzie was restrained while the officers searched the farm. The house seemed empty, but the barn soon gave up its gruesome secret. Under a layer of garbage, covered by some hay, the police found the bodies of Margaret and Sarah McQuillan. Their hands and feet were tied, and their heads were wrapped in cloth. Both had been shot multiple times in the chest.

At first, Lizzie claimed to know nothing. She said that if something bad had happened, she didn't know anything about it.

But then she started to act very peculiarly.

She started picking at her clothes, claiming she could see potato bugs crawling all over her. She tugged at her hair and started talking to herself.

A question began to form in the minds of the police, the public, and the legal authorities, and it was a question that would follow

Lizzie for the rest of her life - was she truly insane, or was she faking it?

Lizzie was taken into custody and locked up at the jail in Burlingham while the search for evidence continued at the Halliday farm. Paul's children were worried about their father's fate, so one of his sons and a friend snuck into the farmhouse early one morning to see if the police had missed anything. In the kitchen, they noticed that some of the floorboards didn't match the others.

They decided to pry them up - just in case. Beneath the boards, the soil looked fresh and loose. One of them used a crowbar to poke around into the dirt. Its point sank into the ground until it met resistance, but this was no rock or brick. It was something soft. Spooked, they ran to fetch the police.

The family's fears were confirmed in less than an hour - Lizzie had buried Paul under the kitchen floorboards. The badly decomposed corpse had multiple bullet wounds in the chest and had been struck so hard in the head that the left eye had been knocked out of its socket.

On September 8, Lizzie was charged with all three murders and held for trial at the Sullivan County jail in Monticello, New York. Hundreds of people lined the streets to watch when she arrived. The jailers hurried her into a cell with no problems, but she'd let out a "deafening shriek" every now and then, so everyone knew she was there.

During her first few months there, she tore at her clothes, ripped her blankets to pieces, refused to eat, spoke incoherent monologues, and answered questions with bizarre replies that made no sense. But many believed she was faking it - it was all just too much. Some said her crazed behavior only occurred when someone was watching. When she thought she was alone, Lizzie usually just sat on her bunk "moodily lost in thought."

On September 12, the *New York Times* reported, "Mrs. Halliday Not Insane." By November 7, the headline had changed to "Mrs. Halliday Was Insane." No one seemed to be able to make up their mind.

It became a matter of public debate, with lawyers, judges, and doctors weighing in on the subject. Dr. Carlos F. McDonald told the Medical Society of the State of New York, "Public delusion is that the insanity dodge is a thing which succeeds very frequently. It is wrongfully put forth in a certain number of cases, but it is a well-known fact that it seldom succeeds where it is wrongfully offered."

Lizzie received national attention while in jail, with one sensational story after another appearing across the country in tabloid newspapers. The *New York World* portrayed Lizzie's case as "unprecedented and almost without parallel in the annals of crime."

She was interviewed by the World's Nellie Bly, the intrepid woman reporter already famous for her investigations into the Women's Lunatic Asylum on Blackwell Island and the lurid baby-buying business in New York City. She used her celebrity to get an exclusive interview with Lizzie in her cell.

During the interview, Lizzie concocted a crazy story about the night of the murders, claiming she had been drinking moonshine with Paul Halliday and the McQuillans when, out of nowhere, someone chloroformed her. When she woke up, she found that

Paul, Margaret, and Sarah had all been murdered. She had no idea what had happened.

Nellie knew that she was getting nothing but lies from Lizzie about the murders. Still, she did get her to reveal information about her previous marriages, which Nellie was able to confirm.

The revelation that she had been married five times before she wed Paul Halliday was shocking to many, but there was more. When it was discovered that two of those husbands had died less than a year after their weddings and that Lizzie had tried to poison a third, it led to much speculation in the press. "Whether these men died natural deaths or were murdered, is not known," the *New York Times* noted.

Before leaving the cell, Nellie flatly asked Lizzie if she had committed the murders. But Lizzie shook her head. "Some other time," she muttered. "My head feels bad now."

Nellie got up to leave but stopped in the doorway to ask a final question - did Lizzie repent for her crimes?

Lizzie smiled at her. "God will send you back to me," she responded.

And Nellie, with a "little chill" going through her body, left the jail.

Lizzie grew increasingly violent as she waited for her trial to begin. She refused to eat, attacked the sheriff's wife, and set fire to her own bed. When none of that got her transferred to an asylum, Lizzie tore a strip of cloth from the bottom of her dress and unsuccessfully tried to hang herself from the cell door. Five days after the attempted hanging, she smashed the window of her cell and cut her throat with the broken glass. Her wounds weren't life-threatening. Lizzie told the doctor that treated her, "I thought I would cut myself to see if I would bleed." After this, she was chained to an iron ring in the middle of the cell floor.

Skeptics continued to insist that Lizzie's madness was all an act. Others thought her suicide attempts were genuine because Lizzie believed her trial was happening soon. It wasn't - it had been postponed until spring, but no one had bothered to tell Lizzie.

Her trial finally began in the Sullivan County Oyer and Terminer Court in Monticello on June 18. As a gaunt, quiet Lizzie was brought into the courtroom, a crowd formed outside to catch a glimpse of her. Her lawyer, George H. Carpenter, offered an insanity defense, while the prosecution attempted to establish revenge as a motive for killing the two women. Lizzie knew the women were McQuillans and didn't care that they had nothing to do with what happened in Philadelphia.

The defense admitted everything - the bullets matched the gun, rings the police found belonged to Sarah McQuillan - but insisted that the blood on the carpet was not caused by murder. Her attorney said that Lizzie wasn't very clean and "did not take the usual precautions taken by women." In other words, the stains were period blood, and this argument went right along with the public opinion of Lizzie that she was uncivilized, unclean, and practically feral.

George Carpenter knew that she couldn't prove Lizzie was innocent, but he thought that he might be able to prove she didn't know right from wrong. She was, he was convinced, clearly insane. He even brought in an asylum superintendent and three doctors to confirm her insanity.

During the trial, multiple doctors stopped by Lizzie's cell to examine her for signs of lunacy. They often found her chatting with the Holy Ghost. Once, she lunged at them with the lid of her toilet in hand, ready to club anyone within reach. She gave nonsensical answers to the most basic questions they asked her.

Her age? "Nineteen skunks."

Her address? "I washed your shirt."

Her father's name? "You took my property."

Carpenter did all the arguing on his client's behalf because Lizzie never spoke a word in her own defense. She sat silently, brooding as the trial went on around her.

Carpenter asked the jury to see the randomness of the McQuillan murders as proof that Lizzie didn't know what she did. But the prosecutor argued that the jury should consider "exterminating the prisoner as an enemy to society." She wasn't insane, he said, noting that in her daily life, she was able to function in normal society, feeding herself, dressing herself, and behaving normally. She only "became insane" when she was in trouble for her other actions.

The jury only took a few hours to reach its verdict. Lizzie was found guilty of murder in the first degree on June 21, 1894. She became the first woman ever to be sentenced to death by electrocution in New York State's new electric chair.

Lizzie covered her face with a handkerchief and said nothing. George Carpenter wept.

Once Lizzie's death became a very real thing, the public suddenly began to question the fairness of it - especially since no woman had died in the electric chair before. It struck many as too harsh. Within days, people began petitioning Governor Roswell P. Flower to appoint a commission to look more closely into the question of Lizzie's sanity.

In July, the governor named three doctors to the panel. Newspapers applauded him for this humane act while still questioning whether Lizzie was insane or simply faking her psychoses. The doctors examined her for a month. They noted her rapid pulse, "extreme emaciation," possible symptoms of diabetes, and her "excessive menstrual flow." They noted that she often complained of being numb all over and how they saw flies land on her face that she didn't brush away. She developed a habit of stuffing bits of her dress into her nose and ears. She drooled constantly and cursed at people without being provoked. She had a morbid obsession with the number 13 and repeated it over and over again. One doctor transcribed some of her ramblings:

*He broke a spine of my ribs. You've got that bear sewed up in me. It's you that done it. You sewed them up in me. You broke three of my legs. You pitched me down from the garret. You put a coat of shingle nails over me. They don't want you in their house. They're going to saw off my nose. Take them that snakes off me. You brought them in a basket. You tied them around me.*

The physicians acknowledged that Lizzie was intelligent enough to plan and execute multiple murders - but saw that she was unable to resist impulse. There was no doubt in their minds that Lizzie could not control her deeply violent nature. They couldn't say for sure if Lizzie recognized the "nature and consequences" of her crimes, but they were positive she lacked the "power to choose between committing them and not committing them."

They declared her officially insane.

Governor Flower commuted her sentence, and Lizzie was sent to the Matteawan State Hospital for the Criminally Insane, where she would spend the remainder of her life.

Lizzie thrived at the asylum. When she arrived, she was raving about bugs and muttering incoherently, but the superintendent sat down with her and told her that if she wanted to be treated well at the hospital, she needed to behave as best she could. Lizzie listened and began taking better of herself, stopped cursing at the nurses and attendants and even started doing small chores.

Because Lizzie was still a celebrity of sorts, journalists made the trip to the asylum and reported back that the murderess was now engrossed in cleaning floors.

Lizzie became friendly with another incarcerated murderess named Jane Shannon, and the two developed a grudge against a young ward attendant named Kate Ward. Lizzie insisted that she had "become sane" and should be sent to a regular jail but that the asylum workers - especially Kate Ward - were plotting against her and keeping her at Matteawan.

Lizzie and Jane hatched a plot. One day they snuck up behind Kate in a bathroom. As strong as ever, Lizzie threw Kate to the floor and stuffed a towel into her mouth. While Jane held the young woman down, Lizzie began to tear out Kate's hair, scratch her face, and beat her with her firsts. By the time the other attendants realized what was happening, Kate was unconscious.

If they had arrived in the bathroom any later, she likely would have been dead.

Lizzie spent the next month in solitary confinement and was eventually returned to the ward. She had calmed down and began behaving again, turning into a model patient. Lizzie gained 60 pounds after the months of starving herself in jail and was trusted with privileges that no one would have dreamed of giving her when she arrived. She was a different woman than she had been but still of interest to the press. In 1896, she nearly died from a bad case of measles, and the newspapers dutifully covered her recovery.

In 1897, Lizzie became fixated on the idea of having false teeth. She wanted all her original teeth replaced, convinced this would make her more attractive. She began faking toothaches and told the doctors that the only cure would be removing all her teeth. Her mouth was inspected, and doctors found her teeth perfectly healthy, but Lizzie kept complaining. About six months later, Lizzie got her away. She was taken to the town of Fishkill Landing, where a (brave) dentist gave her a shiny new set of artificial teeth. When she returned to the hospital, she spent most of her time smiling widely, eager to show them off.

The following autumn, a group of inmates wrote and starred in a "thrilling drama" of the Spanish-American War. Lizzie watched from a row close to the stage, and even though she'd never shed a tear during her own "drama," she sobbed throughout the entire show, moved by the romance and adventure.

This should have been the end of Lizzie Halliday's story - an ending note of emotion and perhaps even redemption for a woman who had lived such a life of trauma and violence.

But tragically, it wasn't.

Nellie Wicks was a favorite attendant at Matteawan. She was only 24 and had been promoted to the head attendant in the women's department the previous year. She was liked by the other attendants, the nurses, doctors, and even the asylum officials. Nellie had dreams, too. One day saw herself leaving the hospital to study nursing.

One of Nellie's star patients was Lizzie Halliday, now in her mid-40s and so calm and reliable that she was never seen as a threat to anyone. She was now trusted with sewing privileges, giving her access to tools, including scissors.

In the fall of 1906, Nellie announced that she had big news - she was leaving the asylum to go into nurse's training. Everyone was thrilled for her, except Lizzie. She was heartbroken, and she begged Nellie to stay. But Nellie assured her that everything would be fine. She promised she would even come back to visit Lizzie.

As the date of Nellie's departure drew nearer, Lizzie stopped begging, and she started to threaten her, saying that she would rather kill Nellie than let her leave. But no one paid attention to Lizzie's threats anymore. She never acted on them, and she certainly would never hurt Nellie. They had a special bond.

Lizzie was just upset. She would never hurt Nellie.

Then one morning in the bathroom, Lizzie crept up behind her, clutching a pair of scissors that she had taken from the sewing basket. Nellie didn't know anyone was there until Lizzie struck her hard in the back of the head. When Nellie fell, Lizzie snatched her keys and locked the bathroom door from the inside.

Horror followed.

Lizzie stabbed the young attendant 200 times in the face, neck, and chest. Stabbing and slashing at Nellie's body until the walls, floor, and Lizzie herself were drenched with blood.

Other attendants heard Nellie screaming, but it was too late by the time they managed to break down the bathroom door. Nellie died a few minutes later. Instead of becoming a nurse, she earned the dubious place of the first known United States female law enforcement officer to be killed in the line of duty.

She also became the final victim of the "worst woman on earth."

On June 28, 1918, Lizzie Halliday died of Bright's Disease, an inflammation of the kidneys. She was 58 years old and had been in the asylum for almost half her life. There was no one to claim her body, and she was buried in the hospital's cemetery, where the graves are only numbers.

Lizzie's death ended her infamy, and she is now a forgotten memory of a long-ago life of terror.

Or is she?

Matteawan State Hospital for the Criminally Insane began in 1886 when a site was chosen to be the place for an asylum. This location would offer "an abundance of light and ventilation" for about 500 patients.

It opened in 1892, and aside from tighter security, it operated the same as the state's other mental hospitals. Doctors prescribed a program of "moral treatment," offering kind and gentle treatment in a stress-free, highly routine environment. Patients who were capable were assigned to a work program -- cooking, maintenance, and making baskets, rugs, clothing, and bedsheets.

There was also a working farm on the property, which allowed the hospital to remain somewhat self-sufficient regarding food and fresh vegetables for the inmates.

But, as with most of the asylums opened in the nineteenth century, the "good intentions" that went into the asylum's opening paved a path to hell. Conditions deteriorated, overcrowding was common, and there were continued complaints of abuse by custodians.

By the late 1940s, new procedures that included electric and insulin shock treatments began to be employed regularly at the hospital. Lobotomies followed, as did more problems, including closing the Matteawan farm. By 1949, the facility, initially built for 500, housed almost 1,500 men and 250 women.

On January 1, 1977, the New York Department of Mental Hygiene opened the Central New York Psychiatric Center, a special forensic mental health facility, which led to the closing of Matteawan. Some of the former Matteawan State Hospital buildings for the Criminally Insane now serve as part of the medium-security Fishkill Correctional Facility. The rest of the buildings remained empty for years to come.

But were they as empty as everyone believed?

The story soon made the rounds that the remains of the old hospital were haunted. And is it any wonder? Such places almost always seem to be, or so the stories say. As with any place where large numbers of people die - especially those who were disturbed and plagued by mental illness -- a belief in lingering spirits usually follows. The tales always grow larger after people begin exploring the abandoned places and sharing their haunting experiences.

But Matteawan already had a history of ghosts, at least by association.

It was at Matteawan that millionaire Harry K. Thaw spent time after the murder of famed New York architect Stanford White.

White had been murdered over a woman. In 1901, White established a caring relationship with a beautiful young model named Evelyn Nesbit, and White helped her get established with artists and photographers in New York society. Five years later, Evelyn would testify that one evening White invited her to his apartment for dinner and gave her champagne and possibly some drug, and then raped her after she passed out - she was 16 at the time.

In 1905, Evelyn married Harry Thaw, a Pittsburgh millionaire with a history of severe mental instability. Thaw was jealous and thought of White as his rival. One night, while at the restaurant on the roof of Madison Square Garden, Thaw produced a pistol and murdered White for "his wife's honor."

At trial, Thaw's attorney claimed his client was not guilty by reason of insanity, which made him want to kill White. And while Thaw may have been insane, he would state that his urge to kill had come from a mysterious force outside his body - a ghost.

This claim was supported by a medical doctor and member of the American Association for the Advancement of Science named Dr. Carl Wickland. The Chicago doctor's wife was a proponent of Spiritualism and a professed medium. Three weeks after Thaw's arrest, Mrs. Wickland insisted that a spirit voice came through her during a séance and confessed that it had forced Thaw to kill Stanford White. The spirit told the group gathered in the séance room, "I killed Stanford White. He deserved death. He had trifled too long with our daughters."

In addition to that angry spirit, she claimed, another entity also came through during the séance. He identified himself as Harry Thaw's deceased father. He defended his son and claimed that the young man had been sensitive to spirit influence throughout his life. The spirit added that he never understood Harry's actions when he was alive, but, in death, he realized that his son's depraved activities resulted from having "been a tool in the hands of earthbound spirits, evil spirits that ordered death." The ghost went on to add explicitly that Harry Thaw was "obsessed by revengeful spirits when he killed Stanford White."

It was undoubtedly a novel defense and one that played well with the jury. The first trial ended in a hung jury. After the second trial, a new jury returned a verdict of "not guilty, on the grounds of insanity at the time of the commission of the act." Thaw had been saved from the electric chair, but he was sent to Matteawan for a life sentence - which was not what his attorney and his family had in mind. His mother spent tens of thousands of dollars trying to get him declared sane but was unsuccessful.

However, on the morning of August 17, 1913, Thaw simply walked out of the asylum. With the aid of a limousine that was waiting outside the gates, he fled and sought refuge in Canada. The following month, under pressure from the U.S. government, the Canadian Minister of Justice agreed to return him to the United States. He was jailed in Concord, New Hampshire, and fought a long legal battle against returning to New York. He was not sent back to stand trial again until December 1914.

This time, he was not only declared sane but found innocent of all charges. Strangely, the ghosts never seemed to bother him again.

But the ghosts left behind at Matteawan Hospital were still bothering others. Locals began exploring the remains of the old hospital in the late 1970s. It was a period when such places were being shuttered across the country. The buildings were littered with trash and had been left to the elements with broken windows, peeling paint, and crumbling walls.

The old asylum was mostly gone, but the stories were still told about the remaining buildings. There were ghosts that walked those corridors and lingered in the cells. Stories were told of voices, screams, unexplained noises, bloodstained handprints, cries for help, and eerie apparitions.

The old asylum had been a temporary home to many notorious criminals over the years, including Harry K. Thaw and George Metesky, the infamous "Mad Bomber." Escape attempts also offered occasional excitement. In 1933, four patients obtained pistols and held two attendants in a locked ward. State Police were called in, and when one of the patients pointed a gun, he was shot and killed by a trooper.

But there were no inmates as vicious and depraved as Lizzie Halliday. More than any other person connected to the hospital, it is believed that Lizzie has remained behind at this place after her death. She spent more than half her life here, and thanks to her brutal killing of Nellie Wicks in one of the hospital's bathrooms, she perhaps deserves to stay behind at this place of torment more than anyone else.

If being locked away at Matteawan was Lizzie's punishment in life, being trapped at the place that confined her may be a fitting way for her to spend eternity.

# "THE GIGGLING GRANNY"
# NANNIE DOSS

After her arrest, lurid newspaper stories and crime magazine articles would dub Nancy Doss the "Giggling Granny." She seemed so lovable and funny. She was all over the news in the mid-1950s cracking morbid jokes, flirting on camera, and painting a picture of her crimes as nothing more than a few mishaps on the way to finding the right man. After all, she was a silly, lovestruck old lady who never intended to hurt anyone, much less murder a string of husbands.

But there was nothing funny about "Nannie," as she was known by friends and family. She was a killer - a cold, unremorseful murderer.

When she was finally arrested by the Tulsa, Oklahoma, police for the death of her fifth husband, her confession included a genuinely honest and unrepentant excuse for her crime -- "He wouldn't let me watch my favorite programs on television."

On November 4, 1905, Nancy Hazle was born in Blue Mountain, Alabama, to Louisa and James F. Hazel. She was one of five children - she had one brother and three sisters - and both she and her mother hated James, a controlling and abusive father, and husband. He forced his children to work on the farm instead of attending school, so Nannie never got much of an education.

But that was likely not the extent of her problems. At age 7, while the family was taking a train to visit relatives in southern Alabama, Nannie hit her head on a metal bar on the seat in front of her when the train stopped abruptly. For years after, she suffered from severe headaches and blackouts and, as an adult, blamed her mental instability on the accident. She called it "thinking crooked" and would later blame it for the lack of remorse she felt for her nefarious deeds.

When she was a young girl, Nannie's favorite hobby was reading her mother's romance magazines and dreaming about her romantic future. She thought about boys - a lot.

This caused her to become intrigued by the "Lonely Hearts" columns that she found in the magazines. But there seemed to be little chance of Nannie finding love. Her father refused to allow the Hazle sisters to wear makeup or nice dresses or go to dances or social events. He claimed that he was protecting them from being molested by boys.

Nannie's first marriage was likely to escape her repressive family life. At age 16, the cute, gap-toothed, rosy-cheeked young woman married Charley Braggs, her co-worker at a linen factory. Her father approved, but Nannie wasn't sure that she did. Charley was the only son of a single mother who insisted on living with him and Nannie after marriage. To Charley, Nannie was the next best thing to his mother, and he described her as "a pretty girl, good build, and lots of fun."

Nannie quickly became restless in the company of her husband and her oppressive mother-in-law. Even so, the marriage produced four daughters between 1923 and 1927. Nannie started drinking, and her casual smoking habit became a heavy addiction. The unhappy husband and wife suspected each other - correctly - of infidelity, and Charley often disappeared for days at a time, leaving his wife with his mother and four young children.

In 1923, the couple lost two of their daughters to suspected food poisoning. Fearing that Nannie had something to do with their deaths, Charley fled with their oldest daughter, Florine, but left their newborn, Melvina, behind. Soon after, Charley's mother died, and Nannie took a job in a cotton mill to support herself and Melvina.

In 1928, Charley returned home with Florine and a divorcee who had her own child. It was an unusual arrangement that did not last long. Nannie and Charley quickly divorced, and Nannie took her daughters to her mother's house.

Years later, Charley would maintain that he left Nannie because he was terrified of her. He was right to be scared, as it turned out.

Living and working back in Blue Mountain - which had become a part of Anniston, Alabama - Nannie kept from being lonely by reading romance novels and the magazines her mother had loved so much. She pored over the "Lonely Hearts" columns and started writing to some of the men advertised there. One of them was Robert Franklin "Frank" Harrelson, a 23-year-old factory worker from Jacksonville, Alabama. He sent her love poems, and she sent him a cake. They met and married in 1929, when she was 24, and moved in together in Jacksonville with the two girls. After a few months, she discovered that Frank was an alcoholic with a criminal record for assault; however, their marriage lasted 16 years.

Nannie's daughters grew up. In 1943, Melvina gave birth to a baby boy, Robert Lee Haynes. Another baby followed two years later but died soon after it was born. Exhausted from labor and groggy from the ether, she "imagined" seeing her visiting mother stick a hatpin into the baby's head. When she asked her husband and sister about it, they said Nannie told them the baby was dead.

They also thought they had seen her with a pin. The doctors, however, were unable to determine a cause of death.

Did Nannie kill the baby? No one knows.

The grieving parents drifted apart, and Melvina started dating a soldier. Her mother disapproved of him and while Melvina was visiting her father after a particularly nasty fight with Nannie, Melvina's son, Robert, died mysteriously while under his grandmother's care. The death, which occurred on July 7, 1945, was diagnosed as suffocation from unknown causes, and two months later, Nannie collected a $500 life insurance policy that she had taken out on the boy.

In August 1945, Japan surrendered to the Allied forces and brought an end to World War II. Frank was one of the millions who celebrated. After getting drunk, he forced himself on Nannie, which turned out to be a fatal mistake. The next day, she discovered where Frank kept a jar of corn whiskey hidden in the garden. She added a fatal dose of rat poison to his liquor stash, and that evening, he died painfully in his bed. No charges were filed against Nannie for his murder. The authorities just assumed the liquor was bad.

She didn't stay a widow for long.

While traveling in North Carolina, Nannie met her third husband, Arlie Lanning, through another "Lonely Hearts" column. She married him three days later. Like Frank, he was an alcoholic womanizer, although, in this marriage, it was Nannie who often disappeared - sometimes for months at a time. But when she was home, she was a doting housewife and beloved by the community. When Arlie died of what was said to be heart failure, neighbors turned out in large numbers for his funeral. Soon after, the couple's house, which had been left to Arlie's sister, not Nannie, burned down. The insurance money went to Nannie, who quickly cashed the check. After Arlie's mother died in her sleep, Nannie left North Carolina and ended up at the home of her bedridden sister, Dovie. Soon after Nannie's arrival, Dovie also died in her sleep.

In 1952, at the age of 47, Nannie went looking for another husband. She joined a dating service called the Diamond Circle Club and soon met Richard L. Morton of Jamestown, North Carolina. He didn't have a drinking problem, but he was a womanizer. He also turned out to be broke.

Richard worked nights in a pool hall, but he often put on his best suit and went out on some mysterious business during the day. Even worse, when Nannie was away on a trip, she heard that he had purchased a fancy ring as a gift. It had been for someone else because Nannie certainly didn't receive it. That meant only one thing - he was seeing someone else.

Not for long, though.

Richard's death was delayed by the arrival of Nannie's mother, who came to live with the couple after losing her husband. After only a few days in her daughter's care, Louisa came down with unexplained stomach pains and died.

Three months later, in May 1953, so did Richard.

A month later, Nannie married again, this time to Sam Doss of Tulsa. Unlike her other husbands, Sam was hardworking, faithful, and loving. He was a Nazarene minister who had lost his family to a tornado, so he even had a tragic backstory. Unfortunately, Sam was frugal and set in his ways. He disapproved of anything that he found frivolous, like romance stories and the soap operas that Nannie loved to watch on television. And so, in September, Sam was admitted to the hospital with flu-like symptoms, which doctors believed was a severe digestive tract infection. But he survived and was released from the hospital after 23 days on October 5.

On the day he was discharged, Nannie served up a steaming cup of hot coffee that turned out to be the last coffee he ever drank.

Her rush to collect on the two life insurance policies that she had taken out on him proved to be her undoing. His sudden death, occurring so soon after he left the hospital, prompted an autopsy. They discovered enough arsenic in his system to kill a horse - actually, several horses.

Nannie was arrested on the night of November 26, 1954. The plump, jovial, grandmotherly woman was taken to the police station, and many of the officers were taken aback by her cheerful mood. "She talks a lot," said detective Harry Stege, "but not about the case."

At first, she laughed and brushed off questions about poison and autopsies and unhappy marriages while smoking cigarettes and grinning a lot. It took 24 hours of off-and-on interrogations before she started to spill everything. She giggled at the detectives and told them that she wanted to clear her conscience. Sam Doss wasn't her only victim - he was just the latest one.

Nannie then confessed with a smile to all her various crimes. Investigators exhumed the bodies of her husbands, her mother, sister, grandson, and Arlie Lanning's mother. Her mother and her previous husbands were loaded with arsenic. The others appeared to have been smothered. Nothing was ever proven in the cases of her two daughters or her grandchild, but the state already had enough to put her away for good.

In a photo taken just after her long confession ended, Nannie is leaving the courthouse with a homicide captain. She is smiling and looking as though the two of them are on their way to a restaurant for a date rather than jail.

At the first hearing, none of Nannie's court-appointed lawyers would enter a plea on her behalf - they insisted she was mentally incompetent. So, she was given a default plea of not guilty.

Nannie herself continued to flirt with everyone in charge of the case. On her way to the courthouse, she told the prosecuting attorney that she had been cold in her cell. She placed one of her freezing hands on his cheek to prove it. When detectives woke her up from a nap to ask more questions, she laughed, "I don't know why you guys get me up at this hour to talk to me. I've been talking to you for a week." Her lawyers finally had to tell her to stop chatting with the police altogether. They feared she'd slip up, and something else would come up to get her into deeper trouble.

Nannie's preliminary hearing was held on December 15. During the proceedings, the judge decided to turn her over to the state mental health hospitals so that doctors could determine if she was sane or not.

Nannie wasn't upset about the compulsory 90-day stay. In fact, she treated it like a vacation. "Now maybe I will get some rest and won't have to answer so many silly questions," she said. "Maybe those docs at the hospital will teach me to think straight."

It's probably no surprise that Nannie enjoyed her stay at the asylum. Thanks to her "Giggling Granny" celebrity status, she got a lot of attention, and she even celebrated her 50th birthday there. She made sure that she primped and put on makeup whenever one of the staff psychiatrists came to examine her. One of the doctors talked about her behavior to the press, noting that she still suffered headaches from her childhood injury but that otherwise, her health was perfect. "If you had small children," he said, "you'd be delighted to have her as a babysitter."

His supervisors disagreed.

On March 14, a panel of medical examiners declared that Nannie was "mentally defective with a marked impairment of judgment and willpower." They recommended that she be permanently committed to an asylum.

But the prosecution moved ahead with its case. They demanded that she be tried for murder, so she was moved back to jail while her attorneys entered a plea of "not guilty by reason of insanity." A sanity hearing was scheduled for April, and dueling experts began to be lined up by both sides.

Nannie disliked being in jail and wanted to go back to the hospital. "You can't see people in jail," she complained," and I like people." Even so, Nannie managed to charm a few people from behind bars. One man even went so far as to mail her a marriage proposal, but Nannie tore the letter up. "I've had enough husbands," she wisecracked to reporters.

The sanity hearing was what everyone expected - various mental health authorities arguing with each other about whether Nannie was sane or insane.

"Mrs. Doss is mentally defective and is now insane in the legal sense. She has also been crazy for a long time," announced a doctor for the defense.

The prosecutor interrupted him to say that he had five psychiatrists on hand who were ready and willing to declare her sane. One of their reports read: "She is a shrewd, clever, sharp, calculating, selfish, self-aggrandizing female whose aggressive behavior under frustration releases her hostility toward men, particularly her husband."

A superintendent from the state hospital noted that Nannie would giggle "extensively at nothing" for days and then fall into long, dark depressions. If that wasn't insanity, what was?

The prosecution witnesses scoffed at that. Nannie was a sociopath, one of them claimed, and a "shrewd, calculating female who feigned insanity to escape the electric chair - the cleverest criminal I ever interviewed."

At that final statement, Nannie laughed out loud.

This went on for three days, but it only took the jury 15 minutes to decide that Nannie was sane.

Scary but sane.

Nannie agreed with their verdict. "I'm as sane as anybody," she chuckled. "I guess I ought to know better than anybody if I'm crazy. I've never felt more sane in my life." She chewed gum while the verdict was read and put on a big smile for a photographer who snapped her picture.

Nannie's official trial was set for early June. The prosecutor in the case was J. Howard Edmondson, who would later become governor of Oklahoma. The press was gearing up for fireworks when Nannie surprised everyone on May 17, 1955, when she suddenly entered a guilty plea for the murder of Sam Doss. She hoped for a lighter sentence and thought maybe an early guilty plea would earn her some goodwill. It's also possible that she misunderstood the implications of pleading guilty. She wanted to go back to the state hospital and perhaps didn't realize it was too late for that to happen.

She'd been declared sane. There was no state hospital in her future. After a guilty plea, she was now officially a murderer.

Her sentencing took place on June 2. The prosecution urged the judge to consider the death penalty. Nannie sat between her two attorneys, loudly chewing gum when the judge made his decision - life in prison.

It would have been the electric chair, but the judge couldn't stand the thought of executing a woman. He told the court, "This court has never heard of a woman being put to death for any crime in Oklahoma. It may happen someday, and the people of this state would very reluctantly see such come to pass."

Nannie just shrugged. "I have no hard feelings," she said.

The prison doors closed for Nannie on June 4. After that, she dropped out of the news until a reporter interviewed her in September. "I thought everybody had forgotten me," she told him. She mentioned she'd lost eight pounds in prison because all she did was laundry and complained that her headaches were getting worse.

Otherwise, Nannie seemed happy enough, with no desire to return to her old marriage and housework routine. "I'm a funny person," she told him. "If they'd let me out right now, I'd go straight to the hospital at Vinita and be content to spend the rest of my life there. That sounds sorta crazy, doesn't it?"

Nannie did just fine in prison, though she might have preferred the hospital. She got to do everything she didn't get to do living with Sam Doss - she saw movies, watched television, and participated in occasional dances for the ladies only. She loved the jail matron, Mrs. N.F. Whitaker, who Nannie said, "was just like a mother to her."

Of course, remember that she poisoned her mother, so maybe that wasn't the compliment she thought it was.

In 1957, Nannie conducted an interview with another newspaper reporter. Always the "Giggling Granny," she told him: "When they get shorthanded in the kitchen here, I always offer to help out. But they never do let me."

And that's the image that remains of Nannie Doss after all these years - the hilariously murderous grandmas who read romance novels in jail and was obsessed with getting rid of her husbands.

Nannie was smart. She knew how to work the angles. She was clever enough to realize that as a husband killer, she could hide behind a goofy, lovesick persona and possibly escape with her life. If she had appeared in the press as a maniac, she would have never gotten the attention she did - the laughs from cameramen, the jokes with police officers, and the doctor who truly believed she'd make a great babysitter. She used the naivete of Americans to emphasize only the marketable aspects of her shady past. She only killed her husbands, who sometimes doesn't want to do that, right? People ignored the dead children, the helpless mother, and the sinister side of Nannie's personality. They chuckled at the stories that occasionally appeared, marveling at how Nannie kept her signature sense of humor in prison.

That is until she didn't.

Two years after being locked up, Nannie told a journalist that she'd lost the will to live. She wanted to be tried again in one of the other states where she had been charged with murder. "Maybe they would give me the electric chair," she said.

But life stretched on for the killer that no one took seriously. Seven years into her sentence, she faked a heart attack, which got her out of prison until doctors could find nothing wrong with her.

On June 2, 1965 - 10 years to the day she was sentenced to life in prison - Nannie Doss died of leukemia.

By then, her notoriety was gone, and the "Giggling Granny" was all but forgotten.

# "THE TRUNK MURDERESS" WINNIE RUTH JUDD

October 18, 1931, was an ordinary autumn night in Phoenix, Arizona. The thermometer had climbed to 89 degrees that afternoon, the beginning of the "cool" season in the desert community of just 48,000 people. The summer heat had been almost intolerable, and everyone looked forward to the milder days ahead. Most of the country would soon be fending off snow and freezing temperatures, but that kind of winter never came here.

That was why Phoenix had so many tourists in the wintertime - although this winter, the tourists would be coming to town for more than just nice weather.

They would be coming for strictly morbid reasons.

It was an ordinary evening for most people in Phoenix, but not for Winnifred Ruth Judd - who most people called "Ruthie."

The 26-year-old daughter of a Methodist minister hadn't spent her day at church as she had on every Sunday of her life while growing up in Darlington, Indiana. In fact, her church attendance had been pretty lax since she'd left home seven years earlier as the bride of a successful doctor who was 22 years older than she was. But she didn't tell her parents that in the long letters she wrote home to them. Her letters were always cheery and betrayed nothing about how her life had turned out.

Dr. William C. Judd hadn't turned out to be as successful as his wife and her family had expected. He had found work as a doctor for American mining interests in Mexico, working for little money and whatever accommodations the company provided. He changed locations often and never held any post for long. Eventually, he had trouble even getting those jobs, unable to keep any position because he was addicted to narcotics. That fact didn't make it into the letters Winnie sent to her parents either.

Ruthie became skilled at taking care of herself. She had come to Phoenix because its dry air offered relief from the tuberculosis she had been diagnosed with. She had arrived in the city from Mexico in 1930 - without her husband - and without the skills to earn a living. Fortunately, though, she found a six-day-a-week job at Phoenix's first private medical office, the Grunow Clinic. It paid $75 a month. Sunday was usually her only day off, but it was not unusual for her to spend part of that day working at home. She was a medical secretary responsible for typing up reports on exams for the doctors. Her salary paid for her rent and groceries and left her a little to send to her husband. She had to keep doing that until he could land a new job, which, she believed, would be any day now.

She usually did the laundry and cleaned her small apartment on Brill Street with the rest of her Sunday. On some Sundays, though, she had dinner with her two best friends, Anne LeRoi and "Sammy" Samuelson, who lived just a trolley ride away from her. They often pooled their money for something special - fried chicken was a favorite - and Anne would cook. Then they'd turn up the radio and listen to the shows broadcast all over America.

But Ruthie did none of those things on October 18. On that day, she was busy packing. In fact, she had been up all night packing. And now she needed help. She went to see her landlords, a kind couple who lived just across the alley from her apartment.

Violet Grimm knew something was wrong when Ruthie, her tenant, came to the door. She looked tired, and she seemed preoccupied and nervous. Her hand was bandaged with a towel. She told Violet that she had burned it while ironing. She fussed at her and said it should be covered with a salve and appropriately bandaged, but Ruthie insisted it would be fine. She wanted to know if she could use the telephone and, also, could Mr. Grimm help her with some luggage?

Howard Grimm was reading the newspaper when his wife told him that she'd volunteered him and their son for an errand. Ruthie was taking the night train to Los Angeles to see her husband and needed some help loading her trunks.

As Howard would later testify, he didn't mind lending a hand to the pretty young woman who had rented one of his apartments. Ruthie was clean, didn't have loud parties, and paid her rent - sometimes a little at a time, but all $45 was always paid by month's end. She had even become friendly with the Grimms' children, especially his daughter Rita. When the girl had trouble with her Spanish classes, Ruthie had offered to help.

Howard didn't know much about Ruthie, but everything he and his family did know convinced them she could use the help. He hadn't been impressed with Dr. Judd, who had spent some time in Phoenix with his wife before looking for work again. He couldn't understand what the attractive young woman would see in the plain, older man. He suspected that the doctor liked either his booze or his dope, but that wasn't Howard's concern. Ruthie had no such vices. Her biggest problem seemed to be that she was in a tough spot as a woman alone during tough economic times. Even when his contracting business slowed down, he still made enough money that his Violet didn't have to work.

Besides, Howard had a practical reason for helping Ruthie. She was a tiny thing - maybe 110 pounds and not even five-and-a-half-feet-tall - and she'd certainly need help moving anything heavy or bulky.

Like everyone else who encountered Ruthie Judd that weekend, Howard and Violet would never forget the details. Violet later said that Ruthie came to her house twice on Sunday to use the telephone. She didn't hear what number Ruthie requested from the operator, but she did overhear her ask someone to loan her $5. She also recalled that Ruthie seemed nervous and preoccupied - not her usual self.

The train to Los Angeles was scheduled to leave at 8:00 p.m., so Howard planned to collect Ruthie's luggage around 6:30. But when he told his son, Kenneth, about the plan, he found it wouldn't work. Kenneth had a youth meeting at church that started at 5:00. The teenager ran across the alley and asked if Ruthie could be ready earlier. She told him she could.

Ruthie was dressed in a plain, brown suit when the men arrived. She pointed them toward the bedroom, where they found two trunks. Howard was startled by the weight of the black one and let out a groan as it tried to lift it. Ruthie apologized for the weight of it. She said that it contained her husband's medical books, and he'd need them in California if he got the job he was promised. It took both Howard and Kenneth to haul the trunk to their car outside. They tied it to the running board on the passenger side. Kenneth managed the smaller trunk by himself, wedging it between the front and back seats.

Winnie carried out her own battered suitcase and a hatbox. She sat in the front seat as Howard drove. Kenneth climbed into the back.

It only took a few minutes to reach the new train depot at Fourth Street and Jackson. Howard and Kenneth climbed out to help her. Ruthie had promised to give them $1.50 for their assistance, but she only had a $1 bill. She offered to pay them the rest when she returned, and, of course, Howard told her it was fine.

Baggage handler Beverley Stallings worked the evening shift at Union Station when the Grimms' car pulled up in front. Stallings and Kenneth moved the large trunk, and Kenneth fetched the smaller one as Stalling started the paperwork. The trunks were overweight and cost Ruthie an extra $4.48 to get them to Los Angeles. Fellow baggage handler Avis Boutchee collected the additional charges from Ruthie and asked for her signature. He noticed that her left hand was wrapped in a bandage. He attached one copy of the paperwork to the trunks and gave a yellow copy to Ruthie. Only later did he look to see what name she signed - B.J. McKinnell. He had no way of knowing this was the name of Ruthie's younger brother.

Head Porter John Washington noticed the attractive woman sitting alone in the station when he arrived for work at 5:00 p.m. It was nearly three hours until the L.A. train arrived, and the station was nearly empty. He noticed the woman getting up and walking around now and then but always keeping her carry-on luggage in sight.

By the time the *Golden State Limited* pulled into the station at 7:55, Beverley Stallings had taken his supper break. He helped the baggage boys load Ruthie's trunks, along with some other luggage dropped off by local passengers. As always, he was in a hurry because the train was at the station for only 15 minutes. But even in his haste, he noticed something leaking from the largest trunk. He thought it smelled like medicine.

Meanwhile, John Washington, the porter, made a point of helping the young woman onto the train with her carry-on bags. She seemed nervous. Her seat was in the rear of the chair car, third from the right. Washington thought she'd be sitting up for the whole trip but imagined she couldn't afford a berth. He didn't expect a tip, but she did manage to find him a few pennies, which he thanked her for and tipped his hat as he left her.

H.J. Mapes was the baggageman on the train that night, handling the duties between El Paso and Los Angeles. He'd been with the Southern Pacific Railroad for 23 years and had managed thousands of bags, so he knew right away that something was wrong with the large steamer trunk that had been loaded in Phoenix. He noticed a strange smell and then when he looked closer, he was sure that it was leaking blood.

As soon as he unloaded his car in Los Angeles at 7:45 am the following day, he notified district baggage agent Arthur V. Anderson that they had a problem - a contraband deer, he suggested.

Anderson went out on the platform, where the trunks had been loaded onto a flatbed truck. Even in the open air, he could smell the horrible odor. As he got closer, he saw blood running down the side of the trunk. He thought Mapes was right. People were always trying to smuggle deer meat on the train to California. Health officials had demanded that the practice stop, so Anderson tagged both trunks with a pink hold slip, which meant the luggage couldn't be released without official approval.

No one noticed the young woman in the brown suit who left the train that morning except Stella Conley, a maid in the ladies' room. The woman was carrying a hatbox and was followed by a porter with a banged-up brown suitcase. They passed the storage locked along the walls and walked directly to the ladies' room. Stella had to step aside to let them past. The woman asked the porter to place the suitcase behind the restroom door against the wall. She put the hatbox on top of it. She nodded to Stella as she left the restroom and sat down on a bench in the station's large waiting room.

Stella didn't usually let people clutter up her restroom with luggage. That's what the pay lockers were for. But the woman was obviously waiting for someone, so she thought she'd let it pass.

But an hour later, the woman was still sitting there. Stella approached the woman and asked if she was leaving, and the woman simply told her she was not. Stella asked her to check the bags she'd left in the bathroom, but the woman replied that she didn't have the money for a locker. She was waiting for her brother, who was a student at the University of Southern California. She'd sent him a message to meet her, but she wasn't sure if he'd gotten it before going to his morning classes. If he didn't come soon, she'd have to go and get him, and she only had enough money for a streetcar ride.

Feeling sorry for a woman in her predicament, Stella offered to keep an eye on her bags if she had to go and find her brother. She knew what it was like not to have much money.

A few minutes later, the woman got up to leave. She told Stella that if she missed her brother and he turned up at the station, he would be looking for "Mrs. Judd."

"If your brother comes, shall I let him have your bags?" Stella asked.

"No, don't let anyone have the bags until I come back," the woman instructed, and Stella agreed. After she left, Stella tried to move the suitcase farther out of the way so that no one would bother it, but it was so heavy she couldn't lift it. Assuming it would be safe, she left it where it was.

By the time Stella's shift was over at 3:00 p.m., neither Mrs. Judd nor her brother had come to claim the two bags.

George Brooker was the delivery clerk that day at the station. As he'd done every workday for the past four years, he exchanged claim checks for baggage and filled out all the paperwork that went with the job. When he went to take down the numbers on the two trunks on the flatbed, he noticed an awful smell. Something dark was leaking out of one of them. Below the flatbed was a spot where the liquid had dripped that was the size of a dinner plate. He saw that both trunks had been pink-tagged.

Around noon, a Ford roadster pulled up to the loading dock. Brooker didn't recognize the attractive woman who got out of the car, but he recognized the young man with her. His name was Burton McKinnell, and he was a college kid who had helped at the station over Christmas, lending an extra hand with the additional holiday mail and luggage.

The young man handed Brooker two claim tickets, and he took them to the front office. Baggage agent Anderson came out personally to handle the situation with the pink tags. "Who does this baggage belong to?" he asked.

The woman said the trunks were hers, and when asked what was inside, she told him that it was personal things and clothing.

"It must be something else," he insisted. "It wouldn't be a broken bottle of booze, I don't suppose?" He laughed, and the woman assured him it wasn't.

Anderson led the woman and the young man toward the flatbed, and they were about four feet away when he asked if they could smell the terrible odor. The woman acted as if nothing was wrong, saying she couldn't smell a thing. The man, Burton, looked horrified. He could see the stain on the concrete from the leaking fluid and noticed flies swarming around his sister's trunks. "Well, I can smell it!" he blurted out.

Anderson led the woman closer to the trunks and asked her to try again. She finally admitted that yes, she did smell something.

"What could be in those trunks to cause that stink?" Anderson asked her sharply.

"Well, I don't know," she replied calmly. "I can't imagine what it is."

Anderson pointed out the liquid that was still dripping. The woman turned to Burton. "What do you suppose that is?" she asked him, but the young man just stared at her. Anderson said that he didn't notice anything in the woman's behavior that suggested she was nervous or uncomfortable. In fact, she seemed as confused as he was. The young man with her was totally befuddled by the scene.

"Please open the trunks, ma'am," Anderson told her. He said that whatever was leaking would undoubtedly damage the other contents. He didn't want her to file a claim against the railroad for what was ruined later. He wanted to determine the extent of the problem now.

But the woman seemed hesitant, so her companion offered an alternative plan. "It might cause some embarrassment to open the trunks here," he said. "Why not come out to the house and examine the contents there?"

Anderson refused. The woman opened her purse and fished around inside with one hand - the other was wrapped in a bandage - as though she were looking for keys to the trunks. Then she looked exasperated, "My husband has the keys," she finally said, but Anderson later said that he knew she was lying.

Quickly, she said that she'd have to telephone her husband to bring the keys to the station. Anderson offered the use of his office phone, and she made a show of thumbing through the phone book, claiming that she didn't remember her husband's number and couldn't find it listed.

"I'll have to go and get my husband and bring him down here," the woman eventually said. The man with her still looked as if he couldn't figure out what was going on, Brooker thought. He watched as the two of them calmly walked to the car and drove away.

They never came back.

Anderson waited until 4:30 that afternoon, and then he called the police and reported two suspicious bags.

Detective Frank Ryan's shift was almost over when the call came in. He hoped to go straight home after a quick stop at the train station.

But the 10-year veteran detective was in for a long night.

When Ryan joined Anderson on the loading dock, he took one look at the large trunk and knew he was looking at blood. He'd seen too much of it over his last decade with the LAPD. Anderson handed him a set of passkeys, and the detective picked open the lock on the larger trunk.

When he lifted the lid, he saw a piece of rug on top. He moved it aside and found some books and papers. Beneath that layer were fragments of women's clothing, some of it smeared with blood. They were piled on top of an old quilt. Ryan lifted the corner of the quilt and instinctively jerked his hand away.

He was looking at a woman's face.

As he pulled his hand back, the quilt was gripped tightly in his fist. It was pulled aside to reveal the body of a woman who was crammed into the trunk. She had dark hair and was wearing pink pajamas. She was on her side, her head in one corner and her knees drawn up to her chest.

Detective Ryan let the lid of the trunk slam shut with a thud, rushed into the depot officer, and called precinct headquarters for fingerprint men and the morgue.

As he waited for them to arrive, he opened the smaller trunk. Several sheets of paper lay on top, some spattered with blood. A thin cotton blanket was stuffed around the contents. Under it were two bundles wrapped in women's clothing.

He unwrapped them to find a human foot, a leg from the knee down, and a woman's torso from the head to the navel.

Frank Ryan had seen enough. He'd wait for the boys from the lab and wouldn't touch anything else. But he already knew something that made him feel sick - the pieces in this trunk didn't add up to a whole body.

He didn't know it yet, but there were two bags that, with the trunks, still stashed behind the door of the ladies' room.

To explain the contents of the two trunks, we have to turn back the clock to a few days earlier - Friday, October 16.

It was 9:30 p.m., and Anne LeRoi was already in her pink pajamas when Ruthie Judd arrived at the home she shared with her roommate, Hedvig "Sammy" Samuelson. Annie had been wearing her pajamas all evening, which she often did for an "at home" night with her best friends.

Sammy was in bed. She spent a lot of her time there, too weak and sick from tuberculosis to get around much. Her entire wardrobe, it seemed, was composed of various kinds of silk pajamas.

They made quite a pair, and everyone who knew them called them "the girls," which they didn't mind, even though Anne was 32 and Sammy was 24.

Ruthie let herself in through the kitchen back door. She knew the house on North Second Street as well as she knew her apartment a few blocks away. She knew the back door was never latched, just as she knew the front door was only used by "company." Ruthie wasn't company. She was a former roommate and still a best friend.

It seemed natural that the three women had become friends. All were newcomers to Phoenix. All were far away from family and hometowns. Anne was from Oregon, Sammy was from North Dakota, and Ruthie came from Indiana.

The bond between Anne and Sammy was already strong by the time they arrived in town together in 1931. They'd met in Alaska, where Anne had worked as a nurse and Sammy was a teacher. The wet, cold climate of the region had been terrible for Sammy's illness, and they came to Phoenix for the same reason that Ruth had a year earlier - hoping the dry climate would ease Sammy's condition and let her live a normal life. Sammy saved about $400 before she became too sick to work again and lived on that, along with Anne's generosity.

When the girls arrived in town, Ruthie was already working as a medical secretary at the Grunow Clinic. Anne was hired as an x-ray technician right away, working six days a week but earning $125 a month, which was $50 more than Ruthie. They started visiting during coffee breaks, going to lunch together, and spending time in the evenings. Ruthie invited Anne and Sammy to her apartment for dinner, and they asked her back. Soon, they even became neighbors.

Anne and Sammy lived in a duplex on the edge of town, just a few blocks off the trolley line. Ruthie moved in when the other half of the house became available in May 1931. The three women became inseparable.

Ruthie's husband, William, also lived there for a few months off and on. By all accounts, they were a friendly foursome, often having dinner together, playing cards, and listening to the radio. Dr. Judd even had things in common with the girls. He and Anne had both worked at Good Samaritan Hospital in Portland, Oregon, and Anne's parents lived near the Judd family's Oregon farm. He also had two sisters who were teachers, like Sammy.

By October 1931, though, none of the three women had seen Dr. Judd in months. The previous year had been challenging for them, and all their dreams of a "new life" in Phoenix had been dashed.

Ruth's hopes of settling down with her husband were shattered by his drug addictions. Sammy wasn't improving in the desert climate, and worse, Anne had found out that she had also contracted tuberculosis. By June, she was too sick to work and wanted to go home to her family and rest for a few weeks. But she feared losing her job and didn't have enough money to make the trip. Ruthie pleaded with the doctors to hold Anne's job for her and give her some traveling money. One of the doctors was so moved that he wrote Anne a check for $100.

With Anne gone, Sammy moved into a sanatorium so she could get the daily care she needed. Ruth moved into the girls' half of the duplex.

By July, things were looking up. Anne's health had improved enough to return to Phoenix and go back to work, so Ruthie moved Sammy back into the duplex, caring for her friend until the three women were reunited in August.

After Anne returned, the three roommates tried to adjust to living in a one-bedroom house. Not only was it cramped, but they also had very different ideas about housekeeping - Anne was fastidious, and Ruth was careless. Their domestic differences led to several "petty arguments," a mutual friend later recalled.

But that was the least of Anne's worries when it looked as though she would not be able to get her job back. One doctor at the clinic wasn't fond of Anne and had trained a young nurse to run the x-ray machine in her absence. He didn't feel Anne's specialized skills were needed anymore. Ruthie pleaded on her friend's behalf again, though, and soon Anne was back to work.

The three women remained living together for only two months. In early October, Ruthie found her one-bedroom apartment on Brill Street. It was only a couple of blocks from the clinic, and it allowed her to walk to work each day instead of paying the daily fare for the trolley ride from the house.

Ruth would soon come to regret her decision to move.

The three girls had many friends - and many admirers. They were always referred to as cheerful, friendly, and pleasant, but more than anything else, all three were beautiful.

Ruthie was the most petite. She had large blue eyes, high cheekbones, and arching brows. When she smiled, she lit up a room. Her light hair was sometimes blond, sometimes hennaed for a reddish tone, and she kept it in the short, bobbed style of the day.

Sammy might not have been quite as pretty as Ruth, but she more than made up for it in personality. Her illness had not caused her to lose any of her looks either. She was tall and thin with blue eyes and auburn hair that she kept short. She was a voracious reader and maintained a daily journal.

It was common for Sammy to be the center of attention whenever they entertained. Since Sammy didn't go out much, their guests came to them, which meant frequent parties at the duplex. Ruth was often there, even after she moved to her new apartment, and so were other friends that Anne had made in town. There were also plenty of men, including young doctors from the clinic and businessmen from Phoenix and out of town.

A favorite guest was a tall, handsome, broad-shouldered man named Jack Halloran, who the other two girls had met through Ruthie. Jack always arrived with plenty of food and booze, even though Prohibition was still hanging on. He often brought along his friends, other successful businessmen like him who also had families at home but loved spending time with attractive young women. Sometimes the men brought presents, like a brand new Philco radio, or left cash on the table.

Anne was a little larger than the other two girls but was definitely gorgeous. Newspapers would later refer to her as "mannish," but friends called her a "brunette beauty." She was not only the oldest of the girls but the one most capable of caring for herself. She was wickedly smart and realized that while anyone could be a nurse, few had mastered the specialized training for the newest diagnostic wonder, the x-ray machine. She knew this skill would bring job security and better pay than she could make as a nurse.

Anne became the breadwinner in the house and, for that reason, likely made all the decisions. Her biggest worry was Sammy. She constantly talked about Sammy's health problems and fretted that the desert climate hadn't done much to give Sammy back her strength. At least a couple of times each week, Anne would pick up something at the drug store that she thought Sammy would like. This kindness was exclusive to Sammy. To all others, she was the woman in charge. But for Sammy, she would do anything.

It wasn't commonly expressed in those days, but Anne was deeply in love with the other woman. And the feelings were likely returned. With their good looks, wit, and charm, it was probably expected that Anne and Sammy would find suitable husbands and join the ranks of American housewives. But that wasn't in the cards for them, and they would always be just "roommates."

It was something that Ruthie Judd would never understand. All she had ever wanted was to be a good wife and a mother.

She had been an 18-year-old assistant in an Indiana psychiatric hospital when she was smitten by a 41-year-old doctor who headed one of the units in 1923. They purposely ran into each other in the cafeteria many times before he finally asked her out in August. She wanted to go to dinner with him, but she had to deliver a speech about missionary work at her father's church that night. She would go to dinner with him afterward if he accompanied her to church. He agreed, and they began regularly dating until her father married them at his church on April 18, 1924.

Ruthie left home for the first time that same night on a honeymoon trip to Mexico. It was her first train ride, her first night in a hotel, and certainly her first time out of the country. She had grown up very sheltered. She had never attended a circus, carnival, ball game, movie, skating rink, or bowling alley. She had never even been allowed to wear jewelry. Her church did not approve of it.

Dr. Judd took his new bride to Vanegas, Mexico, where he'd landed a job as a doctor for an American-owned silver mine crew.

The next three years in Mexico turned out to be the only happiness the couple ever shared. Ruthie even realized her greatest dream - she became pregnant. But the weather in that part of Mexico caused her tuberculosis to flare up, and she became too weak to carry and deliver a child. Tragically, she lost the baby. A second pregnancy the following year ended the same way.

By the end of 1927, Ruthie was so sick that her husband sent her to a sanatorium in California to get treatment for her illness. In a few months, she was well enough to join him at a new posting in Mexico, but that climate didn't agree with her either. In late

1928, she was back in California for more treatment. She tried joining her husband in Mexico again in 1929 - at yet another job - but this place turned out to be even worse for her, and she moved to Phoenix alone in 1930. Dr. Judd promised to join her, sure he could find a job in a town that needed doctors, but he never did.

Ruthie often made excuses for her husband's drug addiction, claiming he'd been given an overdose of morphine for a wound during World War I. Whether that was true or not, by the time Ruthie ended up by herself in Phoenix, she knew he had a drug problem from which he likely wouldn't recover.

In Phoenix, she first found work with a wealthy family named Ford, caring for an invalid wife and watching the children. It was room and board and $80 a month. Ruthie was just the kind, caring, church-going, no-trouble young woman the family wanted. While living with them, she met their friends and neighbors, including Jack Halloran, who lived next door.

Jack was 44 years old and a local success story. He was one of the most prominent men in town, and he and his wife and three children lived in the nicest neighborhood in Phoenix. He was well-liked, admired, and politically connected - you wouldn't find anyone in the city who'd say a bad word about him.

And then along came Ruthie and a relationship that would destroy them both.

Lured away from the Ford family by a political job that paid $125 a week, Ruthie left the family - only to get fired after her new boss lost the election. Luckily, she was soon hired on at the Grunow Clinic, where she made friends with Anne LeRoi and Sammy, by extension.

Her husband remained in and out of her life for the next year or so, skating into town after losing another job because of his drug problem and then taking off again to look for another. Ruthie loved her husband, but she had little hope that her marriage would work out.

Ruthie avoided her problems in letters home to her parents, but she often painted a vivid picture of unhappiness for her brother, Burton, with whom she was close. To her husband, though, her letters were filled with her undying love, and she often begged him to return to her in Phoenix.

But she knew she was wasting her time and her letter-writing efforts.

Ruthie's friend Anne hadn't had much better luck. She had married William Mason in 1925 while still in nurse's training in Oregon, keeping the marriage a secret so she wouldn't be kicked out. The hospital found out anyway, and she was asked to leave. The marriage lasted for 18 months, and they parted on good terms.

Little is known about her second marriage to LeRoi Smith, but it didn't last either. Anne kept his first name as her last name when she moved to Alaska. William Mason saw her once after her second divorce when she passed through Seattle. "She had a girl with her that she was taking to Arizona to Alaska," he later recalled. He and friends in Phoenix would always say that Anne and Sammy were "very, very devoted" to each other.

Anne was surprised on the night of October 16 when Ruthie walked in her back door. Twice that day at work, Anne had asked Ruthie to come to supper. Another friend, Evelyn Nace, would stop by, and the four of them could play bridge. Anne had tried everything, but Ruthie declined, saying she was behind on work and planned to take some of it home with her.

This was partially true, but she couldn't come because she planned to spend the night with her secret boyfriend, Jack Halloran. They had been involved for nearly ten months, but Ruthie's friends had no idea.

Ruthie was well aware that Jack and his friends spent a lot of time at the duplex bungalow, but he'd told her that Ruthie was the one he wanted regardless of his other flirtations. But this didn't do much to curb her jealousy. While she had roomed with the girls, she realized that Jack was responsible for more than bringing bootleg liquor to their parties and handing out the occasional gift. He also frequently slipped them considerable sums of money. She'd seen him flirt shamelessly with both Anne and Sammy. She was jealous of them and knew they were jealous of her in return - or so she thought. Ruthie was blind to the way the two girls felt about each other.

But Jack hadn't shown up for that date that night, and Ruthie was irritated, deciding that she wouldn't be home if he finally decided to come over. She took a short trolley ride to see her best friends instead.

Evelyn Nace had arrived earlier than Ruthie. She also worked at the Grunow Clinic and had a casual friendship with Anne and Ruthie. She didn't meet Sammy until that night.

Anne put dinner on the table but didn't eat. She said she wasn't feeling well and sipped tea while Evelyn and Sammy ate. Tired of sitting in the kitchen, Sammy said she was too weak to sit up for bridge, so the three women moved into the bedroom. There was enough room between the two single beds to set up the card table, and they played bridge for about 40 minutes. They talked and laughed, and the party broke up around 9:30. Both Anne and Sammy walked Evelyn to the door and said goodbye.

Ruth arrived just a few minutes later, explaining that she'd gotten her work finished earlier than she'd planned. She should stay the night, the girls said. It was already late, and the trolleys would stop running soon. Saturday was a workday, plus they had a big day ahead of them - they were all going to look at a house that Ruthie hoped would be their new home.

For months, Ruthie worked with a realtor to find a large house to buy. Her parents were thinking of retiring and moving to Phoenix to be near Ruthie. They'd sell their home in Indiana and use the money for their down payment.

Ruth, Anne, and Sammy had come up with an additional plan. The girls would also move in if the house had a separate entrance and large enough rooms. Anne and Ruthie's rents would cover the house payments. Ruthie was especially anxious for the deal to work out. She missed her parents and wanted them close to her. The realtor had told her only yesterday that he'd found a house that might be perfect. Ruthie had arranged to borrow a car, so they could all go to see it.

Ruthie decided to spend the night on the pullout couch in the living room. Anne loaned her a pair of pink polka-dotted pajamas, and they all clustered for a talk in the bedroom before they turned the lights out.

It was an unremarkable Friday night for the three women. They had been together like this hundreds of times. There was nothing to suggest that this night would be any different.

But by the time this night was over, Anne and Sammy would be dead, each with a bullet in their head. Anne's body would be stuffed into the bottom of a steamer trunk, and Sammy's body would be cut into four pieces.

And Winnie Ruth Judd would be a murderer.

After the two trunks had been opened at Los Angeles' Union Station, the police traced the license number on the car to Burton. They went to his Beverly Glen home, but he wasn't around. They found him in Santa Monica at the home of this brother-in-law, the perplexed Dr. Judd. The doctor was shocked to learn that the police were looking for his wife. He couldn't imagine that she had committed a crime. Why were they trying to find her?

But Burton already knew. While driving away from the station, Ruthie admitted to him that there were bodies in the trunks.

"What?" he cried out. "Who?"

"The less you know, the better off you are," his sister replied. When the car stopped at the corner of Sixth and Broadway, Ruthie begged a few dollars from Burton and vanished into the crowd.

The police started a search, one that the newspapers would call the largest manhunt in the history of the West. Hundreds of officers in California and Arizona looked for her. Nine blond women who matched her description were detained and questioned. They grilled her husband and her brother for hours. They interviewed her landlords and neighbors back in Phoenix, everyone she worked with, and even remotely connected to the three women. They looked into her personal life and the lives of her victims.

And they fed it all to eager reporters who passed the story on to the obsessed public.

Few crimes had ever seen the barrage of coverage devoted to Winnie Ruth Judd, and few criminals have instantly become a household name across the country. The public's fascination was a morbid mix of disgust and glee. The tabloids had a field day. Two-inch headlines screamed about the "Velvet Tigress, "the Blond Butcher," "Wolf Woman," and, of course, the "Trunk Murderess."

Phoenix papers were obviously obsessed with the stunning hometown crime, and entire news staffs were assigned to cover the story. But the fascination of Los Angeles papers rivaled even those in Phoenix. They could claim it was a "hometown crime" since the bodies were discovered there. The newspapers offered huge rewards for stories and information.

Everyone was searching for Ruthie - but she had disappeared.

On Monday night, October 19, it was announced that the police had found the missing parts of Sammy's body. Someone had noticed the old suitcase and hatbox behind the station's ladies' room door, and after the excitement over the bloody trunks, station officials called the police. Inside, they found Sammy's torso from her waist to her knees, wrapped in pajamas and a blanket. In the hatbox, they found an empty black surgeon's bag, surgical dressings, women's undergarments, makeup, a .25 Colt automatic pistol, and a box of cartridges. The discovery sparked another round of "extra!" editions of the city's newspapers.

Ruthie was still missing, but detectives and reporters were unearthing the aftermath of the murders.

Evelyn Nace spoke about her last evening with the girls and how both Anne and Sammy seemed happy and without any sense of apprehension when she left them at 9:30 p.m.

An hour later, a neighbor, Jennie McGrath, was awakened by three gunshots coming from the direction of the bungalow. She said there was one shot, then a pause, followed by two more in quick succession. She looked out the window but didn't see any lights on at the duplex. She didn't investigate any further. Another neighbor, Gene Cunningham, also reported hearing the shots, but he didn't check them out either. Instead, he went back to bed.

On Saturday morning, the clinic secretary, Mrs. Ernest Smith, took a call from Ruthie, who said she would be arriving to work a little late. Shortly after, a woman who claimed to be Anne LeRoi called to say she wasn't coming to work because she had to make an emergency trip to Tucson. Mrs. Smith angrily told the caller she was already late, and that Dr. Louis Baldwin would be very unhappy with the situation. She was right. Dr. Baldwin took the call and demanded that Anne cancel her travel plans and come in to work. They had a full schedule of x-ray patients that day.

Mrs. Smith was still on the line. "That wasn't Mrs. LeRoi," she told the doctor after he hung up. "I think that was Ruth Judd."

When Ruthie arrived at the clinic later that morning, Mrs. Smith confronted her about the call, but Ruthie denied making it. No one believed her, especially after they got a look at her. Evelyn Nace remembered her as looking "white as a ghost and nervous." Others thought she looked "untidy" and as if she "had been up all night."

The most shocking information came from Richard Swartz, a driver for the Lightning Delivery Company. A woman called his office Saturday night and asked for a trunk to be picked up at the bungalow and delivered to the train station. He found the house dark and a single trunk sitting in the living room when he arrived. It was so heavy that he needed help from two of his assistants to lift it. When he asked what was in it, the woman said it was books. Swartz warned her that a trunk that heavy couldn't be shipped as luggage. He said she then hesitated for a long time, looking confused, and then directed him to deliver her and the trunk to an apartment on Brill Street.

Ruthie had apparently moved Sammy - or the pieces of Sammy - into the smaller trunk and the suitcase in which she was later found. The police found a satchel of surgical instruments in her apartment, leading them to believe the woman had been dismembered there.

When detectives searched the bungalow, they became convinced Anne and Sammy had been killed in the bedroom. Both mattresses were missing. The corner of a bedroom had been "crudely hacked out with a pair of surgical scissors." There were blood spatters under one bed, covering the floor and splashing up as high as the baseboard. There was no blood on the walls.

The police later found one mattress - with no bloodstains - in a vacant lot, miles away from the bungalow. The other mattress was never found. The bloody piece cut from the bedroom rug was found inside the bloody trunks.

But why had the murders happened at all? Ruthie's recent move to her own apartment was cited as proof of "friction" between the three women. Bits and pieces of letters written to family and friends were widely quoted to demonstrate the growing animosity that officials claimed had broken the friendship - but really, they only show that the housekeeping styles of Ruthie and Anne clashed. The girls were much better friends living separately. One letter written by Sammy even notes, "We get along so well but it shows there has to be a lot of tolerance which comes from love."

There had to be more.

Internationally known detective William J. Burns, who wintered in Phoenix, commented on the case for the local newspaper. Based on his experience, he told the reporter, "I feel that the motive is the deepest mystery in the crime. The fact that the murderer or murderers in this case sought to hide their crime by shipping the bodies to Los Angeles indicates that the mind of the criminal was inflamed. It was not at all a calm individual who killed the two women. The trunk murder case was handled very clumsily, and it is quite possible that the crime was committed without much deliberation."

Was Ruthie insane? Or was she a killer who carefully premeditated and orchestrated the death of her best friends, as the prosecution in her case would tell the jury?

Or more intriguing was the theory suggested by a few detectives and newspapermen that Ruthie hadn't committed the murders at all. She had just badly tried to cover them up.

Did Ruthie Judd have an accomplice?

As the manhunt continued, the Phoenix papers reported the latest bits of news about the accomplice theory. It was reported that the police found "startling" evidence at the bungalow that proved there was an accomplice, but they never spelled out what it was. Either the police never told reporters what they'd found, or the newsmen decided to keep it a secret. Detectives were quoted about making progress in the case and were confident they would soon identify the accomplice.

But then, officials abruptly changed their minds. The police and the county attorney backtracked crazily, telling the media that regardless of their earlier theories, it was clear that Ruth Judd had acted alone.

There was no explanation in the newspapers for this change of mind. No one even tried to explain the evidence that detectives supposedly had. The police simply said they'd be wrong - it was Ruthie, by herself, all along. She had killed Anne and Sammy and then had tried to ship their bodies to Los Angeles.

But was it the truth? Or was the theory discarded when it began pointing toward the person who was the most obvious choice of suspects - Jack Halloran, Ruthie's secret boyfriend and one of the most prominent men in Phoenix?

As always, Jack Halloran was busy the week the girls were killed. He had a lumberyard to run. He had meetings at the Phoenix Country Club, where he was on the board of directions with the town's major attorneys, politicians, and business people. The Community Chest campaign was preparing for a charity drive, and Jack was head of its industrial division. His family was back from their summer cabin, and the children were busy at school. A pal named Ed Ryan was in town from El Paso, and that always meant a party.

And, of course, his spare time was always filled with Winnie Ruth Judd.

Jack Halloran - successful businessman, community leader, family man, on the board of the Chamber of Commerce, member of the Knights of Columbus, president of the Southwest Golf Association, and Elks Club member - was also a serial philanderer and what was known locally as a "summer bachelor."

It was a tradition in Phoenix. As soon as the temperatures started hitting the triple digits, every business person in town sent his wife and children away to someplace cooler. Jack had a cabin in the mountains. Legend has it that as one train left the station with the wife and kids, another brought in the "summer wives." Those not imported were local girls - like Ruthie, Anne, or Sammy. Most families spent the summer in the mountain town of Prescott, about 100 miles north and conveniently linked by rail line. Business people could take the train on Friday nights to spend the weekend with their families, then return early Monday morning in time for another work week and the ladies waiting for them in the desert heat.

The freedom afforded the summer bachelors allowed affairs to happen, but they were never supposed to become long-term. There were two rules - nobody was supposed to get caught, and the girlfriends were required to disappear in the winter.

Jack Halloran, it seemed, was about to get caught - and all thanks to a murderer.

Jack's activities that week can be pieced together from reports from the police and from detectives who later looked into his story. He was busy that week organizing a big hunting party for the weekend. He planned to go to northern Arizona with some doctors from the Grunow Clinic and a few friends. Ruthie dreamed about going along too but knew their affair would be exposed. She did know a nurse at the clinic from northern Arizona, though, who supposedly knew the best hunting spots.

Jack was happy to hear this and asked Ruthie to set up a dinner with the nurse on Wednesday night. But he got drunk with friends instead and didn't show up at Ruthie's apartment until after 9:00. She wasn't happy that he'd blown off their dinner date and kicked him out. But first, jack sweet-talked her into rescheduling the date for the next night.

As he was leaving, Jack made a flirtatious remark to Maude Marsha, a pretty schoolteacher who lived in an apartment next door to Ruthie's. She was offended and ignored him, but when she got inside, she scribbled down his car's license number - just in case she ever needed information about a pest that was bothering her.

Things went better on Thursday. Jack picked up Ruthie at her apartment, and then they picked up Lucille Moore at her home. Lucille was a young woman who had moved to the "big city" from a small farm community and didn't have many friends in town, aside from Ruthie and Anne LeRoi.

They were supposed to return to Ruthie's apartment with a bottle of tequila, and Ruthie was going to make huevos rancheros, a Mexican dish she'd learned to prepare while south of the border with her husband.

But on the way back, Jack announced that he needed to stop at Anne and Sammy's place. Ruthie protested, but Jack insisted they stop. Ed Ryan and another friend were at the bungalow, and he needed to pick them up. Ruthie and Lucille could wait in the car. He wouldn't be long.

Jack parked in the driveway next to the bungalow, leaving Ruthie and Lucille in the car. A few words spoken during the next few minutes would become the centerpiece of the prosecution's case against Ruthie.

Lucille later told the police that Ruthie asked her, "What do you think of Jack?"

"I think he's nice."

"He's better than that," Ruthie replied. "He's perfectly grand. Anne and Sammy think so, too. You know, I used to live here with Anne and Sammy, but we had a little difference and I moved away - in fact, that's what I moved over, our difference was about Jack."

To Ruth's dismay, both Anne and Sammy came out of the house. She rushed from the car and embraced them both, ignoring Lucille. The girls insisted that everyone stay at their home for supper. A new doctor at the clinic was already inside, and they'd make a party of it. But Ruth declined. Supper was already set at her apartment, and they had to leave.

Jack and his friends piled into the car, and they drove off. Lucille later remembered that she was uncomfortable when they got to Ruthie's apartment, and her husband wasn't there. It seemed improper for Ruthie to be entertaining men when she lived alone. She asked to go home, but Ruthie insisted it was all innocent fun and these were just friends. She convinced Lucille to stay.

Lucille never did get over her uneasy feelings that night. She had assumed that Ruthie, being married, was faithful to her husband. She'd never met Jack but knew who he was and that he had a family. She was disturbed by the "considerable affection" between the two of them.

Around midnight, Jack and Ruthie drove Lucille home - and her life would never be the same again.

Late Friday night, schoolteacher Maude Marshall was awakened when someone dropped Ruthie off at her Brill Street apartment. Maude had gotten home only an hour or so before, and Ruthie's apartment had been dark. She heard a heavy car pulling into the driveway, pausing only briefly. Someone got out and went into Ruth's apartment as the car pulled away. Maude assumed the awful man who had tried to flirt with her two nights earlier had dropped Ruthie off at home.

By the time Maude became mixed up in the case, Anne and Sammy were already dead. The police established they had been killed about 10:30 p.m. Medical experts would eventually conclude that Anne's body was placed in the trunk within six hours of her death before rigor mortis set in. They also discovered that the dismemberment of Sammy's body occurred within a few hours of death.

The police came to Maude's door after the trunks were discovered, and she told them she *assumed* the car she heard on Friday night was the same one she'd seen on Wednesday night. She didn't see it on Friday; she'd only heard it, so that she couldn't say for sure. But she did hand over the paper on which she had written the car's license number. The police had no trouble tracing it - the car belonged to Jack Halloran.

Even though Maude couldn't say for sure it had been the same car, her story did alert them to a significant element of the case - that Ruth Judd had no car, so someone was driving her around in the hours after the murders.

But Maude was not the only one who told the police about Jack Halloran's possible whereabouts that night. Dr. R.B. Raney, who lived across the street from the girls' bungalow, was out late on

Friday night, celebrating his birthday. When he came home, he saw two cars parked at the bungalow. One was large gray car, but he couldn't recall the other. Raney said he was called almost immediately after getting home for an emergency operation at St. Joseph's Hospital and returned home again around 1:00 a.m. He said the car was just then turning around in front of the bungalow and driving away without its headlights on.

The police now had cars at both the bungalow and Ruth's apartment in the early morning hours of Saturday, but this never became part of Ruthie's trial.

They also learned that Jack's gray Packard was seen parked at the bungalow "for hours" on Saturday afternoon by several neighbors. They gave the information to the Phoenix press, which never identified the owner of the "mysterious car."

It was all in the witness statements but never came out at trial. In the 1930s, the police were under no legal obligation to reveal what they had uncovered in an investigation. They told the press what they wanted to tell them, and they told defense attorneys nothing at all.

Considering what officials suspected about Jack Halloran, it seems baffling that they allowed him to reveal Ruthie's "motive" for the murders, but that's what happened.

It was all because of a kiss, the papers announced.

Halloran admitted that he was at a drinking party on Thursday night and that he had kissed Sammy. Ruthie was also at the party and saw the kiss. She wasn't the only one. Jack said that Lucille saw it too, as did the new clinic doctor, H.J. Brinkerhoff.

But Lucille told the police that she never attended any party at the bungalow. She'd never even been inside, only in the driveway. And the only kiss she'd seen that night had been Ruthie kissing Jack at her apartment - and Jack hadn't done anything to stop her.

Jack's story further fell apart when Dr. Brinkerhoff was questioned. Being new in town, he was happy to have dinner with Anne and Sammy. He said that at about 6:00 p.m., three men had arrived who were obviously old friends of the girls. One was named Jack, another was Mr. Ryan from El Paso, and Brinkerhoff never got the third man's name. Ryan set up a radio, and then Jack left, returning later to pick up the other men. After they left, the young doctor said he had a pleasant dinner with the two women. They spent the evening alone, and he left between 10:30 and 11:00. He never saw Jack kiss anyone.

When the "deadly kiss" angle - the newspapers called it that - didn't work out, investigators switched to general jealousy as the motive. Ruthie was insanely jealous, believing that Jack loved the other girls more than he loved her.

What became the most commonly accepted version of the event began on Friday night. Ruthie was at home, fuming over her friends' affairs with Jack. She snapped, grabbed a gun and her husband's surgical tools, and went to Sammy and Anne's bungalow. She killed them both, and not knowing what to do with the bodies, she cut them up and stuffed them into her traveling bags.

On Sunday, she - along with one trunk that contained Anne and two cases of Sammy - boarded the train for Los Angeles. When it arrived in L.A., the pungent stench and bloody trail left by Ruthie's luggage got the attention of the station agent. He confiscated the bags and demanded that they be opened. Ruthie claimed that she had no keys for the trunks and then fled the station.

The agent called the police, and detectives arrived to crack open the luggage and discover the gruesome contents. A search immediately began for Winnie Ruth Judd.

But what about Jack Halloran?

Naturally, he denied having anything to do with the murder. His only sin had been in associating with the girls. "I am guilty of no greater fault than being indiscreet," he said. He later issued a lengthy statement to the Phoenix papers blasting the "sensational" coverage of the Los Angeles papers that called him a "millionaire playboy."

They might have had it out for him in L.A., but Phoenix's newspapers were much kinder. Most of the information that the police learned about him was never revealed, and it was made clear by editors that they didn't want anything negative reported on Jack Halloran. Even the county attorney, Lloyd Andrews, balked when asked by an L.A. reporter for a comment about Jack's involvement in the murders: "That's nonsense. Jack Halloran is a friend of mine. He's a fine fellow."

Former U.S. Senator Paul Fannin later stated, "I knew him well and never believed he was involved. He was very highly respected. He and his family were very embarrassed by it. He made the mistake of being associated with them - going to parties and things of that nature, but he in no way was involved in any sense. He was a good friend of mine, and I always respected him."

Everyone liked Jack. He was an esteemed member of the community - he wasn't a single woman, living on her own, barely making enough money to make ends meet, whose best friends were a couple of party girls known for entertaining a variety of men.

Jack was a great guy. Just ask anyone.

Winnie Ruth Judd, on the other hand, was a killer.

Jack Halloran was never officially named as a suspected accomplice of Ruthie Judd, and he would never be arrested or even seriously questioned.

The same wouldn't be said for Ruthie.

Ruthie finally gave herself up on October 23, 1931. When she left her brother on the day she arrived in Los Angeles, she vanished by walking 20 miles to an abandoned building on the grounds of the La Vina Sanatorium in the hills above Altadena. She had once been a patient there. She hid in the building for three days, sneaking into the kitchen at night for food. She hid until the infected wound in her hand began to throb unmercifully. By the time she received treatment, it was badly infected. But Ruthie saw an ad in the newspaper, paid for by her husband, begging her to give herself up.

Ruthie called Dr. Judd's attorney, Richard Cantillon, who told her to phone another attorney, Patrick Cooney, the next day. When she did, Cantillon and Dr. Judd were also there. Judd pleaded with her and finally convinced Ruthie to give herself up.

She met her husband in the lobby of the Biltmore Theater, and they walked to Alvarez and Moore, an undertaker's establishment at Court and Olive Streets. Dr. Judd treated Ruthie's hand. When the police arrived to arrest her, Ruthie was resting in bed, looking pale and frail. Her fashionably bobbed hair needed to be washed. Her dress was soiled, and her face was gaunt with hunger.

When Ruthie was taken into custody, she sobbed, "I had to shoot her, I had to shoot her!" This didn't make sense to the police and reporters at the time, but it soon would.

Ruthie was extradited to Arizona, where she would be tried for murder. As a defense, she said that she had argued with the girls and that Sammy got hold of a gun and shot her in the left hand, causing her injury. They struggled, and the weapon fell. Anne grabbed an ironing board and tried to hit her over the head with it, but Ruthie got to the gun, shot Sammy, and turned the gun on Anne. She was still coming with the ironing board, and Ruthie had to shoot her.

She hadn't wanted to do it - it was self-defense.

Her left hand was purple and swollen, gangrenous and painful. She cradled this proof of her "dramatic plea of self-defense," as papers soon called it, during her arrest.

Ruthie had admitted to being a killer but not a murderer. It was no crime to kill someone in self-defense. But what about the rest of it? People who kill in self-defense don't cut up their victims and hide them in trunks. They don't travel hundreds of miles to dispose of bodies. No, they call the police.

The police and prosecutors were convinced the gunshot didn't happen at the bungalow. They believed that Ruthie shot herself in the hand later, either by accident or on purpose, as she concocted her self-defense story. While searching her Brill Street apartment, detectives found an empty cartridge shell that matched the bullets that killed the girls.

Besides, no one had seen a bandage on Ruthie's hand on Saturday when she was at the Grunow Clinic that day. And just as obviously, a woman with a gunshot wound in her hand could not have packed the trunks with the victims' bodies.

Ruthie was either lying or, as one detective put it, she was "nuts."

Ruth Judd's trial began on January 19, 1932. Ruthie's version of events was that the murders were committed in self-defense after the other women had attacked her. Her lawyers, meanwhile, claimed she was insane. The prosecution maintained that it had all been premeditated - the work of a jealous woman. What Ruthie was thinking during the trial remains unknown.

She never took the stand in her own defense.

On February 8, 1932, she was found guilty of murder and sentenced to death by hanging on February 17, 1933.

By this time, Ruthie had managed to drum up a lot of sympathies and a lot of support. There were accusations of shoddy police work, suspicions about an accomplice, a belief that she really had been defending herself, and her lawyer's continued assertions that she was mentally ill.

Public opinion across the country was on her side. Thousands of people - including First Lady Eleanor Roosevelt -- petitioned the state of Arizona to reconsider the death penalty in her case. Many complained of the strange twists and turns in the case. Some argued that Ruthie's testimony might be needed later if any accomplices ever turned up; some maintained it was inconceivable to execute a woman, and some begged that she be spared for the sake of her elderly parents.

But a handful wrote to support the state's plan to hang Ruthie. As one woman wrote, "If women are allowed to give way to their passions thinking public sentiment will ensure them leniency, we could all cut and slash and shoot on the least provocation."

It was painfully clear to Arizona business leaders, politicians, and residents that the negative publicity from the case was the last thing the state needed. Arizona's booster campaigns declared it a place where good people raised healthy families in a warm climate. How could they explain executing a woman with so much public support?

There was only one option available. Arizona law at the time allowed the state prison warden - appointed by the governor - to call for a sanity hearing for death row inmates.

Just days before her execution, a panel was formed for the hearing. Her mother testified to a long history of family insanity at her sanity trial, stretching back for generations. Ruthie willingly performed her role in court, pulling her hair, tearing her clothing, and staring into space as she muttered in response to voices.

Prison Matron Ella Heath told the jury that she thought Ruthie was "absolutely insane." She said that the other female inmates in the state prison were "all afraid of her." Mrs. Heath described how Ruthie had beaten herself on the head with a shore, thrown herself on the floor, and torn at her hair, many times without apparent reasons except that some word or incident had excited her. A minute later, she said, she would be laughing.

Ruthie was spared the noose, but she was sentenced to lifetime confinement in the Arizona State Mental Hospital.

With a story this bizarre - that's not the end. Not long after Winnie arrived at the asylum, she escaped. And then she escaped again, and again - for a total of seven times.

Her last escape was in 1962, and she stayed on the loose for seven years, living in Northern California under an assumed name - Marian Ruth Lane. She quietly worked as a live-in housekeeper for Mrs. Ethel Nichols.

Gone was the blond beauty who loved to drink and dance and murdered her best friends. A soft, matronly woman was in her place with kind eyes and an easy smile. She was loved, trusted, and lived in a lovely apartment behind a beautiful home on a street of opulent houses. Mrs. Nichols was generous and sweet to her. She paid her $400 a month, plus room, board, and Ruthie's social security. She bought all of Ruthie's clothes for her, her uniforms, and her aprons. The Nichols' loved to entertain, and Ruthie became the favorite tea cook in the neighborhood.

At the age of 60, Ruthie went back to school in her spare time. She enrolled in night school at the Oakland College of Assistants. She was offered a job in a doctor's office but decided to stay with the Nichols family.

When Mrs. Nichols passed away, her daughter, also named Ethel, and her husband, John Blemmer, owned a farm north of San Francisco. There was a small guest house on the property, and Ethel suggested it would be a perfect place for Ruthie to live out her retirement. The family adored her and wanted to keep her around. Ruthie stayed at the house where she had lived for so many years until it sold and then moved to the country. She was then 64 years old.

She was still unpacking and settling into the house where she planned to live the rest of her life when it all unraveled. The police finally caught up with her in 1969.

The Blemmers hired famed attorney Melvin Belli to represent Ruthie. He stated that it was outrageous for anyone to punish this woman further. He unsuccessfully fought her extradition back to Arizona and then attacked the length of time she'd already served for her crime, praised her rehabilitation, and did everything he could to paint her in a good light after all the years that had passed.

Finally, in 1971, Arizona Governor Jack Williams granted her a pardon.

The Blemmers welcomed her home with open arms, and Ruthie returned to her quiet life as Marian Lane. She passed away in her sleep in 1998 at the age of 93.

What happened that night in Phoenix that left Ruthie's two best friends dead? We'll never know for sure. Ruthie always admitted that she had killed them, but whether it was self-defense or not remains a mystery.

Did she have an accomplice who helped her try to get rid of the bodies? Maybe - or even probably. It seems difficult to believe she would murder her two friends and then cut one up into pieces so that she could more easily fit in her luggage by herself. But the murders did happen, and so did the dismemberment. Ruthie may not have acted alone, but she was there.

Why did she haul the bodies to Los Angeles to get rid of them when she lived in a town surrounded by hundreds of miles of open desert, canyons, mountains, and wild spots where they would have never been found? Why did she take them as luggage on a train? And what did she plan to do with the bodies when she got there?

Honestly, we'll never know.

The story of Winnie Ruth Judd will always contain an element of mystery for which no amount of searching will ever solve.

But the story isn't over quite yet.


In the aftermath of the murders, the Phoenix bungalow became a macabre tourist attraction as Ruthie's case became a media sensation. People flocked to the duplex at the corner of North 2nd Street and Catalina, hoping to get a look at the place where Ruthie had committed murder and stuffed her friends into a trunk.

The duplex began its life in the 1920s as a rental, and it remained a residence for nearly a century, going through a long succession of owners. In 2016, there were rumors that it would be demolished, and it was surrounded by chain-link fencing. But the property was soon purchased by a local attorney, who turned it into his law offices.

And perhaps that's for the best because its time as a family home was never a happy one.

Memories of the past are never far away inside the bungalow. There are original fixtures that survive on both sides of the duplex. Among them are the bathtub where Ruthie may - or may not - have vivisected one of her victims before packing her in a shipping trunk, the original oak floors, and the fireplace mantles and light fixtures from the original decor.

And those items, as well as the house itself, may hold some of the residues from those days gone by. The house is not considered to be "haunted," at least not in the traditional sense, but there is something that has lingered here, making its presence known for decades.

Locally, the bungalow gained a reputation as "the house where love dies." Couples often bought it together as their dream home, and then things turned sour, ending in arguments, bickering, and even divorce.

Coincidence, or merely a high divorce rate? This house seems to have a worse track record than others in the neighborhood. There is something rumored just to be "bad" about the place, and no amount of distance between the murders that happened there, and the present day seems able to make it go away.

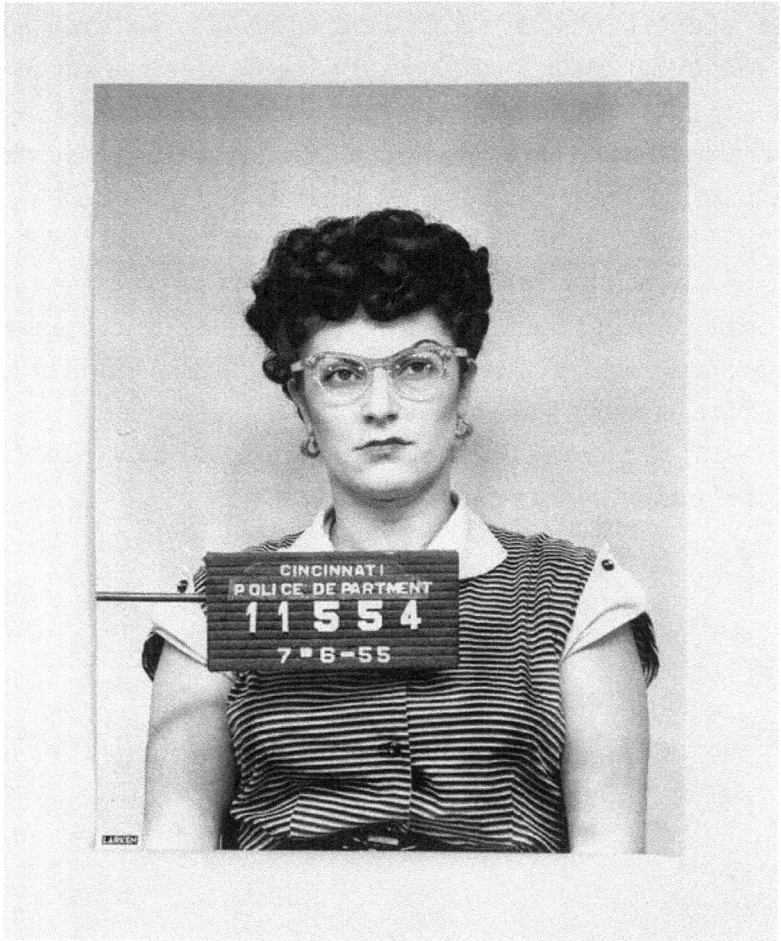

# PART TWO:
# DESPAIR

# "GENERAL INDIGNITIES"
# ELSA LEMP WRIGHT

When Elsa Lemp was born in St. Louis, Missouri, in 1883, she was the youngest child in an American dynasty. With 18 years between herself and her oldest sister, Anna, she was always the baby of the family and lived a very different life than her older siblings. She was beloved by all of them, but instead of becoming spoiled as many last-born children do, she became an independent, resilient young woman who made the most of her short and often turbulent life.

Elsa was only 23 years old when her mother died in 1906. Her mother had inherited her husband's vast estate when he died two years earlier, and it was divided among the children when she passed away from cancer. This made Elsa the wealthiest unmarried woman in St. Louis when she claimed one-seventh of the $10 million estate. Under the terms of her mother's will, Elsa received an additional $100,000 when she married.

An additional windfall that may have eventually caused her murder.

Even though Elsa's death was officially called a "suicide," questions have remained ever since whether she was the one who fired the fatal bullet that pierced her heart on March 20, 1920.

If she wasn't, it might explain why her spirit has never rested in peace.

The Lemp story in America began in 1838 when Johann Adam Lemp established a store that sold household goods and groceries near the St. Louis riverfront. In addition to the store, he also began making small amounts of vinegar and beer.

The beer became very popular because it was unlike anything else in the city - or the country -- at the time. It was a lager beer, named for the brewing and aging process of the beer, and the word means "to rest or store." After this beer was made, it was placed in barrels and then taken to a cool, dark place to age for a few months.

Adam introduced lager beer to St. Louis. He was one of the first brewers to make this kind of beer in the United States. It was quick to catch on in the city, primarily thanks to the influx of German immigrants in the 1840s and 1850s, and soon not only did other brewers begin making their own lager, but Adam became so busy he needed to find a larger place to make his beer. He also got out of the grocery business and began focusing on beer-making.

One of the best things about making lager beer in St. Louis was the natural limestone caves beneath the city. They were the perfect dark space for lagering. Adam bought the property over the entrance to a cave at what is now Cherokee Street and DeMenil Avenue in 1844 and began transporting barrels of beer from the brewery downtown to the cave.

His Western Brewery became the largest in the city, and he finally had great financial success. The company continued to grow in the 1850s and would soon dominate the beer business in the city.

Adam's son, William, had remained in Germany with his mother while his father achieved success in America. He eventually came to America in 1848. By then, his father had a fortune, so William was educated in the finest schools and went to work in his father's brewery.

In 1861, William married Julia Feickert, the daughter of a St. Louis businessman. Then, on August 23, 1862, Adam Lemp died from cirrhosis of the liver. At the time of his death, he was a respected and well-liked man and the owner of the largest brewery in the city.

After his father's death, William began an immediate expansion of the company. He purchased several blocks around the entrance to the cave on the city's South Side and hired architects and workers to start construction of a massive brewery - the largest in the city. The Lemp brewery became a marvel of modern technology. William was fascinated with mechanics and new innovations. The factory was completely electrified, fireproof, and provided hot water to nearby homes and buildings.

Beneath the brewery were three levels of underground chambers, including artificial cellars and the natural cave. Depending on the time of year, there could be as many as 50,000 barrels of beer in storage.

The Lemp brewery became the first in the city to use artificial refrigeration - eliminating the need for the caves - and the second brewery, after Anheuser-Busch, to pasteurize and bottle its beer. All Lemp beer was bottled right there in the factory at a speed of 12,000 bottles per day.

By 1877, the Lemp Brewery was the largest in St. Louis and ranked 19th in the entire country. To give you some perspective, Anheuser-Busch was ranked 32nd at the time.

By the 1880s, Lemp beer was shipped from coast to coast by railroad. It was the first brewery in America to make the change from a regional brewer to a national one. At first, they used ice in the boxcars, but later they had their own refrigeration. William bought his own railroad to ship beer from the factory to the riverfront.

By now, the Lemps were fabulously wealthy - so rich that it's hard for us to imagine just how much money they had. And their wealth continued to grow.

By the 1890s, the brewery employed more than 700 men. Lemp beer was being shipped all over the country and to Canada, Mexico, Central and South America, the Caribbean, Hawaiian Islands, Australia, Japan, Hong Kong, London, and Berlin.

In 1899, William introduced their most famous label - Falstaff – named for Sir John Falstaff, a comical Shakespeare character who was a fun-loving buffoon who could always be counted on to have a good time. His picture soon appeared on advertising posters and cards, becoming one of the first "spokespersons" for beer in America.

By the turn of the century, the company was still the largest in St. Louis and the 8th largest in the U.S. The family's fortune was getting larger and larger, but at this time of great happiness and success, the Lemp family's troubles were about to begin.

William and Julia Lemp's first child died in infancy, but they went on to have eight more who lived to adulthood -- Anna, William, Jr., Louis, Charles, Frederick, Hilda, Edwin, and Elsa.

Born in 1873 and named for William's best friend, Frederick Pabst of Milwaukee brewing fame, Frederick was chosen to be William's successor. After graduating college, he attended a training school for brewers in Germany, and after getting married, Frederick began working side by side with his father at the Lemp Brewery. Although he had three older brothers, Frederick had the same passion for the brewing art that his father had, and he planned to take over the company when William retired. The others all had interests that had little to do with beer.

Unfortunately, though, in the summer of 1901, Frederick became sick. He became so ill - believed to be from heart disease, but no one knows for sure - he temporarily relocated to Pasadena, California, hoping that a change in climate would help. In December, William and Julia came to visit, and Frederick seemed much better. They returned to St. Louis, believing he would be coming home soon. But he wouldn't.

Frederick suffered a relapse on December 12 and died at age 28. He left a young widow and a one-year-old daughter behind.

The family received the news by telegram, and William was utterly crushed. He broke down, his secretary said and cried like a child. William was never the same after Frederick's death. He constructed a large family mausoleum in a cemetery outside the city as a tribute to his beloved son. At first, the rest of the large structure was empty - but it wouldn't stay that way for long.

Frederick's death was just the first in a series of tragedies.

William wallowed in his despair and depression, refusing to leave the house and avoiding the brewery, friends, and family. He spent most days sitting on the steps of the family mausoleum, talking to his dead son. This went on for nearly two years, and then finally, William started to seem more like himself. He returned to work, he began hosting dinners at his mansion near the brewery again, and his trips to the cemetery became a little less frequent.

And then it all came crashing down.

On January 1, 1904, William suffered another crushing blow with the news that his friend, Frederick Pabst, had died. Just as he was after his son's death, he plunged into a black depression, and by February 13, 1904, he couldn't stand anymore.

That morning he rose from bed, showered, shaved, was dressed by his valet, and went downstairs to breakfast. Instead of going to the office, he returned to his bedroom, where he shot himself with a .38-caliber Smith and Wesson revolver.

More suicides would follow in the years to come. Both William, Jr., who reluctantly began running the company, and Charles, shot themselves, and both did so in the family home where their father also died.

Before either man died, however, the Lemp brewing empire continued to rise to great heights during the 1904 World's Fair and during the years that followed. It would be Prohibition that doomed the company. Many breweries closed when it became illegal to buy, sell, and manufacture beer and liquor in America. Many of them reopened when Prohibition was repealed 13 years later, but not the one that belonged to the Lemp family.

It would be largely forgotten today if not for the suicides, tragedies, and untimely deaths that haunted the family and the many ghosts believed to be haunting their former mansion on St. Louis' South Side.

But there also remains a mystery linked to the Lemp family that has never successfully been solved. Most dismiss the death of Elsa Lemp as another of the family's suicides, but some doubts linger about what really happened to Elsa on that morning in 1920.

They linger just like her restless spirit does.

Elsa was a bit of a terror growing up. She was head-strong, a free-thinker, and a rebel against the Victorian standards of the day. As a young woman, Elsa famously did whatever she wanted. She said what came to mind, smoked in public, drank, and didn't care what people thought. And you had better believe that nobody could say or do anything to Elsa without incurring the wrath of her father or older brothers.

She was unafraid of speaking her mind or voicing her opinion - at a time when women were usually considered to be practically a piece of furniture - and she frequently did these things during important meetings that her father held at their home. And she usually did it just to shake them up. She also shared her brother Billy's love of firearms, and she was said to always carry a pistol with her on long train rides so that she could lean out the window and shoot at telephone poles when she was bored.

Elsa joined the suffrage movement in the 1910s, working hard for women's right to vote. She became the founder of the first suffragette society in St. Louis and hosted scores of meetings, parades, and rallies.

She also became fascinated with Spiritualism, which was in its heyday. She held many séances at the family mansion. She became acquainted with a middle-class homemaker named Pearl Curran, who was making quite a sensation in St. Louis with her alleged spirit communications with a ghost named Patience Worth. Curran had first contacted the spirit through a Ouija board, but she later began to receive direct messages from her and put those messages on paper. The relationship between Pearl and Patience Worth produced numerous writings, poems, and even several novels --- works that the largely uneducated Curran would never have been able to produce on her own.

Another of Elsa's close friends was Helen Lambert, whose husband Jordan was the heir to the Lambert Pharmacal fortune, the inventors of Listerine. Elsa attended seances at the Lambert home, performed by a company secretary named Will Hannegan. Strange occurrences during the seances were widely reported in the city's newspapers, and Helen later penned a book about her supernatural experiences.

The most eligible heiress in the city became even wealthier in 1910 when she married Thomas Wright, the president of the More-Jones Brass and Metal Company. The ceremony was a small but opulent affair. Elsa's dress, which she paid for herself, and her wedding ring, were Worth originals. After the wedding, the couple took a year-long honeymoon, traveling to Cairo, Bangladesh, Calcutta, Bombay, and Nairobi. When Elsa traveled, she took along 28 pieces of Louis Vuitton luggage. When they returned to St. Louis, the couple moved into a beautiful home in Hortense Place, one of the private neighborhoods in St. Louis' Central West End. Elsa's independent nature and her husband's repressive and misogynistic views did not mix well, and their marriage was a stormy one from the start.

They had frequent screaming matches that often turned violent. Elsa hit Wright with a vase during one such episode, opening a large gash on his forehead. Wright was unfaithful to Elsa almost from the start of their marriage. Once, she caught him in bed with one of the maids and chased him down the street wielding a fireplace poker. After finding him in bed with yet another woman, she got into her Pierce-Arrow automobile and rammed it into his prized Duesenberg three times. It was not uncommon for the staff to find broken pieces of crockery and glass and splintered furniture when they came on duty in the morning.

Elsa had one child, a little girl named Patricia Lemp Wright, and tragically, she was stillborn. Elsa blamed her husband for the baby's death. They finally separated in 1918.

On February 1, 1919, Elsa filed for divorce. In her petition to the court, she stated that her husband had destroyed her peace and happiness by his conduct and had long since ceased to love her. She also stated that Wright treated her with coldness and indifference and absented himself from their home to avoid her. According to the papers that were filed, all these things caused her great mental anguish and impaired her physical health. Elsa did not go into specifics about the events of her married life. Whatever it was that occurred, the case was expedited so that within an hour after it was filed, a divorce was granted on the grounds of "general indignities." The question of alimony was never mentioned in the courtroom, but it was understood that a settlement had already been reached.

Elsa spent the next year alone, traveling and visiting with friends and family. At some point, though, she reconnected with her former husband. She and Thomas traveled together for a time and eventually reconciled. On March 8, 1920, they were remarried in New York City and then returned to St. Louis and their home in the Central West End. They found their house filled with flowers from friends and well-wishers.

By all accounts, the fighting and unhappiness of the early days of their marriage seemed to be a thing of the past. The household staff didn't mention anything out of the ordinary occurring in the home after Elsa and Thomas arrived from New York, and yet, by the morning of March 20, Elsa Lemp Wright was dead.

Her death was officially ruled a suicide. It was an easy enough mistake for the police to make. According to her husband's account, Elsa had been the only one in the room when the gun was fired. Besides that, her father had killed himself in 1904, so perhaps it ran in the family.

Or perhaps it didn't.

Unfortunately, the only version of events for the night of March 19 and the morning of March 20 came from Thomas Wright, who turned out to be a very unreliable source. In the hours and days that followed Elsa's death, he provided a story that still leaves many unanswered questions.

Thomas later told the authorities that the night of March 19 was a restless one for Elsa. She slept very little and was out of bed many times, suffering from bouts of indigestion and nausea. These ailments caused her periods of severe depression. Today, her problems would likely be diagnosed as Irritable Bowel Syndrome or as symptoms of acute anxiety. The fact that she was suffering as she was such a short time after her second marriage to Thomas suggests that she may have been having serious doubts about the reconciliation.

Keep in mind that Elsa blamed Thomas for the death of their daughter, Patricia, the stillborn baby that Elsa had entombed in the Lemp family mausoleum. And this was only one of the traumas that she had experienced at the hands of her husband. It's possible her stress began to build when she returned to the home where the events that led to their divorce occurred.

But whatever the cause of her suffering, Elsa was awake for most of the night. The next morning Thomas stated that he asked her how she felt, and Elsa replied that she was very tired and would remain in bed. "I told her that was wise," he recalled, "and I went into the bathroom and turned on the water. I remembered I had forgotten to take a change of underwear and went into our room and got it from the closet."

Moments after he closed the door, he heard a sharp cracking sound over the noise of the running water.

Thomas explained, "I had just closed the door when I heard a noise. It was a sharp noise. I thought my wife was trying to attract my attention. I opened the door and said: 'Did you call me? Did you throw something?' There was no reply. She was lying on her back and seemed to be looking at me. As I advanced, I saw a revolver at her side."

But it apparently didn't stay there.

When the police arrived, they asked Thomas why the revolver was found lying on a nearby couch and not in the bed. He shrugged, "Perhaps I picked it up and tossed it on the couch where it was later found."

Thomas saw a bloodstain on the front of her nightgown. Elsa had shot herself in the chest. He said that Elsa tried to speak to him but could not. He could offer no reason for why she would have shot herself. "I never heard her threaten to take her life," he said. "She always seemed happy except when she had sick spells such as she had last night. She had nausea and ate scarcely any dinner."

One of the maids, Martha Westin, recalled what happened next. "At about 8:45, I heard Mr. Wright scream my name, that something terrible had happened... I saw Mr. Wright come running from his room. I went in there and found Mrs. Wright still alive, with her eyes partly open." She saw the revolver lying on the couch.

Martha later told the coroner's inquest that she knew about Mrs. Wright's illness, but she never complained or threatened to take her life. She had also never heard anyone threaten Elsa's life. However, Martha was aware of the revolver found in the room. She told the police that Elsa had possessed the pistol for a "long time" and that she always kept it in a drawer in the night table beside the bed.

Elizabeth Bender, the Wrights' cook, testified that she was in the kitchen when one of the maids ran in and announced that Elsa was dead. "She's been shot!" the other woman cried.

Another maid, Minnie Stover, said that she heard Thomas excitedly calling Martha Westin, Elsa's personal maid, and went to the room to see that Elsa had been shot. She said that she had last seen Mrs. Wright the previous evening at dinner and that she had seemed nervous. When asked if Elsa complained, Minnie replied, "No, she never complained. She was one of the sweetest women I knew. I never noticed anything unusual about her. The conversations between her and Mr. Wright were always pleasant."

Kate Reuckert, the upstairs maid, reported that Elsa "was laying on the bed, she wasn't struggling or anything; and she took one long breath, and I took hold of her arm and tried to rub her. I thought there was life in her and with that Mr. Wright came in, and she took two long breaths after Mr. Wright came in." Elsa tried to speak but couldn't, and a few moments later, she took a last shuddering breath and died.

Thomas stated that no note or letter was ever found, and initially, he said that he was not aware that she owned a gun. This seemed difficult to believe based on the testimony of Martha Westin, who said that Elsa had owned the revolver for a "long time" and kept it in the night table between their beds.

But at some point on March 20, Thomas changed his story and now said that he did know about the pistol. He then claimed that she laid it on the table between their twin beds each night as a protection against burglars.

So, which was it?

Had he never seen the revolver before, or did he see it every night when she placed it on the night table between their beds? It seems a strange thing to have forgotten about. If you were married to a woman who had repeatedly tried to kill you when she caught you cheating on her, you would definitely keep an eye on the pistol that she placed on a table between your beds.

On another strange note, when Deputy Coroner Dever arrived at the house for the inquest, he noted that the revolver was back on the night table where Elsa allegedly kept it each night.

The weapon had now moved all over the room - from the night table to the bed, from the bed to the couch, and now from the couch back to the table again. It had also been handled repeatedly by Thomas Wright and others. The police eventually arrived at the scene, but there is no record that the gun was checked for fingerprints. By 1920, this was a common police technique. In fact, the St. Louis Police Department had begun using a fingerprinting technique as early as 1904. They had been trained by a Sergeant from Scotland Yard who had been on duty at the World's Fair, guarding the British Display.   And yet, no one collected fingerprints at the Wright house that day.

After the discovery of Elsa's body, two telephone calls were placed. One to Dr. M.B. Clopton, the family physician, and the second to Samuel W. Fordyce, a family friend who was - probably not coincidentally - an attorney. Circuit Attorney Lawrence McDaniel said that he was notified about Elsa's death a few minutes after 9:00 a.m. Through his notification, the city coroner received information about what was already being called a "suicide."

A doctor and two lawyers had been called, but no one bothered to telephone the police.

The police were never notified by anyone connected to the family and did not learn of Elsa's death until 10:55 a.m. - more than two hours after it occurred. They might never have been contacted if not for an accident as Edwin Lemp was rushing over to his sister's house. Edwin was having breakfast with Associate City Counsel William Killoren when he received a telephone call from Samuel Fordyce, urging him to come to his sister's house. Shaken by the news of his sister's death, Edwin asked Killoren to accompany him to Hortense Place. As they were driving there, Edwin inadvertently struck and injured Mrs. Lucille Hern with his car at the intersection of Locust Street and Jefferson Avenue.

Mrs. Hern was crossing Locust Street from north to south when a traffic officer signaled for east and west traffic to proceed through the intersection. Mrs. Hern became confused and ran back toward the north curb, stepping in front of Edwin's car. She was taken to the hospital with minor injuries.

When the police arrived at the accident scene, Killoren told Chief Martin O'Brien that "something was wrong" at Elsa's house in Hortense Place. O'Brien passed on the message to the Newstead Avenue Police Station, which served the Central West End, and officers were dispatched to the Wright house.

Wright became "highly agitated" under the scrutiny of the police investigation that followed. His only excuse for not contacting the authorities was that he was bewildered and didn't know what to do. He was questioned at the scene for more than two hours but was never taken into custody - or, it seems, even suspected of playing a part in his wife's death.

A coroner's inquest was convened in the Wright home at 2:40 p.m. Testimony was heard from Thomas - who "appeared nervous and sobbed frequently" - the maids, and the police officers who eventually arrived at the house. Police Sergeant Burke was the first to testify. He said that he found Elsa in her night clothes, lying in bed when he arrived. There were no signs of a struggle. One of the maids told him that she had entered the room and found Mrs. Wright "still alive and gasping."

Patrolman August Klein testified that he arrived at the house at 11:20 a.m. and that Thomas told him that he and his wife had retired early the previous night and that she had not been feeling well. She had gotten up several times during the night because of her illness. When he got up at about 8:20, Wright told Klein he went to her bed, kissed her, and asked how she was feeling. To this, she replied, "All right." When Wright returned to the bedroom after hearing a "muffled report," she was alive and looked at him but apparently could not speak. Then Wright discovered the revolver and summoned the maid. Klein told the jury, "I asked the maids where the revolver was found and they said on a couch, 10 feet from the bed. They said they did not know who placed it there and Wright said the same."

This was the third time that Thomas changed his story -- not to mention another suspicious mention of Elsa's revolver.

When Martha Westin testified, she also mentioned the gun. "I heard Mr. Wright scream my name about 8:45, telling me to call a doctor, that something terrible had happened. I didn't hear the shot. I saw Wright come running from his wife's room. I went in and found Mrs. Wright still alive, with her eyes partly open. A little later, I saw the revolver lying on a couch, several feet from the bed."

Martha also added, "Mrs. Wright had often been ill, but I never heard her threaten suicide."

While this last statement from Martha Westin is interesting, it may not be as interesting as one of the most mundane elements of her story - the time when Thomas Wright called to her. According to Wright's testimony, he had awakened at 8:20 a.m., spoke to Elsa, and then went into the bathroom and started his bath. Moments later, he returned to the bedroom to get fresh underwear and then closed the bathroom door behind him. After a few seconds, he heard the gunshot. He claimed that he called to Martha just a few seconds after seeing that Elsa had shot herself. Could the events he described have taken 25 minutes? It seems very unlikely.

Thomas Wright was either very confused, or he was lying.

In the end, I'm not sure it really mattered. A verdict of suicide was planned from the very beginning. When the coroner's jury of six men arrived at the house, they were not even kept there long enough to hear the testimony from the witnesses. After they were shown the body, they wrote their signatures on a blank verdict sheet and then were dismissed. Deputy Coroner Dever filled in the blank with the verdict after the testimony had concluded.

There was no investigation of the scene, no fingerprints taken from the gun, and the different versions of Wright's story, along with the weird gaps in the time of death and discovery, were never questioned. It was simply assumed that Elsa had committed suicide. She had been known to suffer from depression. Besides, her father had killed himself "during a temporary aberration of the mind," so his daughter had probably done the same - or so the authorities decided.

But was it true? There was no real evidence that Elsa took her own life. She did suffer from depression and anxiety - the result of an unhappy marriage and her daughter's death - but according to everyone who knew her, she had never seemed suicidal. The only witness to her "suicide" was her husband -- who had never seen her revolver before, or he had seen it every night - and who didn't call the police after finding her body but called his attorney instead. Wright became agitated when the police questioned him. Was it because he was upset about her death, or did he have something to hide?

In almost every suspicious death investigation involving a wife, even in 1920, the husband is initially suspected. In this case, though, the police ruled out foul play and assumed that Elsa had committed suicide. Was it because of Wright's money and connections, or were the police misled into ruling out murder?

Those questions will likely never be answered, but of all the deaths that occurred in the Lemp family, Elsa's alleged suicide remains the most mysterious. Many researchers - myself included - do not believe that she killed herself and are convinced that Thomas Wright had something to hide.

Could it have been about money?

Elsa was much wealthier than her husband. While her brothers and sisters did get a small part of her estate and most of her expensive jewelry, Thomas received some of her jewelry, the house, its furnishings, and half of the $836,000 she had in the bank.

It should be noted that he was advanced nearly $150,000 of that amount before the estate had been settled. He had several "business debts" that urgently needed to be settled. Was he in financial trouble when Elsa died?

We must wonder why he tracked Elsa down in early 1920 and convinced her to marry him again. When Elsa sued him for divorce only one year earlier, she charged that he had "destroyed her peace and happiness and had long since ceased to love her." What had changed his mind? Could it have been a loss of his own fortune?

The strange circumstances around Elsa's death suggest there was more to the story than what was told - and what was learned from the lackluster police investigation that followed the tragedy.

What really happened to Elsa Lemp? We will likely never know, but the story isn't over quite yet.

The Lemp Mansion in the Soulard District of St. Louis is regarded by many as one of the most haunted houses in America. Just steps away from the abandoned brewery that made the family wealthy, the house has been through various incarnations over the years as a private residence, brewery office, apartment building, and now a restaurant and lodging for overnight guests.

Through most of those eras, it has been haunted.

There are several ghosts believed to be attached to the place, including Julia Lemp, the matriarch of the family who died of cancer in her bed in 1906, and her son, Charles, who shot himself in his bed in 1949. There may be others, as well. Some say that William Lemp himself still walks the halls, and there have been more reports of knocking sounds, voices, lights turning on and off, phantom footsteps, flushing toilets, and mysteriously running water than you can count.

But none of the ghosts that wander the house are believed to be that of Elsa Lemp Wright.

She remains attached to the place where she died under such mysterious circumstances in 1920. At the house in Hortense Place, her spirit has been encountered in ways that make it clear that the haunting can't be anyone other than the restless spirit of a woman who tried to live her life to the fullest.

The encounters with Elsa's spirit in the house have not been what you might expect from a ghost - there are no opening and closing doors and phantom footsteps in the night. She seems mostly to manifest as a smell. According to past residents, they were sometimes overwhelmed by a floral scent or perfume that suddenly just wafts past them in the hallway or on the stairs. It has been described as a moving scent as if someone had just passed by them. For decades, that smell has been associated with Elsa's spirit.

But that's not all - she is sometimes seen as well. There have been several reports - first- and second-hand - of seeing a pretty, petite young woman with brown hair in various rooms of the house. She is always dressed in clothing of the early twentieth century, and while the stories are not always identical, they all seem to have one thing in common - she appears very sad.

According to a former occupant, an aunt was staying with her family and had no idea of the house's history. One night after dinner, her aunt had stayed up to read after everyone else had gone to bed. The place was quiet, and she was enjoying a book and a cup of tea on the living room couch.

About 30 pages into her book, she heard a noise on the stairs and in the hallway outside of the room. She assumed that someone must have gotten out of bed and perhaps had come down to the kitchen to get a drink. She heard footsteps getting closer, and then they stopped outside the living room. When the woman looked up, though, she saw no one there.

She placed her book on the table in front of her and walked over to the doorway. As she peered down the hall, she spotted the back of a small woman as she went up the stairs. She assumed it was her niece, who was also relatively short and thin.

The next morning at breakfast, she teased her a little. "Why didn't you say anything when you peeked in at me reading last night?" she asked.

"When was this?" the homeowner replied, a little confused.

Her aunt explained that she had heard her in the hall outside the living room and saw her going up the stairs without saying good night.

But her niece just shook her head. "That wasn't me," she told her. "I never got out of bed last night."

After a little more confusion, she asked her aunt what the woman she had seen looked like, and her aunt gave her the best description that she could.

There was no mistaking the figure she'd seen for any other woman in the house - they were the only two women there.

Or perhaps three if you include Elsa in that count.

# "THE LADY OF THE LAKE"
## HALLIE LATHAM

On June 16, 1936, Hallie Latham, a waitress living in Port Angeles, Washington, married her third husband, a beer truck driver and well-known ladies' man named Monty Illingworth. On what was undoubtedly a happy day, she had no idea she had just made the worst mistake of her life - or that she was soon to become a legend in death.

Hallie would have likely never been in the news if not for the discovery of her body, floating in Lake Crescent in Olympic National Park in the summer of 1940. She had been strangled, wrapped in blankets, and tied with heavy rope. But it wasn't the method of her murder that captured the public's attention - it was the condition of her body. Her face was unrecognizable, but her body had not decomposed. In a bizarre chemical transformation, her flesh had turned into a soap-like substance that could be scooped away like jelly.

The newspaper coverage was predictably lurid. The public was fascinated by the story, especially after the murdered woman - unidentified, at first - became known as the "Lady of the Lake." It was the perfect name for a mystery woman found in Lake Crescent, a cold, deep lake known for almost never giving up its dead.

It didn't take long for detectives to discover the identity of the "Lady of the Lake." She had been missing since before Christmas in 1937.

Hallie arrived on the Olympic Peninsula about three years before her disappearance, running away from two failed marriages.

On January 8, 1901, she was born on a farm near Greenville, Kentucky, the fifth child of Finis and Mary "Bunnie" Latham, a farm couple who made a living growing corn and tobacco. One of Hallie's chores, when she was young was to help care for her little brothers and sisters as they arrived. There were 13 of them by 1920. Thanks to this, her formal schooling ended in the eighth grade.

By 1917, hard times had fallen on the family, and Finis and Bunnie decided to pack up and move to the Dakotas, where their oldest sons lived. They piled their belongings into two trucks and left with high hopes for a better life in the west.

The Lathams farmed in a succession of small towns in the southwest corner of South Dakota and then moved to Faulkton, a rural community on the central prairie. The family made a living, but there were a lot of mouths to feed. It was a tough, isolated, and lonely existence, especially for a young woman like Hallie.

She wanted more than a simple farm life, but marriage was then still a dream for a teenage girl. On September 26, 1919, she married Floyd Spraker in Mitchell, South Dakota. Floyd was a down-to-earth auto mechanic who had served in World War I. His family ran an auto service in the town of Wagner, so he had prospects. Things were looking up for Hallie. The newlyweds lived with Floyd's parents in Wagner for a time and then settled near Hallie's parents in Faulkton.

Over the next decade, they built a life together and had a daughter, Doris. Floyd worked as a salesman, and Hallie stayed home to look after the baby, keep house, and grow a garden.

They enjoyed their time together during this time of bootleg liquor and music. Hallie was young with thick auburn hair, a vivacious personality, and easiness with making friends. Floyd was handsome, charming, and friendly and thought he had a perfect life.

But the cracks were already starting to show.

Hallie grew bored as a housewife. She was free-spirited and independent, and being stuck at home all day began to wear on her. She tried raising chickens, then worked as a waitress, and eventually took a job doing hair. But it wasn't enough. Hallie and Floyd's marriage came to an end in 1929.

It couldn't have come at a worse time. The stock market crashed later that year, marking the start of the Great Depression. In 1931 and 1932, droughts devastated the crops across South Dakota.

Hallie moved away and got a job as a waitress in Gettysburg, South Dakota. There, she met Donald B. Strickland, a young man who worked in the restaurant business. Though she was seven years older than Donald at 31, Hallie wasn't bothered by the age difference. She shaved five years off her age on their marriage license, claimed she was a widow, and married Donald on August 8, 1932.

The Depression was still taking a terrible toll on the farms of the Great Plains. Grain prices fell so low that most farmers couldn't make a living. Without work, they didn't have money to eat in restaurants, which impacted Donald's livelihood.

The couple decided to flee the prairie. Hallie had already moved west once to try and improve her life, and now she'd do it again. She left her daughter with Floyd, packed her things, and they drove away. When she made it to Seattle, she had gone about as far as she could go, and life did seem to get better - at least at first.

Like the rest of the country, Seattle had its share of unemployment and homelessness caused by the Depression. Still, hundreds of young people were also finding work in various federal works programs in the Northwest with the Civilian Conservation Corps. They planted trees, built bridges, cabins, and ranger stations, and worked as historians and artists. More jobs opened in 1933 when ground was broken for the Grand Coulee Dam, and thousands of men and their families poured into the state for government work.

Seattle had something that South Dakota didn't - hope.

Hallie and Donald opened a restaurant at the corner of Broadway and East Pine Street downtown. They lived above the diner and worked hard to make ends meet.

They were successful in business, but not in their marriage. It had started to crumble within a year, and the two separated.

Hallie's life was in turmoil again, and she started looking once more for a place where things would be better. Like she had so many times before, she went west. This time, she landed on the Olympic Peninsula, a remote, sometimes inaccessible region bordered by Canada on the north and the Pacific Ocean on the west. It was as far northwest as a person could go and still be in the United States.

It would turn out to be a fateful decision.

Hallie took a job as a waitress at the Lake Crescent Tavern, a rustic lodge with rental cabins on the shore of Lake Crescent. The lodge offered a sweeping view of the lake and was surrounded by heavy forests that stretched as far as the eye could see.

One day in early 1935, Hallie was waiting tables and met a tall, husky beer truck driver named Montgomery "Monty" Illingworth. Born in 1908 in Ruskin, Nebraska, Monty had lived in California before moving to the Olympic Peninsula. Like Hallie, he had been married and divorced and had a daughter, Patricia, and an ex-wife named Esther, who was in constant pursuit of him for unpaid child support.

Monty was a ladies' man with a string of single and married women that he romanced up and down the peninsula. He was good-looking, charming, and friendly. As a beer truck driver, Monty made the daily rounds of taverns and stores in the area, chatting with bartenders and waitresses. He liked to drink, and he liked to have fun. So did Hallie, so the two of them hit it off.

Hallie was in her mid-30s - five years older than Monty - and while beautiful, she was self-conscious about the age difference. She never told Monty that she wore a partial dental plate or had bunions on her feet. Both drank, and they frequently got into alcohol-fueled fights. One night they were drinking at the Maple Grove Tavern when Hallie got into a fight with a woman sitting at the bar. Hallie was convinced that the other woman was eyeing Monty, so she walked over and knocked the woman off her barstool.

But none of this caused Hallie to hesitate in making Monty her third husband.

On June 16, 1936, they were married by a justice of the peace in Seattle. The newlyweds returned to the peninsula and moved into the first floor of a wood-frame house in Port Angeles. Monty was still driving the beer truck, and Hallie was still a waitress, but now her life was starting to take a dangerous course.

Her marriage to Monty was volatile from the start, and things grew increasingly violent. Five months after their wedding, they got into an early morning fight so horrible that police were called to break it up. Hallie often showed up for work with black eyes and bruises on her face and arms. One night, Monty knocked Hallie down in front of her friends and co-workers. No one helped her. Sadly, it just wasn't how things worked at the time.

It remains a mystery as to why Hallie stayed with her brutal husband. Maybe she felt stuck. After all, he was her third husband, and perhaps she was determined to make it work and not fail again. Whatever it was, Hallie stuck with him, and occasionally, she'd fight back, although she was no match for him. Monty was nearly a foot taller than his wife and outweighed her by more than 200 pounds.

They drifted along together, living on the edge. They existed from paycheck to paycheck and spent their money on booze and parties. Monty and Hallie and their rough friends threw wild bashes in each other's homes or got drunk in the taverns along Front Street in Port Angeles.

The drinking inevitably led to violence. Once Monty choked Hallie so severely that she was nearly unable to swallow for a week. A friend had to feed her. Another time, Month punched her in the face, and Hallie bit his arm so hard that he had to pry her teeth from his skin. "I should have killed her," he told a friend after he had knocked her loose.

He didn't kill her - yet. He hit her, choked her, slapped her, and played on her vulnerabilities and jealousy, purposely engaging in behavior that he knew made her furious.

One night, Hallie followed Monty to a nearby hot spring and became enraged when she found him with another woman in the cab of his truck. Another time, she spotted Monty's car in front of a notorious local brothel and stormed inside looking for him. When she found him, he threatened to kill her.

Both threatened to walk out at various times, but neither did. By the time the holiday season of 1937 was approaching, they seemed to have settled into some kind of uneasy truce. They had been married for a year and a half, and things finally seemed to be calming down.

But nothing was as it seemed.

A cold front swept across the Olympic Peninsula on December 21, 1937. The weather forecasters were calling for snow, but Monty announced that he was going out that night anyway. A beer bash was planned at Fort Worden, the nearby military base, and he wanted to be there. He and Hallie fought about it, but he, of course, went anyway.

So, Hallie made plans to go out on her own. She got dressed - underclothes, silk stockings, garters, and a green wool dress with a belt that cinched it at her narrow waist.

Braving the wind, she made her way to the Annex Hotel, a popular hangout for her friends on the waterfront. She climbed the steps to the hotel lobby, where a party was going on. She must have recognized several people who were regulars at the hotel. She and Monty sometimes kept a room there.

Hallie was in the mood for fun and bought a drink - then another and two more. Before long, she had picked a fight with a woman, and the hotel's housekeeper had called the police. When officers arrived, though, they let Hallie off with a warning. She and the other woman agreed to settle down. Around midnight, Hallie and her friends left the hotel and drove to the home of one of the partygoers - where Hallie had more drinks.

She left that house around 2:00 a.m., and a friend walked with Hallie to her car. She got in behind the wheel, started the engine, and the auto lurched away from the curb, clipping another partygoer with the door. At some point, her friend got out of the car, and Hallie drove away down the deserted streets of Port Angeles.

Never to be seen again.

Almost three years passed. On July 6, 1940, two fishermen found a strange bundle floating on the surface of Lake Crescent. It turned out to be the body of a woman.

The corpse was taken to Port Angeles, where a young medical student, Harlan McNutt, examined the body. He had just finished his first year of school and was on summer break when he was asked to look at what the fishermen had found. As a medical student, he had seen dead bodies and even dissected a few, but he had never seen anything like this.

The woman lay on coverings spread on the wood plank floor. She had been hog-tied; her legs, arms, thighs, and waist were bound with rope. She was wearing a belted, green wool dress and stockings with garters.

Clallam County Sheriff Charlie Kemp cut the ropes from the woman's body so that Harlan could get a closer look at her.

He leaned down next to the body and looked closely at her. The upper part of her face, upper lip, and nose were gone. There was no way to tell what the woman had looked like. Because her hands had been exposed, the tips of her fingers were gone, which made fingerprinting impossible.

And then there was the bizarre state of the body.

The dead woman's flesh had turned to "something like Ivory Soap," Harlan said later, describing a condition known as "saponification." The soap-like state resulted from minerals in the lake interacting with the fats in the woman's body.

The lake's near-freezing temperatures had preserved the corpse for years. This made it possible for Harlan to determine that the woman had met a violent death, which was later confirmed by autopsy. Her neck was bruised and discolored, and bruises were all over her body. She had been beaten and strangled.

A medical report noted bunions on her feet, including an especially large one on her right toe. She had brown or auburn-colored hair and large breasts, and the single clue that finally revealed her identity - a distinctive upper dental plate. It was traced back to a dentist in South Dakota who had made the plate for Hallie years before.

The identification came as no surprise. Rumors had been circulating since Hallie's disappearance in late 1937. She had been reported missing by an official from the waitress union - not her husband - which made friends and co-workers suspicious.

When Monty was asked about Hallie, he told people that his wife had run off with another man, but as months passed, even Hallie's close-knit family received no word from her.

Monty didn't seem to care. He went on with his life. He moved to California with a woman he met in Port Angeles - a woman whom he'd been seeing even before Hallie disappeared.

Knowing that he had been abusive to Hallie, investigators were soon on Monty's trail. They found him living in Long Beach, California, where he worked as a bus driver and was living with Elinore Pearson, the attractive daughter of a wealthy Port Angeles lumberman.

On October 26, 1941, he was arrested and taken into custody by Los Angeles County sheriff's deputies. He was charged with murder.

Monty was returned to Washington for his trial. It began on February 24, 1942, and was so sensational that it competed for front-page news with World War II. It was a lurid tale of abuse, drinking, betrayal, murder, and a watery grave - much more exciting than fighting overseas to the public.

The trial developments appeared in the newspapers each day, and spectators - all hoping for a seat in the courtroom - arrived earlier and earlier with each passing day. The courtroom became so crowded during the nine days of the trial that people had to be seated in the hallway. Everyone wanted to catch a glimpse of the "other woman," Elinore Pearson, and Monty's devoted mother, Flossie. Some people brought lunches with them. Others brought knitting.

Monty's defense was that the dead woman wasn't Hallie. He swore she was still alive when he last saw her. But the Dr, Albert

McDowell, the elderly dentist from South Dakota, was a credible witness, and he insisted the dental plate found on the murdered woman belonged to Hallie.

Moreover, Hallie's friends identified clothes worn by the dead woman as belonging to Hallie. A clerk from Montgomery Ward, Jesse Knapp, testified that he had sold Hallie the green wool dress. He said Hallie had a small waist, so he often added an extra notch to her belts.

Another critical piece of evidence was the rope used to bind Hallie before she was dropped in the lake. Monty had borrowed 50 feet of rope from Harry Brooks, who ran a resort near the Lake Crescent Tavern, who recalled when he gave the rope to him. Brooks still had the rest of the rope. The fibers matched.

Monty was not exactly a criminal genius.

When he took the stand, he swore that Hallie left him the day after they both returned home from separate parties on that December night. But several witnesses said otherwise, including friends and co-workers of Monty's. Monty had told different stories to each person.

"I didn't kill anybody!" Monty shouted to the crowd in the courtroom.

The jury only took four hours to reach a verdict, with time for lunch included. On March 5, 1942, Monty was found guilty of second-degree murder and sentenced to life in prison at the Washington State Penitentiary in Walla Walla. Unbelievably, he only served nine years of that sentence and was paroled in 1951. He died on November 5, 1974, in Los Alamitos, California.

Some would say that he got off easy - I'd have to agree. My only hope is that Hallie was waiting for him on the other side when he died - and that she was still angry.

# "WEEPING MAY ENDURE FOR A NIGHT"
# NELL CROPSEY

On the night of November 20, 1901, a young North Carolina woman named Nell Cropsey vanished from her family's home in Elizabeth City. After a frantic search that lasted more than a month, Nell's body was discovered floating in a nearby river.

She had been brutally murdered - but by who?

Her lover spent more than a dozen years in prison, proclaiming his innocence, before being pardoned by the governor. Did he kill Nell? And if not, then who did? And why did he commit suicide soon after getting out of prison?

The story of Nell Cropsey remains one of the strange tales of murder in the state's history, and perhaps the unanswered questions that still surround the case are why Nell's ghost still haunts her family home today.

Nell Maud Cropsey was born on July 17, 1882. Her parents, William and his wife, Mary Louise, lived in Brooklyn, New York, but in 1898, they left the city for the southern community of Elizabeth City, North Carolina.

William had been corresponding with a man named John Bartlett Fearing for some time, and Fearing encouraged the family to make the move. He had substantial land around his mansion on Riverside Drive in Elizabeth City and offered to rent comfortable quarters in his home for the Cropseys until they could buy or rent their own.

After their arrival, William began hauling crops for farmers down to the busy riverport and later turned to potato farming. His brother, Andrew, an attorney in Brooklyn, initially paid the rent for him. The family settled into their new home, and the four older daughters - Lou, Lettie, Olive, and Nell - enjoyed some appeal as newcomers and began to attract a few suitors and admirers.

Olive began a relationship with a man named Roy Crawford while Nell was courted by Jim Wilcox, the local sheriff's son - but rumors claimed she was actually in love with another man. The stories claimed that Nell was having an affair with John Fearing, the man her family rented from, who was nearly 20 years older than Nell. Fearing had a reputation as a notorious lothario, recklessly chasing girls and women in town. His wife knew about his antics, but divorce was unthinkable at that time in the small town of Elizabeth City, so she joined the legion of other suffering wives who lived through their betrayals with steely silence.

For Nell, Jim was useful for providing steady social engagements and covering up the truth about her secret affair. It wasn't long before townspeople got used to seeing Jim accompany Nell to shows, events, and carriage rides around town. Jim proved immensely loyal to Nell, despite her often-difficult personality. Slowly, he began to realize just how one-sided their romance actually was. By then, it was too late, though. Jim had fallen madly in love.

Two years passed, and Jim remained a regular caller at the Greek Revival plantation house owned by John Fearing, where Nell and the other Cropseys were still staying.

Soon after that, however, William Cropsey obtained a home for his family called "Seven Pines," located a short distance away from the Fearing mansion on Riverside Avenue. Once owned by Robert O. Preyer, William seized the opportunity to buy it when the Preyers moved out of state. Seven Pines, built in 1891, was one of the most distinctive homes in the city. It was an eclectic Queen

Anne-style home with an impressive wraparound porch, a three-story square tower, and a sharp pyramidal roof.

Soon, Jim became a regular caller there, as well. He continued to offer Nell his time and money, but she remained lukewarm toward his affections. Even her sister, Olive, who didn't like Jim, admitted he had been generous to her, giving her a silver dish at Christmas, a beautiful pin the next, and a fine gold ring on her birthday.

Nell spent only pennies in return. She eventually gifted him a photograph of herself and an umbrella.

But Jim didn't seem to notice. He called at Seven Pines at least three nights each week, escorted Nell to events and performances, and took her riding, sailing, and dancing. They frequented the new soda shop that opened in 1901. They enjoyed the circuses and fairs that came to town and often visited Munden's Roller Skating Rink because Nell loved to skate.

As the cool winds of autumn began to blow, Jim's passion for Nell started to cool with their arrival. He finally began to realize that their relationship had no future and that he had been taken for granted since it began. Nell's iciness toward him had finally driven him to despair. In September 1901, disagreements damaged Jim and Nell's already shaky ties.

At the beginning of October, Nell's cousin, Carrie, visited the family from New York. She and Nell had an especially close relationship. She would later recall walking downtown with Nell and running into Jim. He hurried over to greet them, and Carrie shook his hand, but Nell rudely turned her back on him and studied the display in a department store window. Despite this, Jim continues to call at Seven Pines, unable to let Nell go.

The rift was patched up later in the month when Jim bought circus tickets for Nell, one of her sisters, and Carrie.

Nell's courteousness lasted for about two weeks after that, but his visits to her home became a test of patience and nerves. Nell began to routinely ridicule and scorn him by not speaking directly to him or even walking him to the door after his visits. She openly flirted with other men. Jim nursed his hurt feelings by paying attention to Carrie Cropsey, taking her and one of Nell's sisters sailing and for evening meals at local restaurants. Unknown to him, Nell has been planning to return to New York with Carrie on November 3 for the Thanksgiving holiday and perhaps to stay longer.

On Tuesday, November 19, Carrie accepted an invitation from Jim to go to the roller-skating rink. Jim arrived at Seven Pines and rang the bell, and Nell, angry and perhaps a little jealous, refused to answer it. Carrie went to the door and welcomed Jim inside. The two of them sat down in the parlor with Olive and Nell. A few strained pleasantries were passed between them before Carrie got her hat and coat and suggested they leave.

After reaching the rink, they skated for an hour or so and then started to walk home. Jim bought a bag of apples from a grocer's stand on Poindexter Street, and Carrie ate one as they walked along.

Carrie turned to Jim and asked, "Why is it that Nell dislikes you so much?"

Jim shrugged sadly. "You tell me, and I'll tell you."

"You've had a quarrel, haven't you?"

"No, not a quarrel - she just doesn't care enough about me to go to the door with me, so I'm going to drop her."

"You mean she will drop you?" Carrie replied.

Jim sighed. "That's about the size of it."

When they returned to the house, Nell and Olive were in the sitting room, and without speaking to Jim, Nell said, "I certainly would enjoy a good apple tonight."

Carrie offers apples from the bag that she and Jim brought back, and Nell made a big show of shaking her head and refusing the fruit. Stinging again, Jim put on his hat around 11:00 p.m. and left for the night.

As soon as he departed, Nell took an apple and started eating it. "This is a good joke on Jim," she said.

Unknown to the young women, Jim was still on the porch and could hear them laughing. He also heard it when Carrie said, "Nell, I had to laugh at you when you refused the apple because I know you wanted it so bad."

Jim was wounded again. He had believed that Carrie was his one ally in the Cropsey family, but he realized he was wrong. What he heard next just made him feel worse.

"Nell, you ought to have seen us going to the rink," Carrie laughed. "We certainly did look funny. I am so tall and Jim so short. I felt like an elephant going in there with that little thing."

As the girls squealed with laughter, Jim walked away. He didn't need to listen to the rest.

The following day, though, Jim saw Carrie and Nell's sister, Lettie, harnessing a buggy for a ride into town. He left work and climbed on the back of the vehicle as the women passed by.

"You are a nice girl," he said coldly.

Carrie was startled. "What's the matter, Jim?" she asked.

"Listeners never hear any good of themselves," he replied. "When I went out last night, my cigarette went out, and I stopped to light it and heard what you said."

"I'm sorry if I hurt your feelings."

Jim shrugged and quietly said, "Oh, Jimmie, doesn't care."

Lettie then asked Jim, "Why didn't you come and harness the horse for us?"

Jim sighed as he sadly told her, "I have been a lackey long enough.

The three of them returned to Seven Pines around 5:30. Jim stayed for a half-hour. He struck up a conversation with Olive, but he and Nell ignored each other.

Enough was enough, he thought.

That evening, Wednesday, November 20, Jim returned to Seven Pines around 8:00 p.m. It was a cold night marked by bright moonlight and a chilling wind. Carrie welcomed him at the door, knowing he suffered from a broken heart.

Jim still loved Nell, but brutal truths had peeled away the veneer of their relationship. Nell wounded him at every opportunity, belittling him, ignoring him, and taking advantage of him. He had heard whispers about her affair with John Fearing, but he had dismissed them, choosing to believe the stories were nothing but neighborhood gossip. It was time to end things, he thought, once and for all.

In hindsight, we must wonder what Jim could have ever seen in Nell in the first place if she treated him as poorly as he would later claim. He had allowed her to treat him miserably for more than three years, and he simply accepted it as the cost of being in love with her.

Or so he said. Or so he believed.

But what if Jim was wrong? What if Nell never considered them anything other than friends? Perhaps she really was in love with John Fearing, as the rumors claimed, and used Jim as a cover for her relationship - or perhaps she just never considered Jim as a romantic partner at all. Could Jim have taken the whole thing more seriously than Nell ever did? Maybe he imagined some great love between them that was never there.

If that's true, then the tragedy of Nell Cropsey soon took a horrific turn.

Jim greeted Carrie when she opened the door. He carried the small umbrella that Nell had once given him as a gift, and he hung it from the hat rack in the front hallway. Jim then found several of the Cropseys and another guest, Roy Crawford, in the dining room after the evening meal. Roy frequently called on Nell's sister, Olive.

Jim sat down in a chair near the door from the dining room to the hallway. Nell was sewing at a nearby table but ignored him.

The clocks ticked, and one by one, members of the family retired for the evening, leaving Jim, Roy, Carrie, Olive, and Nell in the room. Jim was quiet throughout the evening, occasionally taking his watch from his pocket and checking the time.

Jim finally spoke up and asked if there was water from the pump in the kitchen. Olive rose to get a glass for him, but Jim stopped her with a blunt comment, "I don't want your glass - you might poison it."

Carrie said that Jim then began to smile as if what he said had been a joke. If so, it was a sharp one. "What are you smiling about?" she asked him.

Jim looked perplexed. "Was I smiling?" he asked. "I didn't know it."

A little later, Carrie recalled that someone mentioned the subject of suicide by drowning. It might have been something from the newspaper, she admitted later. Jim said that he almost died in the river one time but remembered it as an almost pleasant sensation. "I would not mind drowning," he stated.

Nell barked out a short laugh. "Drowning is one thing I would never want to do because my hair could come out straight. I would look a fright. If I die by my own hand, I want to freeze to death."

Carrie, unsettled by the morbid conversation, excused herself at about 10:30. She climbed the stairs to her bedroom above the sitting room and recalled later that she paced around for 10-15 minutes, troubled by the talk of death. She remembered looking out the window and seeing a buggy passing by the house in the moonlight, then she blew out the lamp and went to bed.

Downstairs, a strained, awkward conversation continued for another half hour. Shortly after 11:00, Jim pulled out his watch and looked at it. He stood up, suddenly deciding to leave. The others also stood, likely relieved that the night could be over.

Before Jim left, though, he turned to Nell with his hat in his hand. "Nell, can I see you out here for a minute?" he asked. It's the first thing he'd said directly to her all evening.

Nell looked at Olive but said nothing and joined Jim in the hallway. Olive walked over and closed the hall door, then returned to the dining room with Roy.

Jim later said that he walked out onto the front porch with Nell, who was wrapped only in a sweater. She was dressed much too lightly for the cold temperatures and icy wind, but she walked with him anyway.

Outside, Jim claimed that he ended their relationship by returning Nell's umbrella and photograph. He told her that he would not be coming back again. According to Jim, she was unprepared for his rejection and began to cry. He told her to go back inside, or she would catch her death in the bitter cold. He then walked away, leaving Nell crying on the porch.

Was his story true? We'll never know, but I feel that it's just as likely that Nell didn't cry when Jim left that night. I think it's very possible she was relieved. She might have thought that Jim wouldn't bother her anymore, and she'd be free from the lovesick man for good.

But we'll never know if it happened the way Jim said or how I imagine it did - because Nell Cropsey was never seen alive again.

A half-hour passed between the time that Nell walked out into the hallway with Jim and Roy Crawford left the Cropsey house. He saw no one outside, so he assumed that Jim had walked home and Nell had gone upstairs. Olive assumed the same. She later said she was slightly irritated to see that Nell had gone upstairs to bed and left her to close the house by herself.

When Olive went to the room she shared with her sister she got dressed in the dark, not wanting to wake up Nell. She felt in the bed next to her and was surprised to find that Nell wasn't there. She assumed that Nell was still with Jim and went to sleep.

Around midnight, the Cropsey's dog suddenly began barking loudly. The entire household was awakened and went out onto the front porch to see the cause of the disturbance. There was no one there, but at that point, Olive realized that Nell had never come to bed. Her sister was missing.

Mrs. Cropsey was terrified, and her husband tried to calm her by going out to search the neighborhood. Along with Nell's brother, Will Jr., William took a lantern and searched the property and along the nearby river. Finding nothing, they headed straight for the Wilcox house a short distance away. William, not knowing the state of the relationship between Nell and Jim, thought it might be possible the couple had eloped.

He knocked on their door around 1:30 a.m., and Tom and Mattie Wilcox, Jim's parents, discovered the need for the early morning intrusion. Mattie roused Jim from sleep, and he told his mother that he had left Nell at home. The last time he'd seen her, Jim said, she was standing on the front porch. After this statement, he turned over and went back to sleep. Mattie passed along his few words to William and her husband, the former sheriff.

William and Henry then hurried off to the home of Crawford Dawson, the current police chief. He promised to dress and investigate the matter and send the Cropseys back to Seven Pines.

Crawford did as he promised. Along with one of his officers, he went to the Wilcox home, and they, along with Tom Wilcox, woke Jim from his sleep again. He told Jim that he wanted him to go to the Cropsey home with him.

Jim agreed and got dressed. As they walked over to Seven Pines, Dawson pressed him for answers.

"What do you think of this case?" he asked Jim.

"I don't know what to think."

"When was the last time you saw Miss Cropsey, and where was she?"

"I left her standing on the front porch."

"Did she seem to be in any trouble?"

"Well, yes, I left her crying."

"What was she crying about?"

"I gave her back her picture, and she said, 'I know what that means.' She began to cry, and I turned off and left her. I came home."

Dawson frowned. He asked Jim, "Have you had any quarrels - any lovers' quarrels, or anything like that."

Jim let out a short backing laugh. "Well, no. Nothing more than she laughed in my face, and I told her the laugh would haunt her in the afterlife."

Jim may have then realized that this statement didn't sound the way that he likely wished it would have and quickly explained the discussion they'd had recently about suicide and drowning.

And that didn't sound much better.

As they walked, they passed a bridge, and Jim suddenly remembered that he had stopped at this spot earlier that night to chat with an acquaintance, Leonard Owens. He had run into him just after leaving the Cropsey house.

They arrived at Seven Pines just after 3:00 a.m., and Jim seemed nervous when the family confronted him with unfriendly faces. Nell's mother, Mary, was the first to speak up. She gripped Jim's arm tightly. "Jim, for my sake and your mother's sake, tell me where Nell is!" she begged him.

Jim seemed stunned by the question. "Mrs. Cropsey, I don't know," he answered. "I will swear and kiss a Bible, I don't know."

Despite more tearful pleas from Mary and Olive, Jim maintained that he knew nothing about Nell's whereabouts.

No one believes that Nell ran away. She had been excited about her upcoming trip to New York. None of her belongings were missing. Her clothing and suitcases were still in the closet.

By morning, with no further clues, Chief Dawson went to the Wilcox house and arrested Jim on general suspicion in the disappearance. However, Mayor Tully Wilson ordered his release, saying that Dawson lacked credible evidence to justify holding him.

Roy Crawford was questioned, as was Leonard Owens, the friend that Jim met on the roadway. Roy claimed to know nothing, and Leonard confirmed the meeting, just at the time that Jim said it occurred.

Oddly, based on the time that Jim left the house and met with Leonard by the bridge, Roy Crawford should have passed them on his way home since he left a little while after Jim did.

But he didn't.

A massive hunt for Nell Cropsey began. Law enforcement officers, volunteers, and trained bloodhounds combed the area, searching the forests and swamps. There was no sign of the missing girl.

Jim's parents asked Deputy Sheriff Charles Reid to go with their son to Seven Pines and try to smooth things over with the Cropsey family. Mattie suggested that Jim could "touch the hearts of the Cropseys" by showing concern for Nell.

On the way to the Cropsey home, Deputy Reid suggested that Jim tell everything he knows about Nell, at least for the sake of her distraught family and his own mother. But Jim insists that he told all that he could tell, and so his second visit to Seven Pines after the disappearance does not go well.

Mary questioned him again. "I don't know where she is," Jim insisted.

"You say you left her crying?"

"Yes."

"Had you ever seen her crying before?"

"I don't know what Nell was crying about unless she became upset when I told her that I was going to quit her."

Mary sobbed, mostly because Jim seemed so indifferent to Nell's disappearance. It didn't help that Olive spoke up and said that she doubted Nell would cry because she'd already lost interest in Jim if she had any in the first place. Carrie agreed, and Jim left.

Mary and Olive spoke with reporters and friends about the case and about Jim's seeming disinterest in Nell's disappearance. Rumors surfaced that painted an ugly picture of the relationship between Nell and Jim Wilcox. Friends told the police about fights they'd had and Jim's unhappiness with Nell in recent months.

Weeks passed with still no trace of the missing girl. Chief Dawson hired an acclaimed private detective named Hurricane Branch to investigate the case. Branch was from Virginia and traveled to Elizabeth City by train. It was not uncommon in those days --when small towns had no detective bureaus and before the advent of the state police - for policemen to hire private operatives to assist them. In this case, though, Hurricane Branch got no further than the local police department did.

As the days passed, the river was dragged for any sign of Nell's body, but nothing was found. Some believed that Nell had drowned herself in the river in a fit of sorrow over the end of her relationship with Jim. Of course, they didn't know how little interest Nell had in that relationship.

Others claimed that Nell fell into the river from a pier at John Fearing's house, where she had gone to meet him for an illicit rendezvous.

Many others still believed that Nell was alive, and searches were made of empty buildings, warehouses on the river, and - primarily because racism was alive and well - of "negro houses" in the southern part of the city.

No matter what they believed about the ultimate fate of Nell Cropsey, however, most believed that Jim Wilcox knew more than he was saying. He was now refusing to speak to the police at all. The Cropsey family spoke about him to the newspapers, with Mary saying that she "did not fancy Jim so much." Olive said that Jim was "changeable. Sometimes he would hardly speak to me for three or four days, and then he would come back and bring flowers. Nell and Jim had been going together about three years, but I knew they were not engaged. She said she didn't care for him, and I think she didn't care for him, and I think she liked another better."

More time passed, and no trace of Nell was found. The Cropsey family had started to fear the worst.

William Cropsey swore out an affidavit against Jim for abduction, and on Tuesday, December 3, Jim was forced to face a preliminary hearing at the crowded county courthouse. It lasted four hours, and in the end, Jim was held on a $1,000 bond for action by a grand jury. He didn't have the money, so he had to wait in jail until a grand jury could be impaneled to hear the case. Meanwhile, he was fired from the Marine Railway Company where he worked, "pending the establishment of his innocence."

After the hearing, William Cropsey spoke to reporters, "Jim Wilcox knows where my daughter is," he claimed. "I do not think that Nell killed herself. I think she was carried away forcibly and that Wilcox knows by whom. The girl had no sweetheart whom I regarded seriously. She had no secret from her sister and mother. There could not have been an elopement. I think she was gagged and carried away in a buggy or a boat. Had she committed suicide, the body would have been found."

The search continued, attracting interest from newspapers all over the country. An expert diver from Norfolk was brought in to search the bottom of the river, but there was no sign of Nell's corpse. A clairvoyant named Madame Snell Newman publicized that she'd had ghastly psychic visions of Nell dying at the bottom of a well. The police, along with two New York reporters, traveled to two old wells in the area but found nothing.

Strange letters and telegrams poured into Chief Dawson's office from people who claimed they'd seen Nell, usually in the company of a man, usually a much older one. These messages came from cities and towns all over Virginia and North Carolina.

On December 21, William Cropsey received a letter from Rocky Mount, North Carolina, claiming his daughter was being held in that area by a "negro woman" who was keeping her for a man who had not returned. The girl would not give her name, saying she was afraid her father would kill the young man who placed her there. Chief Dawson contacted the police in Rocky Mount but with no results. Two local men went to check out the story and returned disappointed - the story wasn't true.

By now, the town was bitterly divided about the guilt of Jim Wilcox. Both factions - including William Cropsey and Tom Wilcox - had published letters in the newspapers, blaming Jim or defending him. "Many people appear a damn sight more anxious to convict my son than to find the missing girl," Tom wrote. "They seem to start out with the promise he is guilty, and they are trying to get more evidence against him than to locate Miss Cropsey. Jim and his friends are anxious to find the girl. They have already given up good money to help the search, and they are willing to give more if needed."

More than a month passed before Nell was finally found.

On December 24, William Cropsey received another letter. It was postmarked from Utica, New York. The anonymous letter writer suggested that Jim left the house when he said he did on November 20. Around the same time, Nell investigated a barking dog and encountered a man stealing one of the family's pigs. When Nell threatened to call for help, the thief struck her in the head and then took her away in a rowboat.

The letter included a detailed pen and ink drawing of the shoreline in front of the Cropsey house and marked an X where Nell's body could be found in the Pasquotank River. It ended with one sensational line:

"Your daughter will appear in front of your house tomorrow."

She didn't, but on December 27, Nell's body, floating face down, was found in the river exactly where the letter writer had predicted. That spot - along with the rest of the river -- had been searched many times without success, causing many to surmise that the killer had taken the girl's body from a hiding place and dumped it into the river after the mysterious letter was sent.

The news of the discovery spread quickly through town, and it was estimated that at least 2,000 people gathered to watch the body being brought ashore.

The body was dressed in a red shirtwaist top and black skirt. Her right shoe was still clinging to the body. Her left shoe was gone. Her hair had fallen and was matted over her face - just as Nell feared would happen if she drowned.

Her body had been found by two fishermen, who had tied her to a stake to wait for the police. They had quickly summoned Dr. Isiah Fearing - John Fearing's cousin - who served as the coroner. He impaneled a six-man coroner's jury to help reach a conclusion about the girl's death.

An autopsy was hastily held in a small outbuilding behind Seven Pines. The doors were left open for light. A crowd watched as Nell was stripped naked and placed on a crude table. They found that her internal organs were normal and that there was no water in her lungs. There were no broken bones. She had not been raped and, in fact, was a virgin, which cast doubts on the rumors about an alleged affair with John Fearing. The coroner did find a bruise and clotted blood on her left temple. It appeared that she had been struck there, which could have led to her drowning - if she drowned. Dr. Fearing had a hard time explaining why she had no water in her lungs, and he eventually concluded that the contusion had been her cause of death. It had been caused by her being struck with a "heavy, rounded object." She had been hit hard and was dead before her body was placed in the river.

Of course, most assumed that Jim Wilcox was the killer. He was arrested again and, this time, charged with murder. Death threats poured into the police station, promising that Jim would be lynched for his crime. On December 28, a mob appeared at Seven Pines, begging William Cropsey to lead them in lynching Jim. He didn't go - but later stated that he regretted not doing so.

A funeral was held for Nell Cropsey on December 28. More than 1,500 people packed into the Methodist church. She was later buried in the New Utrecht Cemetery in Brooklyn, New York, which had been home to the Cropsey family.

On December 30, a Charlotte newspaper reported that the jail holding "young Wilcox, who was arrested for alleged participation in Miss Cropsey's death, lies only a stone's throw from the church. Wilcox knew the funeral was in progress but showed no emotion and merely inquired if a large crowd had attended. He retains much of the easy manner that has characterized him all through.

"Public sentiment is strong against Wilcox."

Jim was indicted for the murder of Nell Cropsey on March 11, 1902. He waived his right to a preliminary hearing and went straight to trial. The attorneys sparred for more than a week, and then the jury began deliberating on March 21. The judge instructed them not to violate their oaths as impartial jurors by bowing to "frenzied public opinion."

This had to be said because reports were still circulating in various newspapers about the possibility of mob violence.

On March 22, 1902, the jury returned. Outside the courthouse were knots of seething men, some with ropes, whispering about what might happen if the jury failed to find Jim Wilcox guilty. When the bell rang to signal that the jury had a verdict, several hundred people packed into the courthouse to hear the jury's foreman pronounce the verdict - "guilty of murder in the first degree."

Jim was sentenced to hang on April 25, but before he could go to the gallows, his case was declared a mistrial by the North Carolina Supreme Court. He was tried again for murder in 1903 and was found guilty of second-degree murder this time. He was sentenced to spend the next 30 years in prison.

Jim Wilcox fared as well as he could in prison. Several efforts were made to gain his release, but each one failed. In 1910, his mother, Mattie, passed away, and his father, Tom, died in 1915.

In 1918, Jim's case took another turn. A new governor Thomas Walter Bickett was elected and, after practicing law in a nearby county, knew that Jim had served almost 16 years of his sentence without a single blemish. He began investigating the case on his own and even visited Jim in his cell. He soon began to believe that Jim was innocent of Nell's murder. Shortly after the two men spoke, Governor Bickett pardoned him, and he was released from prison. He returned to friends and remaining family members in Elizabeth City, where he was greeted warmly by some and with contempt by others, who refused to believe he was innocent.

After Jim got out of prison, he met with newspaper editor W.O. Saunders, who was planning a book about the Cropsey case.

Whatever Jim had to tell him was apparently so shocking that Saunders made immediate plans to start on the proposed book.

But it was never to be.

A short time after the meeting, Jim committed suicide with a shotgun blast to the head. Soon after, Saunders was killed in a car accident. The notes for his book were never found. Whatever Jim Wilcox told Saunders at that meeting will never be known.

And Jim's death was not the only tragedy connected to the case.

Olive Cropsey never married. She struggled with her sister's death for years and eventually became a recluse. She died of natural causes, shut off from society in 1944.

Olive's former suitor, Roy Crawford, fled from North Carolina to Oklahoma. In 1908, he shot himself. Those who knew him said that he was mentally ill toward the end and were not surprised he'd committed suicide.

In 1913, Nell's brother, Will, also killed himself. He drank a bottle of carbolic acid, leaving behind a wife and a five-year-old daughter named Nell.

John Fearing, the alleged secret lover of Nell Cropsey, continued his escapades in town long after Nell's death. He died of natural causes in 1923.

Nell's father, William, gave up farming after his daughter's death and died of natural causes in 1938. He was buried in the local cemetery, just steps away from Jim Wilcox's unmarked grave.

Nell's mother, Mary, passed away a decade later in 1948.

The Cropseys all went to their graves without ever knowing the truth behind Nell's death. It's a mystery that remains unsolved after all these years.

But, of course, not the only mystery. We will never know what happened to Nell Cropsey that night in 1901, and perhaps this is the reason why her spirit refuses to rest.

Even at the time of Jim's trial, many tales were going around about communications with Nell's ghost. A spirit medium named Norman Whitehurst claimed that he had a conversation with her during a séance. "Nell spoke to me," Whitehurst announced, "and she said 'Jim Wilcox killed me, but it was my fault - I provoked him to do the deed. He struck me in the heat of passion, struck me harder than he intended and killed me. Go and do your best to save his life.'"

Unfortunately for Jim, these "communications" did nothing to spare him a trial and 16 years in prison.

There have been more reliable encounters with Bell's spirit, though.

For the past century, those who have lived at Seven Pines have reported strange occurrences. Lights go on and off, doors open and shut, water rushes from the sink even when no one turns the handle, and strange cold gusts of air waft through the house without explanation.

Some reports also include sightings of a pale young woman who has been seen walking through empty rooms, in hallways, and on the front porch. People passing by on the street have seen the same pale figure looking wistfully from an upstairs window.

One resident claimed to recognize Nell when she awoke and saw the murdered girl standing at the foot of her bed one night.

Will the enduring mystery of Nell's death ever be solved? It seems unlikely after all these years, which means that the unfortunate young woman is just as unlikely to find the peace that she still seeks.

Her lingering presence reminds us that she never truly received the justice that she deserved and because she still walks, she is never forgotten.

Her sad story is told over and over as we recall the tragic tale of her ghost. Dead men - or in this case, a dead young woman - really do tell tales.

# "THE WOMAN WHO LOST HER HEAD"
## DOROTHY EGGERS

Early on the morning of January 2, 1946, two motorists were driving up a steep hill in the San Bernadino Mountains of California. They had already climbed 3,000 feet over the last four miles, and their engine was overheating. They found a wide turnoff and stopped to refill the car's radiator with water.

Steam rolled out from under the hood as they rolled to a stop. The driver popped the hood and carefully opened the radiator with a handkerchief wrapped around his hand. He took a large jug from the backseat and placed it on the ground in front of the car. He just needed to wait a bit for the motor to cool down.

The passenger had opened his door and stepped out to stretch his legs. He walked over to the road's edge and looked out over the valley below, admiring the view.

And then he looked down into a ravine directly below, where he got another breathtaking view - a green and white quilt tied with rope. The bare legs of a woman were protruding out from it.

As soon as their automobile had cooled down, the men rushed to the nearest place they could find and called the police. The sheriff, the coroner, and eight deputies from the San Bernadino County Sheriff's Department were on the scene within the hour. With climbing equipment, they entered the ravine and retrieved a woman's body.

Or at least part of a body.

Her torso, legs, and arms were attached, but her head and hands were missing. Someone had removed them with a saw.

The gruesome discovery was just the start of a bizarre series of events that included an unlikely suspect, a confession made and then retracted, a claim of insanity, spirit voices, and the road to the gas chamber.

Once the body was pulled up from the ravine by sheriff's deputies, the coroner was able to take a closer look at the remains. There was a bullet hole almost precisely in the middle of the woman's chest. Another one was found on her left side, just below the armpit. The woman was nude, which allowed the investigators to surmise that she would've had red hair if her head had been present. Besides an old scar on the left side of her leg, the only other identifying feature on the body were bunions on her feet that were so severe they would've required medical treatment in the past. Her age was estimated to be about 35.

The killer - or whoever had dumped the woman's body - had left little evidence behind. There were a few prints at the turn-out, suggesting a car had been parked there, the woman's body had been carried from the car to the cliff, and then she had been thrown into the ravine. It had happened within the last 24 hours. But the location of the body did offer one clue - the killer was not from the area. Anyone who lived nearby would have known plenty of places to hide a body in the area other than the side of a busy highway.

The story of the headless woman was splashed across the front pages of area newspapers later that day. Radio stations broke into their regular broadcasting to inform listeners of the horrific discovery. Within a few hours, the sheriff's department was deluged with hundreds of telephone calls from people asking for more details or requesting to see the body. By the following morning, tips, calls, and inquiries had come in from all over the western United States.

Many of the calls were serious, others were from the morbidly curious, but there was one man who didn't call - a man whose wife was missing.

His name was Arthur Eggers. He was a 52-year-old clerk who worked at the Temple City substation of the Los Angeles County Sheriff's Department. The shy, unassuming man with gold-rimmed glasses and receding hairline decided that he had better tell someone he hadn't seen his wife for the last three days. All this fuss about a woman's body being found reminded him that the police likely ought to know.

Or so he told the officer who took his report.

Arthur's wife, Dorothy Eggers, was a 42-year-old vivacious redhead. She was loud, fun-loving, and restless. She dominated her small, quiet husband. The cops who had worked with Arthur for the past 14 years knew the Eggers had a difficult marriage. Some of the men felt sorry for him, while others figured that Arthur had bitten off more than he could chew when he'd married Dorothy in the first place.

Arthur speculated that his wife had run off with another man when he filed the report. He'd last seen her on December 29, he said.

Filing that report turned out to be Arthur's first big mistake.

As part of the investigation into the missing woman's identity, the San Bernadino Sheriff sent out a bulletin to ask law enforcement officers throughout the region to check their missing persons files for any of the features that matched the body found in the mountains. Despite her missing head, the coroner measured the woman from her shoulders to her feet and estimated her height to be between five-foot-seven to five-foot-eight inches.

When deputies at Temple City received the bulletin, they checked their files. The only missing person that was even close in description to the dead woman was Dorothy Eggers, but there was a problem - Arthur claimed that his wife was only five-foot-two-inches-tall. The deputies, who were friendly with Arthur and Dorothy, knew this wasn't correct. Some of them had danced with Dorothy at department social functions and knew she was taller than that - at least as tall as the dead woman. They politely asked Arthur if he thought his wife might be the unidentified woman in San Bernadino.

Arthur scratched his chin. "Yes, I thought of that. That's why I filed the official report, for the record. I went over there last night and took a look at her, but it isn't Dorothy, thank god."

It didn't take long for them to discover Arthur was lying.

While Arthur did go to the San Bernardino coroner's office, he never actually looked at the body. He just stood around for a few minutes and then left. The "mistake" about Dorothy's height and his lie about seeing the body raised some suspicions, and detectives had no choice but to start a secret investigation of their co-workers. Arthur was treated as he'd always been in the office. Meanwhile, they began digging into what turned out to be the couple's complicated private life.

Investigators learned from her friends that Dorothy had grown tired of her husband of 18 years. Arthur was boring, mousy, and quiet. Dorothy wanted excitement and found it by running around with other men. She didn't make any effort to hide her affairs from Arthur. They also learned that Dorothy hadn't been seen since December 29, which Arthur agreed was the last day he'd seen her.

Family and friends also confirmed that Dorothy was five-foot-seven-inches tall, weighed around 145 pounds, and had recently had surgery on one of her bunions. She'd also recently received a local chiropractor's treatment for a spinal condition. Both doctors were called in, and both identified the headless woman as Dorothy Eggers.

And then the case became even more damning for Arthur. On January 19, a new deputy at the Temple City substation told his colleagues that he had recently bought a 1940 Plymouth sedan from Arthur Eggers for $800. Unknown to the deputy - but well-known to the other cops at the station - it was Dorothy's car, not Arthur's. When the title was transferred to the new owner at the courthouse, Arthur told the deputy that his wife was outside in his sedan. But the deputy later recalled the woman was much younger and more slender than Dorothy. It turned out to be the couple's 19-year-old niece, Marie. She lived with the Eggers, along with her younger sister, Lorraine.

When the Plymouth was examined, police found the trunk had recently been cleaned - but not well enough. They found traces of Type-A blood - the same blood type as Dorothy's. A search of gun records showed that Arthur owned a .38-caliber revolver, the same caliber of bullet that had killed the unidentified woman. Detectives searched his house when Arthur was at work and found more Type-A bloodstains in the couple's bathroom.

Arthur was not exactly a criminal genius, which is ironic considering his father was the former sheriff of San Francisco County.

He was finally arrested on January 22 on suspicion of murder. Over the next five days, he was questioned repeatedly about

Dorothy and the dead woman found in the mountains. Arthur confessed to forging Dorothy's signature on the title to sell the car but denied killing his wife. He also admitted that he gave away all her clothing to charity but said he only did it because he assumed she was not returning. It was also discovered that he sold his wife's engagement and wedding rings on January 4, using a fake name and address. Arthur maintained that he did these things because Dorothy had run away with another man.

He was taken to see the headless body and grudgingly admitted that it might be his wife. Deputies noted that he displayed no emotion as he looked at the headless corpse and was surprisingly calm when talking with them.

"I'd say that was her. I'll claim the body," he shrugged.

When asked why he didn't say this the first time he claimed to see the body, he had an excuse for his actions. "I lied for the benefit of my wife's aged mother," he said. "I wanted to put her mind at ease."

Arthur had his own theory about the murder. He was sure that she had been murdered by one of her lovers. "I wouldn't hurt a hair on her head," he told deputies. "I wouldn't kill her. I wanted her to raise the children."

Arthur was talking about his nieces, but after hearing their uncle's connections to the murder, Marie wanted nothing to do with him. She even confronted him in his holding cell about the green and white quilt that had been wrapped around her aunt's body. In front of detectives, she announced that the quilt had not only been on her bed but that she had also seen it on Arthur and Dorothy's bed.

"The girl is lying," Arthur snapped.

He continued to be held in jail on charges of grand theft related to the fraudulent sale of his wife's car. It was the only way the authorities could hang onto him without a murder confession.

For four hours on January 27, Arthur was given a polygraph test, but he was too nervous and too jumpy to give detectives anything other than inconclusive results.

He continued to plead innocent until a retired deputy named Robert Jones came to see him. The two had worked together for a long time, and Arthur respected him. Jones told him that he knew he was guilty but wanted to help him. "Get this off your chest and lay it on the line," he said to Arthur.

The other man sighed heavily. "Okay, Bob, I did it. I'll tell you anything you want to know."

In his confession, Arthur told detectives that he returned home from work around 1:00 a.m. on December 30. As he approached, he heard the front door slam and saw a man leave the house, walking quickly away. Suspicious, Arthur went into the house through the back door, turned on the lights, and found his wife naked in their bedroom. She was still on the bed, where she had obviously been having sex with the man who'd just left.

Arthur claimed that his wife told him that she was going to leave him and run away with the other man. "I had suspected her for a number of years," he said. "I started to boil over."

Dorothy called him names, he told detectives and asked him what he was going to do about it. He grabbed a pistol from the dresser and started chasing after the man he'd seen leave. But Dorothy jumped up from the bed and grabbed him before he could leave the room. They began struggling over the gun, and the fight spilled over to the bathroom, where they both slipped and fell to the floor.

When they did, the gun accidentally went off.

Arthur then explained that he tried to cover up the crime by putting Dorothy's corpse in the bathtub. He then dismembered her with a portable electric saw, wrapped her in the quilt, loaded her in his trunk, cleaned up the mess, and drove her out to dump in the ravine off State Route 18.

No matter what Dorothy had done, Arthur insisted that he still loved her. "I'm sorry," he sobbed. "I didn't mean to kill her. I will always love her."

On the morning after his confession, Arthur led investigators up the mountain road to where he'd dumped the body. Newspaper reporters followed close behind and snapped dramatic photos of the little man showing how he threw his wife's headless body into the ravine. He also drew a map that directed them to where he had tossed the gun and the saw.

The report about the examination of the saw was a gruesome one, describing "a fatty, greasy substance and human blood" on the blade. There were also numerous "bits of tissue, bone, and fatty debris" stuck in the saw's teeth. One large fragment of human bone was also forcibly wedged into part of it.

Test bullets fired from the gun matched the bullets found in the body.

Since he had been arrested, Arthur had continually lied to the police. When he finally confessed, he kept lying, trying to make himself seem less guilty - if that was possible. His story of where had concealed Dorothy's head and hands changed frequently, and he seemed to relish keeping investigators guessing about where they might be found.

After detectives and 400 Boy Scouts spent several hours searching for the head and hands through brush about 20 miles from where Dorothy's body was dumped, Arthur changed his story. "Well, it's almost too horrifying to tell, but here's the truth," he grinned. "I burned Dorothy's head and hands in the incinerator at home."

However, when investigators went to his house and collected ashes for testing, they found no bones or teeth. Arthur knew that - as the detectives did - teeth could withstand fire, so he came up with a new lie. "Dorothy had plastic dentures and I guess they must have melted completely," he shrugged.

As they sifted through the ashes looking for charred bones, detectives asked Arthur when he had burned the body parts. "Why, in the morning, of course. It's against the law to burn anything at night!"

Captain Gordon Bowers, the sheriff's department's top homicide investigator, was fed up with Arthur. He told reporters, "He has lied so much that we are going to get his story straight once and for all. He has told some truths but most of his details are self-preserving lies in his attempt to escape a first-degree murder charge. He is trying to show there was no premeditation on his part."

When asked about the integrity of Arthur's confession, Captain Bowers told the press that his story, like most of Arthur's story, was mostly fiction. "If the slaying took place as Eggers said it did, that meant the couple's adopted children and a roomer, slept through the fight and the shooting in the small bungalow."

Lester Loomis rented a bedroom from the couple and didn't hear anything that night, and neither did the Eggers' two nieces.

He also added that even if Dorothy's head and hands were never found, the district attorney would still take Arthur to trial. "We no longer need to establish corpus delecti," he added. "We have practically given up searching for them."

Despite Arthur's confession - and all the discrepancies that conflicted with the known facts that detectives had put together - he pleaded not guilty and not guilty by reason of insanity at his preliminary hearing. The dual plea was not unknown in California, but it was an odd one to make. It was sort of like saying, "I didn't do it - but if I did, I was crazy at the time."

By late February, Arthur had changed his story again - he had not killed his wife, and the body found in the mountains was not even Dorothy. She was still alive and had faked her death and disappeared to frame him. To keep this story going, Arthur refused to pay the funeral expenses for the dead woman from the ravine. She was no relation to him, he maintained.

Even though he was ducking funeral bills, Arthur did manage to do something right after his arrest - he hired an aggressive defense attorney. James Starritt was a chubby little man who wore loud ties and had a mop of curly hair. During his client's grand jury indictment, Starritt went after the prosecution with bold claims, arguing the confession was inadmissible because it was hearsay - it had never been put into writing. He also condemned the indictment itself, which failed to mention that Dorothy was even missing. "That body may be the headless horseman of Sleepy Hollow for all this transcript shows," Starritt quipped.

When Judge William McKay denied his motion to block the indictment, Starritt appealed to a higher court. He argued that Dorothy was not missing, and without a head and hands to identify her conclusively, the state had no case. Starritt failed with the higher court, too, but it delayed Arthur's trial until May 1946.

But Starritt had another trick up his sleeve. Judge McKay accepted his motion to set aside Arthur's confession because he said that the police had gone too far in their tactics to get it. His ruling cast doubts on its admissibility at trial because it was "given under circumstances not in accord with ethics or pure principles."

Without the confession, the police had to rely on forensic evidence. When all put together, it seemed overwhelming. There was the blood-type match from the trunk and the bathroom, the ballistic comparison with Arthur's gun, the samples found in the saw, the green and white quilt found wrapped around the body, hair from the body that matched that found in Dorothy's hairbrush, and the positive identifications from her doctor and chiropractor.

But remember, there was no DNA evidence in those days. There was no way to conclusively say that the body belonged to Dorothy without a head and fingerprints. Was it likely that it did? Of course, all it took was for a good defense attorney to raise reasonable doubt, and the trial could be over.

The murder trial of Arthur Eggers began on May 6, with the prosecution approving potential jurors based on how they felt about the death penalty. As he listened to this, Arthur flinched. Reporters noted his anxiety.

The state's case, heard in the courtroom of Judge Clement Nye, was as strong as predicted. Forensic evidence was offered efficiently and effectively to the jurors, and Dorothy's nieces became primary witnesses. Marie testified about how Arthur had made her practice signing Dorothy's name so he could transfer the title to her car to a deputy. She also identified the quilt wrapped around the corpse as one that had been on her bed the year before.

Lester Loomis, the Eggers' boarder, was called to the stand and denied that he was ever intimate with Dorothy but testified that Arthur told him he had looked at the body from the ravine and told him it was not his wife.

Finally, a neighbor testified that she had seen Arthur vigorously cleaning the trunk of his car on January 3.

During the defense's opening arguments, Starritt condemned Dorothy as a "harlot who had violated the sanctity of the Eggers home" and said that she had been shot by accident during an argument.

He told the jury, "Our evidence will prove that Mrs. Eggers was a domineering, forceful woman who was not averse to attending dances alone and picking up strange men. For a long time, Eggers heard rumors about his wife's unfaithfulness. When he saw with his own eyes the truth of these rumors there was a blinding flash in his mind, and he grabbed a gun to defend the sanctity of his home. In the struggle, Mrs. Eggers, who was strong physically, was accidentally shot."

But Starritt did make it clear that the woman's torso found in the mountains was not Dorothy Eggers. He announced that he would call a witness whose testimony would exonerate Arthur as the one who dumped the unknown woman in the ravine.

While his attorney was outlining his case, Arthur sat in his chair with his eyes closed, giving the impression that he was dozing off.

With little evidence and no experts to put on the stand, the defense's star witness was Arthur Eggers. But Starritt knew that if there was anyone who could convince the jury his client was crazy, it was the client himself.

Starritt guided him in his testimony, telling the jury that his marriage had been a happy one until one or two years ago. Around that time, Dorothy told him that she was beginning the "change of life," and she had been challenging to get along with ever since. He heard rumors that she had been going to dances whenever he worked late and that she was picking up men there. Arthur said he ignored the rumors because he trusted her.

But, boy, did he turn out to be wrong, he added.

Just before Dorothy's disappearance, the couple argued about Christmas presents. She ridiculed him for not getting something for their boarder, Lester, and called Arthur a "cheapskate."

Starritt then steered him toward the night in question. Arthur said that he was returning home from work in the early morning hours of Sunday, December 30, when he heard the door slam and saw a tall man run off down the street.

"I went into the house and found my wife in the bedroom, nude," he told the jury, "I told her I was going to stop such goings-on and got my gun from the dresser drawer. Dorothy grabbed me and we struggled in the bedroom. She pushed me into the bathroom and we both fell down. The gun went off. Next thing I knew, I was crying, and I heard these voices."

According to Arthur, he was sitting on the toilet seat, crying and scared, and then he went outside to his car and got inside. As soon as he started the engine, mysterious voices began whispering to him:

*She is in back. She is in back.*

He started driving, and he kept driving as the voices continued to call out to him. Finally, he stopped the car and looked in the trunk, but it was empty. "I thought it was all a bad dream, but when I went back to the house, Dorothy wasn't there," he testified.

This way, Arthur had two options - one, his wife wasn't dead and had fled the house while he was out, or two, that he killed her and dumped her body, but he was so crazy that he didn't know he'd done it.

"Did you intend to harm your wife?" Starritt asked him.

Eggers jumped to his feet and raised his hand as if taking an oath. "No!" he righteously declared, "As God is my judge, I never had any thought of killing my wife. I loved her."

"Do you know where she is today?"

Arthur appeared to be deep in thought. "Sometimes I think she is dead. Sometimes I think she is alive and laughing at my predicament. But the body I saw in San Bernadino *was not* my Dorothy!"

After the prosecution finished with Arthur, Starritt called his surprise witness, who testified that someone else threw the body into the ravine. Lloyd Cuthbert explained to the jury that he came to the assistance of an unidentified man with bloody hands changing a tire near where the body was found on the night in question.

While the courtroom buzzed with excitement, the prosecutor called his own "surprise witness" - the man with the bloody hands. Former U.S. Marine Fred Matuskey testified that yes, he had been changing his tire along the highway, and his hands were bloody. He was on his honeymoon following a wedding four hours earlier, and he had cut his hands while removing the traditional tin cars that were tied to the back of his and his wife's "just married" car.

After that blunder, James Starritt rested his case.

The jury's verdict of "guilty" came as no surprise to anyone in the courtroom but Arthur Eggers. He stood blinking as the verdict was read but showed no other emotion. When it was finished, he cried out to his attorney, "How could they? It wasn't Dorothy's body! I know it isn't Dorothy's body! This is absolutely unfair!"

Although the jury had rendered a guilty verdict, a legal snag occurred when the foreman sent a note to the judge and asked if the sentence could be set as life without parole, even though a first-degree murder charge always meant the death penalty at that time. The jury didn't want to send Arthur to the gas chamber.

But the judge said that wasn't possible. He then ordered them to decide on the defendant's sanity. Before that hearing could begin, though, one of the jurors stated that she had a "closed mind" on the sanity question, and the foreman told the judge that if the same jury were retained for that question, "it would be a hung jury."

Judge Nye dismissed the jury and was forced to impanel a new one. It was a huge blow to the defense since a new jury would not have the experience of witnessing Arthur's bizarre antics in the courtroom and on the stand. Starritt attacked this situation and called for a mistrial, which was overruled.

On June 4, Arthur was back in the newspapers and calling attention to himself by formally resigning from the Los Angeles County Sheriff's Department. In a letter, he wrote to Sheriff Eugene Biscailuz, "I will always hold the highest regard for you and your department." He ended the letter requesting that his remaining sick leave and vacation pay be added to his commissary account at the county jail.

Arthur's sanity hearing began one week later. It lasted for two weeks, and three psychiatrists testified that he was sane. Arthur went on the stand to speak for himself.

"Do you think you're sane?" his attorney asked him.

"Of course, I'm sane!" Arthur shouted.

One of Arthur's sisters, Etta, gave jurors the impression that insanity ran in their family. Their father, Frederick Eggers, who had been the sheriff of San Francisco County, had become convinced that Governor Friend Richardson - who was dead at the time -- was about to appoint him as warden of San Quentin. These hallucinations went on until their father also passed away.

When Arthur heard this testimony about his father, he sprang to his feet, pointed a finger toward the sky, and yelled, "Let his spirit rest!"

After he was ordered to sit down and be quiet, Etta added that her brother had suffered several falls as a child, one of them leaving him unconscious for seven or eight hours. She implied that brain damage had been caused, making Arthur act strangely and kill his wife.

But the new jury didn't buy it. On June 29, they decided that Arthur was perfectly sane when he murdered Dorothy and dismembered her body.

Of course, his only reply to the verdict was, "That still isn't her body," he blurted out. "Someday, somewhere, she'll show up and make fools of the prosecutors. She's probably waiting to hear what happens to me."

But that was never going to happen. One month later, what was left of Dorothy was buried in Valhalla Cemetery in North Hollywood.

And Arthur was on his way to the gas chamber.

Over the next two years, Arthur's new attorney, Berwyn Rice, tried everything to postpone the inevitable. He made motions, filed appeals, and even begged Governor Earl Warren for a last-minute stay of execution. It was denied.

On Friday, October 15, 1948, Arthur was strapped into the steel chair inside San Quentin's gas chamber, and 15 minutes later, he was dead.

To this day, Dorothy Eggers' head and hands have never been found.

# "VICTIM OF THE KILLER PRIEST"
# ANNA AUMULLER

On February 26, 1913, a Catholic priest named Hans Schmidt married a young woman named Ana Aumuller in a secret ceremony that he performed himself. If this sounds a little out of the ordinary to you since Catholic priests are forbidden to be married or even have sexual affairs, you'd be right.

But Hans Schmidt was no ordinary priest. He was so out of the ordinary that he illegally married, impregnated, and then brutally murdered his wife. He was eventually sent to the electric chair for his crime and, to this day, remains the only Catholic priest ever to be executed in the United States.

But there was no question that he deserved it.

Little is known about Anna Amuller's history, but we do know that she met Hans Schmidt while working as a housekeeper at the rectory of St. Boniface Church in New York City. In 1913, she was only 20 years old. She had been born in Oedenburg, Hungary, where she lived until coming to America. Her father died unexpectedly when she was a child, and Anna was raised by an aunt, who sent her to Catholic School at a very early age.

As a teenager, Anna was very bright and pretty, with sparkling blue eyes and pouting lips. She was also friendly and fun-loving, making her one of the most popular girls in school. She never had trouble attracting boys. She had musical talent as well and learned to play the piano. Shortly after finishing school, her aunt decided to send her to America, where she imagined the young woman would continue her musical training.

When she arrived in America, though, Anna found that the possibilities for immigrants without much money were few. She stayed with friends of her aunt for a time - Joseph Igler and his wife, Marie - and when Igler managed to get her a job at the church, she moved out.

Anna went to work as a housekeeper at the St. Boniface Rectory, and there, she met Hans Schmidt - and her life would never be the same again.

As you won't be surprised to learn, Schmidt was an unusual child. He was born in the German town of Aschaffenburg in 1881, one of 10 children. All of them took notice of his unusual behavior, which could be amusing one moment and terrifying the next. His father, Heinrich, was a well-known railroad official and liked by everyone in town. With help from a large garden and several farm animals, he made a decent living and provided plenty of food for the large family.

However, his mother, Gertrude, was a sour, poorly educated woman who instilled one thing in her son that would last throughout his lifetime - religious zealotry. She had abandoned her role as a wife and mother long ago to spend her time praying all day. Overwhelmed by the task of motherhood, she turned to the Catholic Church, dragging her protesting children with her as she spent the days on the hard pews.

Only Hans accepted it without question.

He immersed himself in the religious trappings of the Church, becoming obsessed with it. He memorized lengthy passages from the Bible while still a small boy, said several rosaries each day, and when he was nine, built a homemade altar where he pretended to be a priest and presided over mass. He had several cassocks, which his mother had sewn for him. She often sat in his room with him while he performed. As he stood at his altar, reciting the words of the mass in Latin and holding a chalice high over his head, his mother fell to her knees in ecstasy, convinced he was some sort of holy child.

Around the same time that Hans became obsessed with religion, he also developed a fascination with blood. One of his passions as a boy was to spend his afternoon at the local slaughterhouse watching the cattle and pigs being killed and processed. When his mother prepared dinner at home, she slaughtered the chickens by cutting off their heads. Hans watched this very closely and became transfixed by the killings. Sometimes, he would take the heads of the chickens and play with them in his room. His father once caught him with a bloody chicken head and scolded him for it. After that, the boy was careful to conceal the chicken parts from his father - but not careful enough.

Once he took the head of a rooster and, while it was still bleeding, placed it on his penis until his father caught and beat him.

Blood obviously provoked a sexual response in Hans, as his sister Elizabeth discovered when she bandaged a cut on his leg. Whenever he saw blood, he associated it with sex - but it was not until an incident in the summer of 1891 that Heinrich Schmidt realized his son was very different than other children.

Gertrude had bought three geese at the market and planned to breed them for food and their feathers. One morning she went out to feed the geese and found two were missing. She questioned the children, but all denied any knowledge about the theft.

That same afternoon, Heinrich was at home repairing a fence and saw Hans walking out of the woods. He called out to him, and the boy seemed startled, quickly dropping something on the ground and running away. Heinrich searched through the grass to see what the boy had dropped and found a bloody lump of white feathers - it was the severed head of a goose. He followed a trail of blood and found the bodies of the two missing geese. The second bird's head was missing. Heinrich later found it in his son's bedroom, stuffed into a pocket of his pants. Blood was dripping on the floor.

After that, no one in the Schmidt family looked at Hans the same way again.

As the years passed, Hans continued his obsession with blood and watched as the animals were butchered at the slaughterhouse. Chickens on the farm died mysteriously, rabbit parts were found in the cellar, and the horribly mutilated carcasses of squirrels were found on the property. It could never be proven that Hans was responsible, but the family and the frightened neighbors believed that he was.

In 1895, when Hans was 14, the Schmidt family moved to Mainz, about 30 miles away. At his mother's insistence, he was enrolled in a school that was considered the final step before the Catholic seminary. Hans, his parents believed, was in need of some guidance.

He studied hard and finished all his coursework, but his behavior remained erratic. He wandered the town's streets at night, walking quickly until stopping suddenly for no apparent reason, as if in a trance. After several minutes frozen in silence, he continued on his way without a word. He was found sitting in a freezing bathtub, oblivious to the cold, playing the violin on several occasions.

His teachers, though, considered him a genius, and at the age of 19, he was admitted into the St. Augustine Seminary to prepare for the priesthood. He kept to himself and made a few friends but was hostile toward his colleagues and difficult to control. He was constantly in conflict with everyone, frequently going out without asking leave to take walks, arguing with professors and fellow students, and keeping his own hours of sleeping and waking time, regardless of schedule.

In 1904, he moved to Munich and continued his studies at the university there. He left the college grounds at night and played the violin in the city's taverns and saloons. During the day, between classes, he gave away all the money he'd made the night before and then complained that he had none left with which to buy food.

Hans was arrested in Munich in 1905 and charged with forging graduation certificates for failing students. Most believed he was innocent because of his reputation for generosity, but the authorities had evidence of his fraud. His father hired an attorney, who pointed out to the court that Hans had a reputation for mental instability.

It was decided that the young man should spend some time at the cold-water sanitarium, where he could get some rest and relaxation. Using the baths as a medical treatment, patients immersed themselves daily in cold water, which was alleged to be therapeutic, both psychically and mentally. According to records, Hans stayed there for one month but only took one bath that entire time.

Upon his release, he was sent to do penance at a monastery but could not get along with the monks because he questioned every order they gave him and refused to follow simple directions.

After that, he returned to the seminary. He had been allowed to return in the spirit of forgiveness. He plunged back into his studies, and on December 24, 1906, he was ordained into the Catholic priesthood.

Over the next three years, he served in several different churches, constantly being transferred because of problems with his superiors. He had also broken his vows numerous times with women in his parish, as well as with prostitutes. He often removed his collar and wore civilian clothes to make late-night trips to local brothels and not be recognized as a priest.

His sermons were widely ridiculed, and he performed masses in strange ways or out of order. His strange comments at social gatherings surprised and frightened other priests, who constantly complained about his behavior. Parishioners often witnessed his odd way of acting in the streets, seeing him wander around in a daze and then stand as if paralyzed while people walked around him in fear. In one parish, he was caught stealing donations to the church. He didn't keep the money for himself. Instead, he personally gave it to people he thought were deserving, making it impossible for the Church to punish him as a thief.

So, he was relocated, again and again. Whenever Hans caused enough trouble in a parish, the Church just moved him somewhere else.

By 1909, his career as a priest was in shambles, and he had nowhere else to go - except to America.

Schmidt's first assignment in the United States was at St. John's Church in Louisville, Kentucky. When he first arrived from Germany, he spent a little time in Trenton, New Jersey, but he was quickly shuffled out the door.

The dark-haired young man made a good first impression. His demeanor was friendly, though he was a bit intense, and he had come to the city with a strong letter of recommendation from a German diocese.

Even so, he would not stay in Louisville for long.

On December 8, 1909, a little girl named Alma Kellner disappeared on her way to St. John's Church.

Several people had seen the little girl that morning. A druggist recalled that the eight-year-old paused to look at the cat in the window of his drug store. A mail carrier recalled that she greeted him as she walked by. Many remembered her outfit that day -- a black and white checkered coat with a velvet collar and a red hat.

She went to the church for morning prayers, but when the prayers were over, no one ever saw Alma again.

There was a search and plenty of theories to go around. Some said she was lost, while others claimed she had been kidnapped for ransom because her family owned a successful brewery. Her millionaire uncle, Frank Fehr, offered a reward, but no one claimed it.

Months passed, and there was no sign of Alma. Then in May 1910, a flood in a hidden cellar of the parochial school next to the church offered a gruesome solution to the mystery.

A laborer named Richard Sweet was hired by a plumbing company to pump out the water and clean up the muddy floor in the cellar. He had just started digging when he uncovered a child's shoe. He continued to dig and eventually found a small skeleton wrapped in a carpet.

Dental records would identify her as Alma Kellner.

The coroner examined the body, and he found there appeared to be an attempt to dismember and burn the child. Her head had been split open, the right arm was missing at the elbow, and the left shoulder blade and arm had been sliced off. Most of the bones had been broken and charred.

Only someone familiar with the property would have known how to get into the cellar. A hidden trap door was the only entry point.

Suspicion fell on a new arrival in the parish - not the young priest but a new janitor named Joseph Wendling.

The janitor had grown up in France, where his family owned a farm. After deserting the army, he came to America and settled in Louisville. His wife, also a French immigrant, worked as a housekeeper. Wendling made money through odd jobs and became the new church janitor less than three weeks before Alma disappeared.

A month after the girl vanished, though, Wendling left town. When her body was found in May, police searched his home. They found bloodstained clothing, knives, and even a piece of jewelry that the Kellner family identified as Alma's.

They also grilled his wife, who he had left behind, but she offered no information and insisted she did not know where he had gone. Detectives didn't believe her, and she was arrested as an accessory.

The manhunt for Wendling went worldwide, stretching to France and Germany. Captain John P. Carney, chief of detectives for the Louisville Police, logged almost 15,000 miles chasing leads throughout the United States, Mexico, and Central America.

In the end, a tip from a woman Wendling had romanced led Carney to a boarding house in San Francisco. He found Wendling living there under an assumed name.

Carney took his prisoner back to Louisville, where he was quickly tried, found guilty, and sentenced to life behind bars. But Wendling maintained his innocence and filed constant appeals. He even tried to break out twice but was quickly caught each time.

In 1919, Wendling became eligible for parole, and Alma's uncle, Frank Fehr, appeared at the hearing and voiced his opinion against him being released. He appeared at every parole hearing after that, making it clear that he was opposed to the man who killed his niece every getting out.

After a parole hearing in 1921, Wendling finally gave up and devoted himself to being a model prisoner, learning to work as an electrician, machinist, and radio technician. He finally realized that he would never be a free man.

Then, in 1934, Alma's uncle, Frank Fehr, wrote to Kentucky governor Ruby Laffoon and, in a surprising move, recommended a pardon for Joseph Wendling. He told the governor that he would accept full responsibility for the parole. It became official in January 1935, and Wendling was released.

Fehr set two conditions for the release. One was that Wendling returned immediately to France. The exact nature of the second condition has never been revealed, but it had something to do with a letter that Wendling sent to Fehr.

It was not a confession. During all the years he was in prison, Wendling maintained that he had not killed Alma - someone else had. It's possible that the letter to Frank Fehr revealed the evidence needed to show that the janitor had not been the little girl's murderer.

Perhaps it had named a young priest who had arrived at St. John's Church at the same time the janitor had.

Soon after the body was discovered in the church's cellar, Father Schmidt was quietly moved to New York and assigned to the St. Boniface Church in Manhattan.

He wasn't the only new arrival in the parish. A young housekeeper named Anna Aumuller was recently hired to clean the church and rectory. It wasn't long before she and Father Schmidt were having an affair.

Once again, Hans was moved out of the parish. This time, he was sent to St. Joseph's Church in Harlem, but the distance couldn't keep the two lovers apart. Anna and Hans were married in that secret ceremony -- but their secret was soon revealed in a very gruesome way.

Hans had installed Anna in an apartment on Bradhurst Avenue, and they used it as a place where they could be together. Their "secret marriage" continued for several months, then one day, Anna announced that she was pregnant.

Hans was in shock. He knew that his days as a priest would be over if word got out that he had married a woman and gotten her pregnant. The Church wouldn't just move him to another parish this time.

That couldn't happen. For Hans, the Church was his life. There must be something he could do to stop this.

Around 5:30 a.m. on Tuesday, September 2, 1913, a young woman named Lucy Cure left her home in Brooklyn to go fishing, a passion she shared with her father. She was out in her rowboat when she heard a thud against its side. She leaned over to look and saw nothing - at first.

But then she heard another thump and looked into the blank, murky eyes of a human head. It was floating faceup, trailing a two-foot-long clump of fine blond hair behind it. The mouth was open, revealing a row of clean white teeth. It had been neatly severed at the neck.

Three days later, on Friday, September 5, Mary Bann, age 11, and her little brother were playing along the shore of the Hudson River in Cliffside Park, New Jersey. They were splashing in the water and building sandcastles when Mary noticed an oddly-shaped package floating in the shallow water. She imagined it was a bag of garbage or discarded clothing, but she was curious and went to take a closer look.

Just then, a friend named Alice McKnight called over to her and asked what she'd found. Mary didn't know. She had picked it up and was carrying it up onto the beach. Whatever it was, it was heavy.

When the two girls looked at the bundle, they saw a heavy blue sheet was wrapped around the item inside it several times. It was held together by a length of string, tied in a tangled knot.

They untied the line, and Mary grabbed one edge of the bedsheet and pulled it toward her. The bundle rolled away, flipping over until something popped out.

It was the upper part of a human torso, cut neatly in half just below the rib cage. There were no arms or head attached to it. Several crabs emerged at the bottom end of the chest and quickly curried off the bloody sheet onto the sand.

"Oh!" Mary uttered. It took a moment for realization to set in, and then all the children ran screaming into the woods.

By the time the Hudson County Police had arrived, a small crowd had gathered around the remains. They couldn't help but stare at the macabre sight, yet they stayed far enough away so they couldn't smell the terrible odor coming from the flesh. The mob was pushed back so the police could do their work.

Investigators carefully examined the corpse, which was foul and grayish-green in color. Since there were no hands or feet, no jewelry was found. It had been wrapped in a pillowcase and blanket that matched the bedsheet, but there seemed to be no identification markings on it - or so they initially thought.

After the remains were taken away to the county coroner's office, detectives searched along the Hudson River for several miles in both directions, but no tracks or clues were found.

The wrappings -- which included a bloodstained sheet, a blanket, and a single pillowcase - were taken to the detective bureau and laid out on a table. The blanket appeared to be a common variety, easily available in department stores. The sheet was plain and unmarked. When detectives turned the pillowcase inside out, though, they found their first clue. A cloth tag attached to the lining read:

*Robinson-Boders Company, Newark, New Jersey*

It wasn't much, but it was something. In the meantime, they'd check missing persons and accident reports, looking for a woman who had vanished or had fallen into a boat propeller.

However, the coroner, Dr. George King, knew it was no accident. He soon announced that the young woman - whoever she was - had been murdered.

Two miles from Cliffside Park, the shoreline of the Hudson River extends to Weehawken, where two young men - Joe Harmann and Michael Parkman - were checking traps for blue crabs on the morning of Sunday, September 7. By noon they'd pulled in dozens of crabs and were getting ready to quit for the day when a man began shouting at them. His name was Steven Sullivan and the friend with him, Edward Hamilton, worked for the Erie Railroad.

They were pointing to something in the water near Joe and Michael's skiff. When Michael looked to the stern, he noticed a large bundle partially submerged in the water. It was wrapped in brown paper and tied with a string like that used in a butcher's shop.

He grabbed it and hauled it up into the small boat. Whatever it was, it was heavy. He cut the string, and a load of stones - later weighed at 10 pounds - fell onto the deck. The rock would turn out to be Manhattan schist, a granite that can only be found along the Manhattan banks of the Hudson. It was not found on the New Jersey side of the river.

As Michael continued to tear away the paper, more rocks fell out, and then suddenly, the contents of the package were revealed - it was the lower half of a woman's torso, minus the legs. It was pale white, and the amputation had been cleanly executed. A small amount of blood stained the sheet also contained in the package.

"What do you have there?" one of the men on the shore called out to them.

"You don't want to know," Joe replied. "Really!"

The police were notified, and the torso was taken to the county coroner's office. The upper portion of the torso, found on Friday, was brought in for comparison and proved to be an obvious match. Dr. King called the amputation one of the neatest pieces of surgical work he had seen in a long time. An autopsy on the body revealed that the dead woman was under 30, likely around five-foot-four-inches tall, 120 pounds, and had given birth prematurely a short time before she was murdered.

The police were interested in the wrappings. The linen seemed to match the cloth wrapped around the upper torso, found on September 5. It was a higher-than-average quality sheet, and the letter "A" had been embroidered on one of the ends of the pillowcase. The edges were also embroidered, which indicated it was likely a custom-made piece.

After the Weehawken discovery, the newspapers started calling the incident the "Hudson River Mystery" and speculated about every aspect of the case. It was widely believed that the killer had to be a doctor because the cuts were so neatly performed.

He wasn't a doctor - he'd just had a lot of practice at butchery.

Meanwhile, investigators were chasing what leads they had. The police contacted hotels with an "A" in their name, which might have used those pillowcases. But they knew that was a shot in the dark - the "A" could have been a family name, the name of the killer, or even the victim herself.

A few days later, on September 10, two men - Irving Broander, 56, and his neighbor, Norman Carhart, 66 - were walking along the shoreline in Keansburg, New Jersey.

As they were climbing over a shallow wall of ancient wood pilings, they spotted something snagged at the water's edge. As they moved closer, they got a better look - it was part of a human leg.

A bloodstained shirt washed up on the Hudson shore near Cliffside on the same day. The garment was the same size as the torso and had large blood spots in the front. The heaviest stains were around the neck. The shirt was also possibly charred as if someone had tried to burn it up.

While body parts were washing up on the New Jersey shore, investigators ran down leads from the bedsheets and pillowcases. The search led them to the Robinson-Boders Company, which had made the pillowcase found at Weehawken. After the company reviewed its sales receipts for the year, police learned that only 12 items of that style of bedding had been sold. The sale had taken place over the summer, and the stock was shipped to a furniture dealer in New York City.

Detectives contacted NYPD inspector Joseph Faurot, chief of Manhattan detectives, who agreed to meet with the Hudson County detectives on September 10.

With the bed linens sold in New York - along with the stone in the package coming from Manhattan - it now seemed more likely than ever that the murder had occurred on the New York side of the Hudson.

After meeting with the New Jersey detectives, Faurot felt the next step should be meeting with the furniture dealer who had received the linens from Robinson-Boders.

The furniture store proprietor was George Sachs, who had a store at 2782 Eighth Avenue, near West 147th Street. On the morning of September 11, Faurot sent two of his men - Detectives James O'Neill and Frank Cassassa - to Sachs Furniture Store. The owner found a receipt dated August 26, when a Manhattan buyer purchased a bedspring, mattress, and pillows for $21.68. All the items were secondhand, except for the pillowcases. The buyer identified himself as A. Van Dyke, paid in cash, and asked for the items to be delivered to a third-floor apartment at 68 Bradhurst Avenue, only a few blocks away from the furniture store.

The detectives then made their way to 68 Bradhurst Avenue, a brick, six-story walkup with five apartments on each floor. They found the superintendent, an elderly black man named Carlton Booker, who said that he remembered the delivery and the man who had rented the apartment. He had walked in off the street to inquire about openings, and he spoke with a heavy German accent. He rented the place as soon as he saw it and asked to move in with his wife as quickly as possible. He returned the following day and paid the rent in advance. Mr. Booker wrote him a receipt - the man's name was H. Schmidt.

The detectives called the station house and spoke to Faurot, who told them not to enter the apartment yet. For now, they had found out all they could about the occupant.

O'Neill and Cassassa spoke to some of the other tenants in the building, including a man named Keefe, who lived in an adjoining apartment. He said he and his wife had heard nothing out of the ordinary in the apartment, but Mrs. Keefe said she often saw a man sneaking out of the apartment early in the morning. He always kept his head down, so he couldn't be recognized.

That seemed to be the story with the tenants throughout the building. No one knew the third-floor apartment's occupant. Neighbors had seen a man come and go, usually late at night. Sometimes there was a woman with him, but no one had gotten a good look at her. They occasionally heard voices in the apartment but didn't hear what was said.

The detectives knocked on the apartment door several times, but there was no response. With no other leads, Faurot told them to stake out the place and wait for someone to show up.

O'Neill and Cassassa took up residence in Mr. Booker's apartment for the next three days, watching the street from the front window. Detectives Kevin McKenna and Bill Connolly took turns waiting in a grocery store nearby, where they drank coffee and took turns napping in the storeroom. Faurot stopped by often, reassuring the men and encouraging them about the boring assignment - it couldn't last forever.

On the night of September 13, Inspector Faurot decided to break into the apartment. He sent Detective Cassassa up the fire escape. He peered in the windows, ensured no one was inside, and then pried a window open with a knife. He made his way across the darkened flat and unlocked the door to let the other detectives inside.

And then they switched on a light.

The men were stunned. The walls and floor were covered with blood. Someone had made a half-hearted, messy attempt to clean up - based on the presence of a scrub brush and six bars of soap on the sink - but had done a poor job. A bloody trail remained where the killer had dragged his victim into the bathroom, where he dismembered the body.

They found a large, bloodstained knife. It was lying next to a carpenter's saw with ominous stains along its teeth and dried blood on the handle. No attempt had been made to hide either item.

In the living room, the detectives found handkerchiefs embroidered with the same "A" on the pillowcase. Several pages of a newspaper, dated August 31 matched the paper that the body part had been wrapped in at Cliffside Park. They discovered a spool of wire at the other end of the room that seemed to match the wire that tied that same bundle.

In the kitchen were six empty ginger ale bottles, a sack of granulated sugar, part of a loaf of bread, a glass watcher pitcher, and two drinking glasses. In the cupboard was a gas inkwell. The refrigerator contained nothing but an empty milk bottle. On top of the refrigerator was the receipt from the Sachs Furniture Store.

In the closet was a man's jacket - the only item of clothing in the apartment. When it was examined, they found the name "A. Van Dyke" sewn into the lining, which was the name of the man who purchased the goods from Sachs.

They found a small metal box in the same closet that contained dozens of handwritten letters. Some were in German, some in English. They seemed to be from different women, but all the envelopes were addressed to Hans Schmidt. Many were from

Anna Aumuller, posted from several different addresses. The most recent address was 428 East 70th Street.

Faurot, O'Neill, and Cassassa decided to go to that address while the others continued searching the apartment. When they arrived there, they met Joseph and Marie Igler, who were the friends of Anna's aunt that she had lived with when she arrived in New York. They told the detectives that Anna had gone to work at St. Boniface as a housekeeper but had not heard from her in nearly two years.

It was almost midnight when the detectives arrived at St. Boniface. The doors were locked, and both the church and rectory were dark. They pounded on the door until they saw a light appear inside. Father John Braun, the parish priest, opened the door.

Faurot explained they were there on an urgent matter and needed to speak with him. Father Braun assumed that someone had died and needed last rites, the only reason that the police usually came to his door at midnight, but this was much worse.

Faurot explained that they were trying to find a missing girl and showed the priest Anna's photograph, which they'd gotten from the Iglers. Father Braun immediately recognized her as a girl who had once worked for the church as a housekeeper. She had left St. Boniface some time ago, though. Faurot then asked if he had ever heard the name Hans Schmidt. Yes, he said, he had once been assigned to St. Boniface, but he had not seen him since May 1912, when he left to go to St. Joseph's parish up on 125th Street.

Father Braun explained that it was better that way because he could not get along with that strange man. "I tried to understand him, but I couldn't. The only way I can describe him was that he was like Stevenson's Jekyll and Hyde."

"And what of Anna?" Cassassa asked. "Where did she go?"

"Oh, she decided to go to St. Joseph's, as well. She told me that she didn't want to stay here anymore after Father Hans left."

The detectives immediately left for the Church of St. Joseph of the Holy Family, arriving at 1:30 a.m. They knocked loudly on the door until Quinn, pastor of the church, finally answered. They apologized for the late hour and asked if he knew a Hans Schmidt. The pastor, visibly concerned, said that he did - and that he was in his room on the second floor. He directed the detectives to wait in the parlor. He would go up and get Father Schmidt for them.

Father Quinn knocked on Schmidt's door and called his name several times. Hans finally answered and was asked to come downstairs. Hans imagined that someone had died or was about to die, so he carefully dressed in his priestly attire and hurried down to the main floor. When he entered the parlor, he found two policemen waiting for him.

Hans showed no emotion, even when one of the men showed him a photograph of Anna. He denied that he knew her. He'd never even heard her name, he said.

Faurot knew he was lying, even though the priest seemed confident and unafraid. They knew that Hans and Anna had been together at both St. Boniface and St. Joseph's, and they had a stack of letters that Anna had written to him. But the more that Faurot asked about Anna, the less Hans was willing to say. He continued to lie to the detectives for nearly a half-hour.

Finally, Faurot decided to get aggressive. He threw Anna's photograph down on the table, stepped in front of Hans, and shouted, "Why did you kill that girl?"

The color drained from Schmidt's face, and he started to tremble. All the bravado slipped away from him, and he began to faint. If Faurot had not been standing close to him, the priest would have fallen to the floor. Detective Cassassa helped Hans into a chair. Faurot came over and placed a hand on his shoulder. "Don't lose your nerve," the detective urged him. "Brace up and tell us the truth. You murdered Anna Aumuller. Tell us what happened."

"I killed her because I loved her!" Hans cried out.

Between sobs, Hans said that he had married Anna several months before her death. He said he was thinking of leaving the priesthood to start a new life. On the morning of her murder, he said he went into her room and cut her throat with a special knife that he had bought the day before. After he was sure she was dead, he dismembered the body, packaged all the pieces, and dumped them in the Hudson River. Each time he left the house, he stopped at an empty lot and gathered some rocks. He later used the rocks to weigh down each bundle. He could not say how many times he took the ferry that night, but it was several trips. Each time he dumped one of the packages. Later, he noticed the mattress in the apartment was covered in blood and realized it wasn't safe to leave it there. He tied it up and carried it to the same lot where he had found the rocks and burned it.

Faurot took the priest upstairs, and they searched his room. While Hans was packing some clothing into a bag, Cassassa discovered a marriage license in the name of Hans Schmit and

Anna Aumuller that was dated February 1913. Faurot asked him where they had been married.

"I'm a priest," Hans replied, "so I married us myself."

"You married yourself?" Cassassa asked.

"You wouldn't understand."

"I don't understand any of it," Faurot said.

In the room, the detectives also found some of Anna's clothing, a key, the rent receipt for the apartment on Bradhurst Avenue, and several medicine bottles with Anna's name.

"She never knew what happened," Hans said quietly as he waited for the search to end. "I carried her into the bathroom and finished the job there. I didn't want to make a mess in the bedroom."

"That was considerate of you, Father," Cassassa smirked.

"What happens now? I mean, do I get a lawyer?"

The detectives said nothing. Faurot picked up all the items from the room and placed them in a bag. He glanced across the hall where Father Quinn and other priests of the parish had been watching the events unfold. They all held rosaries in their hands and prayed silently. Hans stopped in the hallway and asked the monsignor, Father Huntmann, to step into the hall. When Schmidt turned to him, lifted his arms, and started to embrace the man, Father Huntmann's face turned white. Hans tried to put his arms around him, but the monsignor pushed him away.

Inspector Faurot told the priests that Schmidt would be charged with murder as Cassassa handcuffed him and led him away.

Father Huntmann wept as Hans was taken away. "Oh God! How did such a thing happen? Did he really do it?"

"You heard him, Father, "Faurot said. "He did it all right. I'll be in touch with you at a later time."

Even with a confession, the NYPD continued to investigate the case. Mr. Booker from the Bradhurst Avenue apartment building identified Hans as the man who had rented the apartment. So did George Sachs at the furniture store. They found the store where he had purchased the knife - H.S. Sterns and Company on Center Street - and continued to question Hans Schmidt about the murder.

They also made a firm identification of Anna's body. Detectives had located a young woman who had worked for St. Boniface Church while Anna did. Her name was Annie Hirt, and she told investigators that she and Anna were good friends, and she would be able to identify her, even if she didn't see her face. Anna had a brown birthmark on her breast that was easily recognizable.

On September 15, Annie was taken to the morgue in Hoboken, where Detective Cassassa waited with her in the lobby while the body was prepared for viewing. Dr. King laid all the separate pieces together. They fit together almost perfectly.

The only thing missing was the head. At the time, the police did not know about Lucy Cure's discovery of the head with the long blond hair.

When Annie walked into the room, she gasped when she saw the body parts, but she knew what to expect and quickly regained composure. She made the identification, pointing out the birthmark that had escaped the doctor's attention until Annie called attention to it.

She also told Detective Cassassa about Anna's relationship with Hans Schmidt. "She often spoke about him," she said. "After she had been out the day before, she always, the following day, spoke about him. She once said in two weeks, she was going to get married. She also said that she had been to the flat with her intended and to the moving pictures and show told me how the rooms were in the flat."

After the identification, the police were satisfied. The body of Anna Aumuller had been found. The Hudson River Mystery had been solved.

Hans Schmidt was indicted on September 23, and he would be staying in the infamous Tombs, New York City's bleakest prison, until his trial. His guilt was so overwhelming that his attorneys immediately began working on an insanity plea. They claimed that Schmidt was overwhelmed with "blood lust" and was too unstable to know right from wrong.

Locked away, Hans spoke with alienists - an early 1900s term for psychiatrists - and reporters. Even a phrenologist, a scientist who believed that the physical shape of your skull could reveal your personality traits, came to examine Hans to see if he was insane. His attorney, Alphonse Koeble, kept looking until he could find enough doctors to declare his client insane. It wasn't hard since the newspapers seemed to be on his side, printing stories about how the priest ranted in his cell while denying that he was mentally unbalanced.

Schmidt told anyone who would listen that he wasn't crazy because whatever he did, he'd done on orders from God. "There isn't much to say about this," he told his lawyer. "God in his own time will clear it up. Perhaps the people will never understand this thing, but God and Abraham know why I killed her. What's the use of talking about it anymore? I married her. I performed the ceremony myself, as I had a right to do. I was commanded to marry her by St. Elizabeth, my patron saint."

When Koeble asked him if he had any regrets, he said he didn't. "Why should I?" Hans demanded. "I was commanded to do it."

The New York District Attorney's office took Schmidt to Bellevue to be examined. They needed a clear picture of his state of mind on the night he murdered Anna. They believed he was a cunning criminal trying to get away with murder.

Alphonse Koeble ridiculed such statements from the prosecutors and the police. Still, he knew that for the insanity defense to be successful, it had to be shown conclusively that Hans didn't know it was wrong to cut his wife's throat, chop her up, and throw the pieces into the Hudson River. It didn't matter that he had acted strangely in the past, liked to cut the heads of geese when he was a boy and was obsessed with the local slaughterhouse. According to New York State law and the criteria established in the nineteenth century, none of that mattered. The crucial part of the insanity defense in American courts was whether the defendant appreciated the wrongfulness of his act and the consequences of his actions.

Hans Schmidt's trial began on December 7, 1913. Koeble worked hard to establish his client's mental state. He brought in family members to testify to his mental problems, which doctors confirmed, and the prosecution seemed unable to change any of their opinions. From the jury's reaction, the attorney was convinced they saw his client as mentally disturbed.

And he was right - almost.

At the end of the trial, two of the jurors voted to send Hans to a mental hospital, the rest to the electric chair. The trial ended in a hung jury. The attorneys had to do it all over again.

The jury was not as forgiving the second time. The one thing that seemed impossible for them to accept was the fact that Schmidt admitted to killing Anna and cutting up her body - and then said he'd returned to his church and performed a mass. It was just too twisted and cold-blooded for them to understand.

Hans was convicted of first-degree murder and sentenced to death. He was taken by train to the Sing Sing state prison, where he'd await his execution.

Behind bars, Schmidt didn't do well. While his attorney filed appeals, Hans paced his cells and tried to come up with reasons why he should be released. Eventually, he retracted his confession and claimed that Anna had actually died during a botched abortion. Not knowing what else to do, he had cut up her body and tried to hide the evidence.

Even his attorney didn't believe him. Koeble simply assured him that his case was being appealed and left him in his cell. Koeble didn't give up. He went all the way to the governor, but there was no one left to listen. The only glimmer of hope came when a request arrived at his office to ask his client about a little girl in Louisville. If Hans Schmidt knew anything about her murder, there might be a way to delay his execution.

But Schmidt refused to talk about it. "God damn it!" he shouted. "Why are they trying to blame her death on me? It was that damned Frenchman, that horrid maintenance man. I met him once, awful man! They convicted him; you know. He killed that girl. Always trying to put things on me. Of all people, after all the good I've done. It's just not fair."

Hans wasn't going to talk about Louisville.

The execution went ahead as planned. He ordered sauerbraten, string beans, mashed potatoes, cheesecake, and coffee for his last meal. He spent his last night in his cell alternating between raving and protesting his innocence and declaring that he had made peace with God.

At 4:00 a.m., the warden gave permission or a mass to be performed in Schmidt's cell. A temporary altar was set up with a chalice, a crucifix, and a small amount of wine. It was the first time that this had been allowed at Sing Sing.

A half-hour later, the witnesses began to arrive. They were seated in the death chamber, facing "Old Sparky," New York's electric chair.

When Father Schmidt was led into the chamber, he paused in front of the chair, reached inside his shirt, and removed a crucifix. He held it above his head, startling the guards who thought he was starting to resist. "One minute! One minute!" Hans cried. "I want to say one word before I go. I beg forgiveness of all I have offended or scandalized, and I forgive all who have offended me."

The guards forced him into the chair, and he prayed loudly as they applied the straps and electrodes to his body. A brown metal cap with a mask was placed over his head, and in a muffled voice, he called out his last words, "My last word is to say goodbye to my dear old mother!"

And then the executioner turned the dial, and thousands of volts of electricity coursed through his body. A doctor briefly examined him and announced the prisoner was still alive. Another jolt followed, then a third. The doctor pronounced him dead at last.

It was 5:58 a.m. on February 18, 1916.

Hans Schmidt remains the only Catholic priest ever to be executed in the United States.

We can only hope that Anna Aumuller was now able to rest in peace.

# "STRANGE LOVE"
# ELENA MILAGRO HOYOS

Key West, Florida, was always home to some of America's great eccentrics. It's a place that, far removed from the mainland of America, serves as sort of the last outpost for writers, dreamers, musicians, and weirdos.

But in 1940, news spread around the island that something very strange was taking place in "Dr. von Cosel's" laboratory and when details were revealed about what it was - it finally realized just what was "too much" even for Key West folks to handle.

The story of what happened in Key West remains one of the most shocking stories of passion in American history. It's the story of a beautiful woman, a very strange man, and a love that managed to defy even death.

It's also one of the most twisted and repulsive stories that I've ever put onto paper, so I'm not sure you'll thank me for this one, but at least I saved it for last.

Maria Elena Milagro Hoyos was born on July 31, 1909, the daughter of a Key West cigar maker named Francisco "Pancho" Hoyos and his wife, Aurora. She had two sisters - Florinda, the oldest, and Celia, the youngest. Elena was in the middle. They grew up in Key West, and there's nothing to say that Elena's childhood was anything other than normal. Her family had been wealthy in Cuba before falling on hard times and moving to Key West to work in the many cigar factories.

Cubans were known for their love of families, and fellow Cubans were treated as relatives. The Hoyos household was no exception. The chaotic home was always filled with uncles and cousins; aunts who cooked; boyfriends, girlfriends, and children always coming and going; and a daily round of laughter, tears, and loud conversation.

The girls all loved the moving picture shows at the Strand, and they loved singing and dancing. They were popular and sought-after partners at the dances held at the Cuban Club on Duval Street.

The Hoyos home was on Watson Street, one street over from White Street, near the intersection of what is now called Truman Avenue. The nearby streets were paved with reddish brick and electric trolley cars traveled by rails that ran down their centers.

Most of the homes near where Elena lived were built around the turn of the century by tobacco barons to house the cigar makers. Both men and women worked in the factories. Each day, they entered the large brick buildings and sat in straight-backed chairs in front of a carved wooden tray to aid them in hand-rolling the leaves. In the middle of the warehouse was a small, elevated platform, surrounded by a railing, where the "readers" with powerful voices would sit and read aloud from newspapers, magazines, and books to relieve the monotony of making one cigar after another.

Elena was a beautiful girl. Her hair fell to her shoulders in black ringlets; she had a bright smile and was the most charming and charitable of her three sisters. She was a popular performer for special events held at the San Carlos Theater and had many friends. She was described as exuberant and full of life, even though her family struggled as so many poor workers did at the time. The girls made mascara from Vaseline and the charcoal of burnt matches and rubbed wet red paper on their cheeks for rouge. A cotton print dress might only cost 50-cents, but they couldn't always afford them.

When she was in her late teens, Elena began to be courted by Luis Mesa, a handsome, mischievous young man who often accompanied her to the theater and dances. Her parents approved, and they were married on February 18, 1926. Photographs of the couple show Elena as a blushing 18-year-old bride in a white lace gown, smiling radiantly as she stands next to her new husband. Luis, grinning, looked equally overjoyed.

Luis and Elena's courtship, wedding, and subsequent months of happiness were the most joyful time in Elena's life. A few months after the wedding, she learned that she was pregnant, making her life seem perfect.

But in truth, it was the beginning of the end of her happiness.

On November 5, Elena miscarried. But soon, things got worse. At first, her family and friends thought Elena's paleness and lack of energy were caused by grieving over the loss of the baby, but they soon realized the cause had to be physical and not the effects of her sorrow. She was taken to see the family physician, and he gave them a tragic diagnosis - it was tuberculosis.

Even though Elena had come down with a recurring cough in the early stages of the disease, the symptoms of tuberculosis aren't usually apparent until it advances to the point that lesions appear in x-rays. Next comes the fever, malaise, and weight loss.

At the time of Elena's diagnosis, tuberculosis was incurable and barely treatable. In Key West, especially in the 1930s, it was the number one cause of death, especially among cigar makers who passed germs to one another in the close confines of the factories. Of the various strains of the disease, the most dangerous one was the kind that Elena had. It was dubbed "hasty consumption" because it quickly consumed those unfortunate enough to contract it.

Realizing the seriousness of the situation, her doctor immediately referred her to the Naval Marine Hospital on the island for a blood test and x-ray.

The hospital in those days was the only medical facility for many miles around, which was why it was open to the public and not just the military. It was a modern hospital dedicated to providing the best care possible, but this did not make Elena and Luis dread going there any less. They rode the trolley out to the base and then walked the rest of the way to the hospital.

Once there, Luis stayed in the waiting room while Elena was ushered back to an exam room. She had taken a seat just moments before a distinguished-looking gentleman with a trim beard and mustache came in to take a blood sample.

And that's when Elena met a German-born radiologic technologist named Carl Tanzler - or as he liked to refer to himself, "Carl von Cosel" - and when her story took its first strange turn.

Carl Tanzler actually had many names.

He was born Karl Tanzler, or George Karl Tänzler, on February 8, 1877, in Dresden, Germany. Little is known about his factual background because his invented one was so confusing and changed often. He grew up in Germany, living in a house with a built-in laboratory that allowed him to develop his scientific skills. Eventually, he graduated from the University of Leipzig with nine degrees.

Or so he claimed.

He traveled to India and Australia, where he did electrical work, bought boats, purchased a South Seas island, and began building a trans-ocean flying plane around the time of World War I. When the war broke out, he claimed that he was jailed by British authorities for "safe-keeping" and was released at the war's end.

How much of this was true, no one knows. Exactly who Carl Tanzler was remains unclear because the veracity of his memories cannot be trusted. Partly truth and partly fiction, they were written by a man whose obsessive love for a woman he considered his "soulmate" warped his sense of reality.

We do know that he had a vast knowledge of science and was fluent in several languages - all of which could have been self-taught - and that he emigrated to the United States from Germany in 1926 via Cuba. He left his wife, Doris, and small daughters behind. The plan was for them to follow once he had settled and could provide for them. He was going to live with his sister in Zephyrhills, Florida.

The boat to the United States from Cuba deposited Tanzler in Key West. There was no one there to greet him. The telegram that he'd sent to his sister had never arrived. After leaving the Custom House by the Navy yard, he tried to catch a train to his sister's house. The last one had already departed, though, so he started walking. He made it 12 miles before a train caught up to him the next morning, and he rode the rest of the way to Miami. From there, he traveled to Zephyrhills, near Tampa, where he planned to start his new life.

In 1927, his wife and children arrived from Germany, but their reunion was brief. Whatever happened, Tanzler walked out and left them with his sister while he pursued his dreams.

It's not hard to imagine that the Tanzlers were not suited for one another. Doris was strong-willed, practical, serious, and half her husband's age. She insisted that once in America, her daughters only speak English and learn the ways of their adopted country. On the other hand, Carl was 50 years old and was an imaginative, impractical inventor, scientist, electrical wizard, and an ingenious liar. He had already started to mix fact with fantasy about his life, and in the years to come, it would only get worse.

Even though he hadn't been impressed with the town when he first arrived, Tanzler drifted back to Key West. He applied at the Marine Hospital and initially took any job they offered. At first, he was an attendant who cleaned up after medical procedures, but somehow, he managed to convince the officials in charge that he knew how to operate the x-ray machine. He soon found himself in charge of the department, operating the devices, doing laboratory work, and collecting blood samples.

It was at the hospital that he met Elena Hoyos, and he immediately fell in love with her. He would later claim that, as a child, he was visited by visions of a dead ancestor, Countess Anna Constantia von Cosel, who revealed to him the face of his true love, an exotic dark-haired woman. That same apparition came back to haunt him many times when he was a young man, including for seven days while living in Australia. She stayed with him while he went about his work and ordinary life. She never demanded anything, but she was always there, even standing by his bed at night while he slept.

He would never forget that face, and years later, he became convinced that the apparition of his "true love" had worn the face of Elena Hoyos.

Tanzler was delighted that she would be returning to the hospital the next day for a chest x-ray. Before leaving for work that morning, he made sure that his tie was on straight, and his clothes were neatly pressed. At the hospital, he prepared his equipment more thoroughly than ever, and after what seemed an excruciating wait, Elena was escorted in.

Tanzler fawned over the young woman. He pretended to carefully examine her charts, even though he had already committed them to memory. He examined her, listening to her heart and lungs, and reassuring her that his x-ray machine would tell him all he needed to know. "Let me say this," he added in his German accent, "I have studied pulmonary tuberculosis and will be able to see any lesions that appear on film. Tuberculosis is a strange disease. If you have it - and we don't know this yet - but if you do, I can treat it. Don't be afraid."

Tanzler then directed her to take off her blouse and undergarments and have a seat in front of his strange device. Elena hesitated, but he assured her that the room would be dark so she would have her privacy. "I will not turn the lights back on until you have put on your blouse," he told her.

Even though the room was dark, a dim red light was glowing on the equipment. Tanzler was sweating as she undid her buttons and removed her clothes. He wiped his forehead with a handkerchief before getting down to business. When he finished, he told her again that he would do everything in his power to make sure she stayed in good health. He would develop the film and see her back at the hospital the next day for the results.

Tanzler's hands shook as he placed the film into the developing tray, still thinking about Elena. His nose filled with the smell of chemicals, but all he could imagine was the scent of her perfume. But his heart dropped when he glimpsed the finished film - there were lesions in her lungs.

She had tuberculosis - and she didn't have long to live.

To add to Elena's misfortunes - losing a child and learning she was seriously ill - not long afterward, her husband, Luis, abandoned her for another woman and left Key West. He ended up in Miami, working as a waiter in a restaurant there. Though he claimed Elena's illness had nothing to do with their failed marriage, he was out into a difficult position - stay and perhaps die of the same contagious disease or leave and have a life.

And he may have chosen wisely. Elena's illness would later claim the entire Hoyos family.

Only Carl Tanzler was happy that Luis was gone. He hated to see Elena suffer but knew that Luis leaving was for the best. He hadn't deserved someone as special as Elena.

There is little doubt that Tanzler exuded brilliance to those who didn't know any better. His theories and analytical skills impressed doctors and nurses at the hospital, although in truth, he was walking a thin line between genius and mad scientist.

For the Hoyos family, who knew nothing of the inner workings of Tanzler's mind, he was a godsend. Pancho and Aurora were beside themselves with worry. They were angry with Luis for abandoning their daughter, but the anger and frustration they felt toward him paled in comparison to the horrible news that Elena was so sick she might soon die.

It wasn't just about her health either. There was barely enough money to get by in normal times - how would they pay for costly medical treatments?

And then along came Count Von Cosel, a medical man with all the answers. He used all his knowledge to attempt to treat and cure Elena with a variety of medicines, as well as x-ray and electrical equipment that was brought to their home. Their daughter's health had become his mission - and he was doing it all for free.

Officials at the hospital knew there was little hope of recovery, but no one discouraged Tanzler's genuine efforts to find a miracle cure for the young woman. He also showered her with gifts of jewelry and clothing and frequently professed his love for her. There is nothing to say that Elena ever reciprocated his affections. She was likely baffled by the attention being given to her by the strange little man.

At first, the family appreciated his kindness - even if they were overwhelmed by it - but in time, they stopped trusting him, and when Elena had appointments at the hospital, she frequently failed to show up for them. Her family started taking her to other doctors and avoiding Tanzler's efforts to treat her.

Tanzler was now reduced to begging - asking Elena to come back to the hospital, continue the treatments, and, most importantly, marry him and go away somewhere as his wife.

But, of course, she couldn't. Elena was dying. Her condition had become critical. Allowing Tanzler to return to their home was an act of desperation by the Hoyos, partly because the weird little doctor still offered hope for a cure.

The other doctors who were asked to treat Elena offered no chance for her recovery. They only offered painkillers to make her as comfortable as possible as she drew nearer to death. The idea of her seeing other doctors made him mad with jealousy, and he was kicked out of the Hoyos' home again.

This time, Pancho and Aurora took Elena and went to stay with family in another part of town. They didn't leave a forwarding address for Tanzler. Unable to find them, he was inconsolable. Then, according to his story, he ran into one of Elena's relatives, who told him where she was. "Elena is now in bed all the time," she told him. "She needs you, but her parents won't let you come. I'll tell you what, doctor, it's a crime."

When he found Elena, she was pale and emaciated, wearing a silk kimono he had given her as a gift. When Aurora got angry with him for being there, he simply said he was there to begin a new series of treatments for Elena and to stand aside. Aurora reluctantly agreed to let him try and help. It was now too late to do much damage.

His new "treatment" was a series of electrical shocks, but he wanted to do this cautiously and not upset the family. He first brought over a small "inductor box" powered by a dry-cell battery to get them accustomed to the voltage. It had a small movable shocking coil with silk cords and brass handles. Elena was able to regulate the current for herself.

The box was only a warm-up for a bigger and better high-power, high-frequency medical unit that he had invented. It had a glass globe on the top that showed the current.

He also worked to improve her mood with more presents. He brought over new things each day. When Elena's bed broke, he purchased a new one. Each day, he carried in gifts and then hooked her up to his machine with electrodes he placed on her chest. The electricity that surged through her body jolted her and made her cry out. She hated it - but Dr. Von Cosel knew best.

When her condition improved slightly, Tanzler was elated. To boost her spirits, he went to a local store and bought her six silk dresses and stockings to go with them. She wasn't ready to go anywhere yet, but he wanted her to have nice things to wear when she did.

But the slight improvement didn't last. On various days in mid-October 1931, Elena's father took her for walks and a ride in an automobile so that she could have some fresh air. Tanzler was fuming when he found out, certain that the outings would harm her.

His intentions were good, but so were those of Elena's family. Both were certain they were doing the right thing. It was inevitable that Elena would die from the terrible disease. Knowing how ill she was, her father, mother, sisters, and relatives were doing what they thought best for her. Except for an occasional outing, though, she spent most of her time in her room, which Tanzler believed was the most beneficial place for her to be.

By Friday, October 23, Elena was exhausted. She drifted in and out of sleep, sweating from fever and struggling to catch her breath. Tanzler still clung to the delusion that he could save her, refusing to admit it was too late.

Despite all his efforts, Elena died on October 25, 1931.

Tanzler wasn't there when she took her last breath. He learned of her death from Mario, the husband of one of Elena's sisters. And when he realized that Elena's father had taken her out for another automobile ride, which he had strictly forbidden, Tanzler was enraged.

His grief over Elena's death became a hatred for her family. They had refused to follow his instructions about rest and visitors. Because they had the nerve to question his motives and abilities repeatedly, he knew he would never forgive them.

Once again, Tanzler was there to save Elena, this time from a pauper's burial. He made and paid for all the funeral arrangements. He selected the coffin and the flowers and made all the decisions required for the final disposition of his beloved. She was dressed in one of the silk dresses that he had bought her, and she was laid out at the Hoyos home, surrounded by flowers. Even in death, she still looked beautiful.

Her service was held at the Star of the Sea Catholic Church, and then a procession entered the Key West Cemetery at the Margaret Street gate. A narrow road led to the Catholic section, where wooden chairs had been arranged for the mourners. Elena's casket waited there for one last eulogy before she was placed in the ground.

When the service was over, Tanzler placed a large canvas tarp over her grave to protect it from the elements. He couldn't stand the idea of her decomposing down there in the dirt. But this was only a temporary solution. He had plans for something more permanent, and as he visited her gravesite day after day, the details began forming in his mind to build her a grand mausoleum.

With permission from the Hoyos family - and the state of Florida - Elena was exhumed and taken to the Lopez Funeral Home, where she could be safely kept while the tomb was constructed.

There was also another reason for taking her there - Tanzler wanted to "re-bed" her body just in case there had been water damage. Or so he said. He really just wanted to see her again. With a little money slipped to the undertaker, he accomplished this in the middle of the night. He cleaned her corpse, sprayed it with a disinfectant and preservative, and wrapped her in layers of clean cotton. He then placed Elena's coffin in a second coffin. He had designed it himself, and it was meant to prevent any further decay of the corpse while the construction on the mausoleum was being finished.

Tanzler would later claim that he had no future plans for the body at this time - but it's hard to know whether to believe him.

It took three months for the mausoleum to be finished, but it was the largest and finest in the cemetery once it was. Surrounded by palm and pine trees, it had an ornate cement dome supported by Greek pillars. On either side of the entrance were pedestals for vases of flowers, and on the small building's four corners were large cement urns for more flowers. The short, wide doors had glass windows and curtains. There was a white porcelain doorknob, and inscribed in the cement wall next to the entrance was:

**ELENA MILAGRO HOYOS**
**BORN JULY 31, 1908**
**DIED OCTOBER 25, 1931**

## R.I.P.
## CT. D COSEL

There was also a Latin inscription on the base of the dome that read *Accersitus ab Angelus* - "Summoned by Angels."

Soon, Tanzler, walking to and from the mausoleum with his ornate cane, would become a familiar figure to those who lived near the cemetery. He faithfully visited the tomb every day for the next 18 months, spending hours sitting outside the door to the crypt.

No one knows what finally pushed Tanzler over the edge. At first, he claimed he could smell her perfume coming from inside the mausoleum. He began having conversations with her, and it was rumored that he even installed a telephone so he could call Elena when the weather was bad and when he was unable to visit her in person.

He heard her voice, he'd later say. He was convinced that he was communicating with her spirit. He claimed that he felt her touch and that Elena's spirit appeared to him when he sat next to her tomb and serenaded her with her favorite song.

And then, she began calling to him and asking him to free her from her stone prison. She directed him as to how her body could be removed from the crypt and safely spirited out of the graveyard. It was Elena's idea, of course. Tanzler was only her willing servant.

So, one night in April 1933, Tanzler crept into the cemetery, removed Elena's body from the mausoleum, and carted it out of the cemetery in a toy wagon. He took her home with him - and that's when things got even stranger.

Tanzler wired Elena's bones together with wire and coat hangers and inserted glass eyes into her head. He used splints to make sure her nose looked "as beautiful as when she was alive." He had to straighten out her arm, which had been folded across her body in the coffin. He did this by counterweights with a cord over a pulley on the ceiling, fastening it to a bandage on her wrist. It applied gentle tension until the arm automatically took the required position below the hip joint.

The cosmetic work went on for some time. As her skin began to decompose, he replaced it with silk cloth that had been soaked in wax and plaster. When her hair fell out, he fashioned a wig from hair given to him by Elena's mother soon after her funeral in 1931. He filled her cadaver with rags so that she could keep her original form, and he dressed Elena in her clothing, stockings, jewelry, and gloves. Tanzler also used copious amounts of perfume, disinfectants, and preserving agents to mask the odor and slow the body's decomposition.

To anyone else, Elena had been turned into a modern-day mummy. To Tanzler, though, she was returning to life. He truly believed that Elena would someday be resurrected.

In the meantime, things were happening that were unsettling Tanzler's everyday life. The commander of the Naval Station of which the hospital was part had died, and a new man had taken his place - one not so appreciative of Carl's many eccentricities. As orderly as Tanzler thought he was, he was not that neat. The new chief was amazed at his unkempt laboratory and put him on notice.

But Tanzler had little time to deal with work - he was consumed by Elena and her care.

He was also too busy for his own daughter, Crystal. In 1934, she died from diphtheria in Zephyrhills, and Doris was deeply grieved. Surely, her husband would come home for the burial of his child. Desperately seeking emotional and financial support, she wrote to Carl and told him of the tragedy.

But he ignored her pleas. He didn't go to Crystal's funeral, nor did he send any money. All that he had was for his beloved Elena. He needed money to build a new "castle" for her where they could live together forever. He was now so deep in his delusional, make-believe world that all his thoughts and sympathy were restored for his poor dead love, whom he had sworn to return to life.

Tanzler's new home was hardly a "castle." From photographs, it appears to be an open shed with metal sliding doors. Located on Rest Beach, it was once part of a local slaughterhouse where cattle were killed so that the blood could run directly into the sea.

He continued to try and improve the place over the next two years, which he called the "happiest of his life." He leveled the floor, added some walls, and separated the space for his laboratory from his living quarters. He installed the million-volt transformer in his lab space that he'd tried to heal Elena with, his homemade x-ray machine, his books, bed, and other essentials. In another room - always kept padlocked - was an "incubator tank" of his own design, which was supposed to keep Elena's body in perfect condition until she could be brought back to life.

There was another reason for preserving Elena's corpse - Tanzler had to do it because he was often keeping her body in his bed.

Unfortunately, the peace and solitude that Tanzler enjoyed at Rest Beach was interrupted in 1936 by workers from the WPA - the Work Projects Administration. In an effort to revive the economy during the Depression, Franklin D. Roosevelt's New Deal had started a massive public works project. In Key West, one of the projects the WPA tackled was the restoration and clean-up of all the beaches, including Rest Beach.

For Tanzler, this meant people were suddenly all around his private and peaceful home. Having this many people around made it impossible for him to put Elena in the incubator tank, which he was convinced was restoring her life. The idea of suspending Elena's treatments to hide her from prying eyes was agonizing to Carl.

Needing another place out of the way, he eventually found another house. This one was about two miles from what's now considered "Old Town" in Key West, and it fit the bill for seclusion and privacy.

Around this same time, Tanzler was laid off at the Marine Hospital. It was not because he was incompetent - crazy, perhaps, but he knew his job - but because of a decreased operating budget. Carl accepted his discharge graciously - he now had more time to spend with Elena.

Away from his fellow workers, Tanzler soon lost almost all contact with the community. His only interactions with townsfolk were when he went to the post office to pick up a monthly check that arrived for him. It was a check that caused a lot of speculation among those who knew about it. Carl claimed it was a monthly payment for a business he'd sold in Germany. Others suggested it was a stipend from the German army or an inheritance, but no one ever really knew for sure.

The laboratory at the new house didn't offer the space needed for Elena's incubator tank, and Carl could not decide what to do next. The only thing he knew for sure was that he needed to protect her from natural destruction. He covered her with new layers of cotton, silk, and wax, trying to ensure she did not deteriorate.

And it's a good thing he did this because, on July 29, 1936, Elena came back to life.

He woke early that morning -- "in the full possession of my senses and faculties," he said -- and looked over to Elena's side of the bed to see the fingers of her right-hand moving. He took her hand in his and "felt how relaxed and soft it became again." He went on to add:

*Immediately thereafter, her whole arm lifted itself up and her hand pressed firmly against my face and lips as she used to do when she was alive, so that I could kiss it. When I kissed her hand, she opened her eyes and looked at me intently. Then, turning herself on her side toward me, she attempted to get up. I was fully awake and became alarmed, fearing that she would collapse and fall, so I spoke to her quietly: "God Bless you, Elena. I am so happy you awakened from your long sleep."*

Carl hurriedly got up and told her to rest. He would make her some beef broth to restore her strength, and then she would be able to get out of bed. He was only away for a few minutes, but Elena had returned to a state of rigidity when he returned. He tried to give her some of the broth, but it simply dripped from her mother, staining the linens on the bed.

Tanzler was grief-stricken, assuming he had done something wrong and missed out on his second chance with his beloved Elena. There was nothing he could do with his electrical appliances - this was now obviously a spiritual problem - so he gathered some flowers and placed them around her head.

Insects had started to torment her body, so after a bath of preservatives and perfume, he gave her another layer of wax and silk.

Now that she was alive, he thought, it was more important than ever to pay attention to her upkeep.

As more years passed, Elena continued to speak to Carl, even as her body withered and decayed. He did all he could to make sure her body was protected, but she slowly fell apart. She never returned to him as she did that day in 1936, but she never completely left him either.

In March 1940, Carl slipped and fell through the deck frames of a boat he was working on and broke several ribs. It was only Elena's voice that saved him, he later said. He managed to get free from the painful position he was in, crawl out of the boat, and walk home. Incapacitated and in agony, he could not rest until Elena instructed him to lie down with his back resting against her body. Only then could he sleep.

Tanzler always believed that his secret had been safe, but his actions had become suspect to many people in town by this time. He bought soap and jewelry and large bottles of perfume - for who? What was he doing with it?

It could have been someone malicious who started the talk, or maybe some children had peeked into the windows of his house - no one knows. But an ugly rumor began circulating in town. Most people just laughed it off, but some took it seriously. In Key West, where everyone knew everything about everybody, it was only a matter of time before Elena's sister, Florinda, heard that her dead sister might not be resting in peace in her mausoleum.

On September 28, 1940, it was discovered that - just like the rumors said - Elena's tomb had been broken into, and her coffin had been tampered with. Tanzler was summoned to the cemetery, where he found Florinda, her husband, an undertaker, and the cemetery caretaker waiting for him. Florinda immediately insisted that the coffin - to which Carl had the only key - be opened.

Tanzler refused.

But he had a good reason. Elena had been dead for nine years. Undoubtedly, it would be a gruesome sight if they opened the casket. The undertaker and caretaker agreed, and for the moment, Florinda was placated.

But that wouldn't last.

And neither would Tanzler's time with his beloved. When he returned home, he told Elena of her sister's behavior, talked to her, and caressed her throughout the evening. He feared that his time with her was coming to an end.

And he was right. On October 1, Tanzler was again called to the cemetery, and this time a crowd was waiting for him. Florinda confronted him and emotionally demanded that Tanzler open Elena's coffin. Carl angrily responded that Florinda should be ashamed of herself for trying to desecrate the grave of an angel. Didn't she care about her sister's safety, he asked, ironically accusing her of attempting to endanger a gravesite that he knew was empty because he'd already opened it.

But Florinda refused to give up this time. "Please open the tomb and let me see Elena inside her coffin or I believe I will go crazy," she said. "If only I could see her to know that she is all right, I'll be satisfied."

Finally, Tanzler sighed. "All right, I don't want you to go crazy, I will let you see Elena. Let's talk this over in peace and arrange it between ourselves. This is not a public affair."

"Where do you want us to go?" she asked.

Tanzler agreed to take her to his home. When they arrived, he ushered her inside.

"Come here and see how beautiful Elena is resting in her bed with her silken garments and with all her jewelry," Tanzler invited her in with a flourish. "Come and see, she could not have it better anywhere."

As she walked up to the bed, Tanzler lifted a curtain, and there she was, his Elena.

In the dark, candlelit room, Florinda could not understand what she was seeing at first. It was nearly impossible to believe the patchwork body with wax and heavy makeup was her sister. She asked Tanzler how long she had been there, and he replied that it had been seven years.

Florinda ran out of the house. Her husband was waiting for her outside, and she told him that they were leaving. They would return to the cemetery, open Elena's coffin, and see what was inside. She refused to believe that what she had seen in the dark, rundown house was her sister.

As the car pulled away, Tanzler went back into the house and sat down next to Elena. He softly stroked her arm and tried to reassure her that everything would be all right.

And it was - for the next five days.

On October 5, 1940, nearly a dozen cars pulled up in front of Tanzler's house - two sheriff's vehicles, a justice of the peace, a funeral car, and several others. When Tanzler opened the door, the sheriff presented him with an arrest warrant that charged him with being in possession of a dead body.

As he was led away, Carl looked over his shoulder at Elena. It was the last time he'd ever see her. He caught a glimpse of her face as men from the funeral home loaded her into a wicket body basket. He stared through the back window of the police car as they placed her into a black hearse.

For better or worse, Carl Tanzler's life changed dramatically when he was arrested. Literally overnight, he went from a solitary eccentric in a small island town to an internationally known figure. "Count Von Cosel" went from obscurity to fame.

When he arrived at the courthouse, flashbulbs from reporters' cameras exploded. Word had circulated around the courthouse that someone was about to be arrested for sleeping with a corpse. The news spread throughout southern Florida and beyond. Reporters and photographers, already there, were in a feeding frenzy, and many more were on the way.

Carl was bewildered by the attention but said nothing as he was booked at the county jail for "wanton and maliciously demolishing, disfiguring, and destroying a grave." It turned out that he was charged with desecrating the tomb - not for stealing her corpse. That wasn't illegal at the time.

Psychiatrists examined Tanzler, but they found him mentally competent to stand trial. The preliminary hearing was the closest that Carl ever got to a trial, though he insisted that he had brought Elena back to life. His spirit spoke to him many times, he told the court, and she had even warned him that trouble was coming and that he should hide her body. There was life still in Elena, Tanzler said, even though her physical body was asleep.

Judge Enrique Esquinaldo, Jr. was seen shaking his head many times during the hearing, especially when Tanzler was on the stand. He finally spoke up, "Sir, you have had her body in your possession for seven years - seven years! - and she appears to be completely dead, lifeless, not alive. It seems to me you don't understand."

In the witness chair, the judge leaned toward Tanzler as he spoke, "Listen to me very carefully. What is left of Elena Hoyos is going to be buried. As the presiding justice of this hearing, that is my decision."

The room was completely silent. Then, Carl spoke up, "Now may I have Elena's body back?"

"No!" Judge Esquinaldo shouted. "No, you may not! You may not have her body back. She is going to be buried. Her only living relative wants her buried. You are no relation to Miss Hoyos. You have no claim to the body."

Tanzler was genuinely shocked. He exclaimed, "You can't do this to me! This isn't justice! Her father gave her to me. I paid for everything, *everything*, the funeral, the caskets, and the mausoleum. She is mine! To take her from me will be the end of everything. You are forcing me to break my sacred promise to Elena!"

Florinda could restrain herself no longer. "Elena is going to be buried in the ground like all her ancestors!" she cried, openly weeping.

"Order! Order in the court!" The gavel pounded as the judge demanded the courtroom to be silent.

"I understand and sympathize with you," he said to Florinda. "Never have I encountered anything like this. You have my sympathy for what you have gone through and the carnival atmosphere surrounding this bizarre affair. Regardless of his guilt or innocence, this court will honor your request to have the body of Elena Hoyos buried. Because of the circumstances surrounding this case, only relatives will be told where the grave is."

While Carl waited in jail on a $1,000 bond, the newspapers were having a field day with the story and turning it into a sensation across the country. Believe it or not, the public mood toward Tanzler was generally sympathetic. Many viewed the eccentric German as "romantic." The general view seemed to be that while Tanzler should probably have his mental condition checked, few felt he deserved to be in jail for an extended amount of time.

Some newspapers blamed Key West's "marked Spanish strain" for the feeling of forgiveness that went around the town. And maybe they were right - well, sort of anyway. A ballad called "The Love of Von Cosel" was written in the wake of the hearing by none other than the brother of Judge Esquinaldo, and it began playing in the saloons of Key West.

In one interview, an unnamed island resident told a reporter that anyone who knew Tanzler knew that he wasn't insane. "He might be obsessed with the thought that he can bring life back to Elena. His love for her is responsible for this. He is not insane. Visit his home. See the electrical and engineering work he has done. This will convince even the most persistent that the man is not insane."

As the newspapers were fanning the flames of the hottest story of the week, the people of Key West were witnessing something they'd never forget.

Even though the judge had ordered Elena's body to be buried, there was one small problem - the Hoyos family couldn't afford to do it. The Lopez Funeral Home was put in charge of the body while it was decided what was to be done, and they decided to put the body on public display. Needless to say, everyone who read the story about Elena and Carl Tanzler wanted to see the famous corpse. Despite the dire warnings of the Catholic Church, few stayed away. It was estimated that at least 7,000 people - including public school kids who were let out to see it -- filed past Elena in her coffin.

While Tanzler waited to see if he would go to trial on the charges filed against him, stories continued to appear in the newspapers. Some claimed he was insane regardless of what doctors said. Others, claiming "inside knowledge" of the case, accused the Hoyos family of knowing that Carl had the body all along. They said he'd been paying them off and only raised a fuss when the money ran out.

But what the rumors were saying about Carl and Elena didn't matter to the courts. The cases against Tanzler were soon dismissed. The statute of limitations for his crime had run out, and he couldn't be prosecuted.

Carl Tanzler was free to go, but he now faced life without his beloved Elena, and as one newspaper noted, "His existence has woven around the memory of a girl for the last several years and no one knows how he will react if he feels he has lost that body forever."

The stories eventually faded, but they might not have if the press and the public had been aware of the information that at least two people in Key West had when the charges against Carl Tanzler were dismissed.

They were the two doctors who performed the autopsy on Elena's body after discovering it in Tanzler's home. For mysterious reasons, they chose not to discuss the case until 1972 - 32 years after the hearing.

The final burial of Elena Hoyos was every bit as strange as Carl Tanzler's behavior had been because those responsible for her third trip to the cemetery didn't want the obsessed scientist to dig her up again.

Three people were entrusted with the burial - Key West Police Chief Bienvenido Perez, Lopez Funeral Home undertaker Benjamin Sawyer, and the cemetery's caretaker, Otto Bethel. They met privately to discuss how the burial would occur, and during these discussions, they made a solemn promise never to reveal the grave's location.

And then things get weird again.

To hide the burial, they dismembered Elena and put what was left of her into an 18-inch square box that could be more easily hidden. The burial took place at 3:00 a.m. on a summer morning in a secluded spot in the cemetery. They placed the box in a shallow hole, covered it over, and replaced the grass so there would be no sign that digging had occurred.

To this day, the spot has never been found.

When Carl Tanzler was finally released in November 1940, he was a broken and penniless man. But there was still a lot of sympathy for him. People regularly came by his home to see where Elena was kept for so long. He began charging 25-cents for a grand tour. This made sure he had food and could afford to rent a room in town.

At first, this pleased him, but it was, in part, his notoriety in Key West that eventually caused him to leave. He had become a tourist attraction and always answered questions from yet another person with out-of-state license plates.

It was agonizing, but he left the town he had shared with Elena and returned to Zephyrhills, where his sister was suffering from health issues and needed his help. There, too, for better or for worse, lived his wife Doris and their teenage daughter. It didn't occur to him that his presence in the town where they lived would be difficult for them. He was not ashamed of what he'd done. Why should they be?

Tanzler packed up three large trucks that he had rented and prepared to leave Key West. However, he had one last thing that he wanted to do before he left.

On the night before the trucks were scheduled to depart, Tanzler put on the same black suit that he had worn when he visited the mausoleum before bringing Elena home to live with him and walked through the cemetery's dark streets. Although he had no idea where Elena was now buried, he believed that her spirit walked beside him as he walked to the graveyard, opened the mausoleum door with the only key, and went inside.

Tears trickled down his face as he removed sticks of dynamite from his coat and wedged them above the wooden door. He set a timer so they could explode in 24 hours, long after he was gone from Key West.

And they did. At 1:40 the following morning, an explosion ripped through the mausoleum. It was heard all over the city, and it tore the small building to pieces. Everyone in Key West knew that the blast had been Tanzler's farewell to the island, but they knew they could never prove it.

It was a final note to a story so strange that it could have only happened there.

But that's not quite the end of Tanzler's story - or Elena's story, for that matter.

Tanzler settled into a life in Zephyrhills that was much quieter than his last days in Kew West. He missed his home on Rest Beach, the ocean, and, of course, his beautiful bride. Still, he was a celebrity, and more than a few people wanted to meet him, especially those who knew his actual wife, Doris. How could anyone give up a normal life to live in seclusion with a corpse" They wanted to know the answer, so they visited Carl and asked for themselves.

He never really answered, though, and they went away almost as bewildered as his wife and his daughter, who had been sheltered from the truth as much as possible.

It might be difficult to believe, but Doris showed great compassion for her husband. She called on Carl at his sister's house and took him to see where his daughter Crystal had been buried. As he stood over her grave, he cried softly as he saw his child's resting place for the first time. He later built a stone monument for her here, topped with a vase-like the ones he'd added to Elena's mausoleum.

In 1944, Tanzler moved out of his sister's house to a rural home in Pasco County, Florida, where he could enjoy some seclusion again. Local residents felt sorry for him, but they really felt sorry for his wife, who, through no fault of her own, was a marked woman, as was their daughter. They weren't simply someone's neighbors; they were the wife and daughter of you-know-who who did you-know-what to that Cuban girl in Key West.

Likewise, relatives of the Hoyos family felt embarrassed that a relative of theirs was involved in such a strange story, even though much of it occurred after she died. To this day, some who are related to the Hoyos family refuse to talk about the incident.

It was also in 1944 that both Florinda Hoyos and her husband, Mario, died. Mario was electrocuted trying to rescue another worker when the crane the man was operating hit a power line. Florinda, who had been ill for some time, succumbed to tuberculosis, the same disease that killed Elena and the rest of the family.

At his new home, Tanzler worked hard to complete his memoirs. He had wanted them published as a book, but the best he could do was when a pulp magazine called *Fantastic Adventures* agreed to print "The Secret of Elena's Tomb" in 1947.

The magazine landed on newsstands in September, and, once again, Tanzler was in the limelight. Doris was horrified, of course, and had one more thing to try and shield her daughter from.

After the money from the magazine sale was gone, Tanzler was destitute. During this final period of his life, Doris proved again what a kind and compassionate woman she was. She met him once a week to talk and give him $2.50 from her $15-a-week salary. It wasn't much, but it allowed him to buy a few staples that kept him from starving to death.

But Carl Tanzler didn't merely exist. He still stayed in touch with Elena, even though her body was long gone. His obsession with her never ended.

During the time that he had her corpse secreted away in his home, he created a death mask of her face from plaster. It was almost as though he knew that he would someday need it. He used that mask as the basis for a life-sized figure of Elena that he kept in his bed until his death on July 3, 1952.

Some accounts of Tanzler's death claim his body was found in the arms of the dummy, but this is merely wishful thinking by those of morbid sensibilities. According to his obituary, he died on the floor of his home.

However, it was noted that overlooking his corpse was a "waxen image, wrapped in a silken cloth and a robe." It seems that his replacement Elena was with him to the very end.

But our story cannot end without a conclusion to the story of Elena Hoyos.

In the years that followed Tanzler's death, tabloid papers, detective magazines, and books occasionally revived the bizarre tale of Count Von Cosel and his bride. As you might expect, the stories were sensational, but they were incomplete.

It would not be until an article appeared on March 5, 1972, in *Tropic Magazine* that the rest of the story would finally be told. It was now 20 years after Tanzler's death and 32 years after his hearing and sanity evaluation, that the author confirmed what had been whispered about all along.

The article included an interview with the doctor who had performed the autopsy on Elena's corpse after she had been retrieved from Tanzler's home. According to the doctor:

*I made the examination in the funeral home. The breasts really felt real. In the vaginal area, I found a tube wide enough to permit sexual intercourse. At the bottom of the tube was cotton, and in an examination of the cotton, I found there was sperm. Then I knew we were dealing with a sexual pervert.*

Why, with all the sympathy given to Carl Tanzler, didn't the doctor reveal what he had found? Perhaps he would have been forced to disclose this information if Tanzler was brought to trial, but he never was. It certainly would have changed the minds of many about Tanzler if they had known that the sordid rumors were actually true.

But that didn't happen. People didn't talk about things like that in print in 1940. Doctors remained silent to protect the public and the families of those involved. What Tanzler had done was never revealed.

But it was Key West - everyone probably already knew.

And what about Elena herself? Was this the end of her story too?

Everyone assumed that Carl Tanzler was crazy when he claimed that Elena's spirit was appearing to him, speaking to him, and making her presence known. But what if he wasn't?

Well, *only* about that part of his story, I mean.

Since Elena's reburial in 1940, stories say that the spirit of a dark-haired girl in a white dress has been seen wandering the grounds of the Key West Cemetery. She seems lost, they say, as if she is looking for something, and perhaps she is.

Perhaps she is seeking the place where her remains were finally placed. Only three men had any idea where Elena was eventually buried and all of them took that secret to their own graves.

Perhaps the ghost of Elena herself is trying to solve a mystery for which a solution will never be found.

# BIBLIOGRAPHY

*American Weekly*

Amundson, Mavis - *The Lady of the Lake*, Port Angeles, WA, Western Gull, 2000

Asbury, Herbert - *The Gangs of New York*, New York, NY, Avalon Publishing, 2004

Bellamy, John Stark, III - *The Corpse in the Cellar*, Cleveland, OH, Gray and Company, 1999

Blum, Deborah - *The Poisoner's Handbook*, New York, NY, Penguin, 2010

Bommersach, Jana - *The Trunk Murderess: Winnie Ruth Judd*, New York, NY, Simon and Schuster, 1992

Brandon, Craig - *The Electric Chair*, Jefferson, NC, McFarland, 1999

*Brooklyn Daily Eagle*

Wenzell, Brown - *Introduction to Murder*, London, Andrew Dakers, Limited, 1953

Buhk, Tobin T. - *The Lonely Hearts Killers*, Jefferson, NC, Exposit, 2020

Cheli, Guy - *Sing Sing Prison*, Portsmouth, NH, Arcadia Publishing, 2003

*Chicago Daily Tribune*

Cimino, Al - *Women Who Kill,* London, UK, Arcturus Publishing Limited, 2019

Collins, Paul - *Murder of the Century*, New York, NY, Random House, 2011

Dash, Mike - *Satan's Circus* - New York, NY, Crown Publishers, 2007

Drimmer, Frederick - *Until You Are Dead*, New York, NY, Windsor Publishing, 1990

Dunstan, William E. - *Nell Cropsey and Jim Wilcox*, Independently Published, 2019

Gado, Mark - *Killer Priest*, Westport, CT, Praeger, 2006

Harlow, Alvin Fay - *Old Bowery Days,* new York, NY, Appleton, 1931

Harrison, Ben - *Undying Love*, New York, NY, St. Martins Press, 1997

Hynd, Alan - *Murder, Mayhem, and Mystery*, A.S. Barnes & Co., New York, NY, 1958

Kaute, Wilfried - *Murder in the City: New York 1910-1920*, New York, NY, St. Martins Press, 2016

Liebling, A.J. - "The Case of the Scattered Dutchman," *New Yorker* Magazine, September 16, 1955

Michelfelder, W. -- "Florida's Dr. Frankenstein and His Love Laboratory". Detective Cases, June 1982

Morrow, Jason Lucky - *Famous Crimes the World Forgot*, Tulsa, OK, Historical Crime Detective Books, 2014

Nash, Jay Robert - *Look for the Woman*, New York, NY, M. Evans and Company, Inc., 1981

*New York Evening Post*
*New York Evening Telegram*
*New York Herald*
*New York Journal*
*New York Sun*
*New York Times*
*New York Tribune*
*New York World*

Perez, B. -- "Police Officer Bienvenido Perez Only Living Person Who Knows Where Elena Buried". *The Key West Citizen,* August 15, 1952

Perez, B. -- "The Mad Scientist of Key West". *Men's True Adventure,* 1952

Schechter, Harold -*Psycho USA: Famous American Killers You Never Heard Of,* New York, NY, Ballantine Books, 2012

Sloan, David L. --*The Lost Diary of Count Von Cosel,* Phantom Press, 2012

Swicegood, Tom -- *Von Cosel,* Ocala, FL, iUniverse, 2003

Tanzler von Cosel, K. --"The Secret of Elena's Tomb". *Fantastic Adventures,* September 1947

Telfer, Tori - *Lady Killers,* New York, NY, Harper, 2017

Traub, James - *The Devil's Playground,* New York, NY, Random House, 2004

*True Crime Detective*

Vronsky, Peter - *Female Serial Killers,* New York, NY, Random House, 2007

Wilson, Colin - *Mammoth Book of True Crime*, New York, NY, Carroll and Graf, 1998

Wolf, Marvin J. and Katherine Nader - *Fallen Angels*, New York, NY, Facts On File, 1986
------------------------------------------ - *Rotten Apples*, New York, NY, Ballantine, 1991

## SPECIAL THANKS TO

April Slaughter: Cover Design and Artwork
Becky Ray: Editing and Proofreading
Lisa Taylor and Lux
Samantha Smith
Brianna Snow
Orrin and Rachel Taylor
Rene Kruse
Rachael Horath
Bethany Horath
Elyse and Thomas Reihner
John Winterbauer
Kaylan Schardan
Maggie and Packy Lundholm
Cody Beck
Tom and Michelle Bonadurer
Lydia Rhoades
Susan Kelly and Amy Bouyear
Cheryl Stamp and Sheryel Williams-Staab
Joelle Leitschuh and Tonya Leitschuh
And the entire crew of American Hauntings

# ABOUT THE AUTHOR

Troy Taylor is the author of books on ghosts, hauntings, true crime, the unexplained, and the supernatural in America. He is also the founder of American Hauntings Ink, which offers books, ghost tours, events, and weekend excursions. He was born and raised in the Midwest and divides his time between Illinois and wherever the wind takes him.

See Troy's other titles at: www.americanhauntingsink.com